Mastering Legal Analysis and Communication

Carolina Academic Press Mastering Series

RUSSELL WEAVER, SERIES EDITOR

Mastering Bankruptcy
George W. Kuney

Mastering Civil Procedure
David Charles Hricik

Mastering Criminal Law
Ellen S. Podgor, Peter J. Henning, Neil P. Cohen

Mastering Evidence
Ronald W. Eades

Mastering Intellectual Property
George W. Kuney

Mastering Legal Analysis and Communication
David T. Ritchie

Mastering Negotiable Instruments
Michael D. Floyd

Mastering Products Liability
Ronald W. Eades

Mastering Statutory Interpretation
Linda D. Jellum

Mastering Legal Analysis and Communication

David T. Ritchie

MERCER UNIVERSITY
SCHOOL OF LAW

CAROLINA ACADEMIC PRESS
Durham, North Carolina

Library of Congress Cataloging in Publication Data

Ritchie, David T.
  Mastering legal analysis and communication / by David T. Ritchie.
     p. cm. -- (Mastering series)
  Includes bibliographical references and index.
  ISBN 13: 978-1-59460-363-1 (alk. paper)
  ISBN 10: 1-59460-363-4 (alk. paper)
  1. Law--Interpretation and construction. 2. Law--Methodology. 3.
Law--Philosophy. 4. Law--Study and teaching--United States. I. Title. II.
Series.

  K290.R58 2008
  340'.1--dc22

2007046385
                    Carolina Academic Press
                         700 Kent Street
                       Durham, NC 27701
                  Telephone (919) 489-7486
                       Fax (919) 493-5668
                       www.cap-press.com

            Printed in the United States of America

to
Courtney and Westley,
for all the inspiration you bring

Contents

Series Editor's Foreword

The Carolina Academic Press Mastering Series is designed to provide you with a tool that will enable you to easily and efficiently "master" the substance and content of law school courses. Throughout the series, the focus is on quality writing that makes legal concepts understandable. As a result, the series is designed to be easy to read and is not unduly cluttered with footnotes or cites to secondary sources.

In order to facilitate student mastery of topics, the Mastering Series includes a number of pedagogical features designed to improve learning and retention. At the beginning of each chapter, you will find a "Roadmap" that tells you about the chapter and provides you with a sense of the material that you will cover. A "Checkpoint" at the end of each chapter encourages you to stop and review the key concepts, reiterating what you have learned. Throughout the book, key terms are explained and emphasized. Finally, a "Master Checklist" at the end of each book reinforces what you have learned and helps you identify any areas that need review or further study.

We hope that you will enjoy studying with, and learning from, the Mastering Series.

Russell L. Weaver
Professor of Law & Distinguished University Scholar
University of Louisville, Louis D. Brandeis School of Law

Acknowledgments

This work would not have been possible without the support and encouragement of the Dean and Faculty at the Mercer University School of Law. In particular, I have benefitted from the advice and guidance of Linda Edwards, Linda Jellum and Jack Sammons. I am indebted to Jennifer Sheppard, Sue Painter-Thorn, and Karen Sneddon for their constant support and friendship. Throughout my career in the legal academy I have had the good fortune to work with amazing mentors: Steven D. Jamar, Zoyad Motola, Jan Levine, Kathy Stanchi, Ellie Margolis, Michael Smith, Kristen Gerdy, Anthony Neidwiecki, Cheyney Ryan and Linda Edwards. I would not be where I am today were it not for them.

I am also deeply thankful for the help provided by my assistant Ms. Barbara Churchwell. Finally, I would like to acknowledge the patience and assistance afforded me by Russell Weaver, the general editor of the series, and by Ms. Jennifer Gilchrist at Carolina Academic Press.

I also need to acknowledge the contributions of several scholars in the field for contributing to my understanding of the concepts I discuss in this book. Their work has played an important role in the formation of my views, but any omissions or inaccuracies are my own. They are (listed with the work(s) I found particularly helpful):

Mary Beth Beazley, *Better Writing, Better Thinking: Using Legal Writing Pedagogy in the "Casebook" Classroom (Without Grading Papers)*, 10 LEGAL WRITING 23 (2004);

_____, A PRACTICAL GUIDE TO APPELLATE ADVOCACY (2002);

BRIAN BIX, JURISPRUDENCE: THEORY AND CONTEXT (3d ed. 2004);

STEVEN J. BURTON, AN INTRODUCTION TO LAW AND LEGAL REASONING (1995);

LINDA H. EDWARDS, LEGAL WRITING: PROCESS, ANALYSIS, AND ORGANIZATION (4th ed. 2006);

_____, LEGAL WRITING AND ANALYSIS (2003);

_____, *The Convergence of Analogical and Dialectical Imaginations in Legal Discourse*, 20 LEGAL STUD. F. 7 (1996);

PATRICK HURLEY, A CONCISE INTRODUCTION TO LOGIC, 1997 (6TH ED.);

LINDA D. JELLUM AND DAVID CHARLES HRICIK, MODERN STATUTORY INTERPRETATION: PROBLEMS, THEORIES, AND LAWYERING STRATEGIES (2006);

Stefan H. Krieger, *Domain Knowledge and the Teaching of Creative Legal Problem Solving*, 11 Clinical L. Rev. 149 (2004);

STEFAN H. KRIEGER, RICHARD K. NEUMANN, JR., KATHLEEN H. McMANUS AND STEVEN D. JAMAR, ESSENTIAL LAWYERING SKILLS: INTERVIEWING, COUNSELING, NEGOTIATION, AND PERSUASIVE FACT ANALYSIS (1999);

GEORGE LAKOFF & MARK JOHNSON, METAPHORS WE LIVE BY (1980);

RICHARD K. NEUMANN, JR., LEGAL REASONING AND WRITING: STRUCTURE, STRATEGY, AND STYLE, 1998 (3D ED.);

HERBERT N. RAMY, SUCCEEDING IN LAW SCHOOL (2006);

DAVID S. ROMANTZ AND KATHLEEN ELLIOTT VINSON, LEGAL ANALYSIS: THE FUNDAMENTAL SKILL (1998);

PIERRE SCHLAG AND DAVID SKOVER, TACTICS OF LEGAL REASONING (1986);

Michael R. Smith, *Levels of Metaphor in Persuasive Legal Writing*, 58 MERCER L. REV. 919 (2007);

_____, ADVANCED LEGAL WRITING: THEORIES AND STRATEGIES IN PERSUASIVE WRITING (2002);

RUTA K. STROPUS AND CHARLOTTE D. TAYLOR, BRIDGING THE GAP BETWEEN COLLEGE AND LAW SCHOOL (2001);

PAUL TIDMAN AND HOWARD KAHANE, LOGIC AND PHILOSOPHY: A MODERN INTRODUCTION, 1999 (8TH ED.);

STEVEN L. WINTER, A CLEARING IN THE FOREST (2001).

Introduction

This book is designed to help you master the analytical and communication skills you will need to become an expert in the legal profession. The topics covered in what follows are selected to help you both grasp key foundational concepts, and introduce you to advanced ideas that are generally only mastered by experts in the legal system. This book is not meant to substitute for the casebooks and course books that you will have in your law school classes. I have tried very hard to craft this material into a helpful resource that will enable you to navigate the many complex and difficult concepts that you will need to learn and master, explaining to you the processes you can use to make that journey. I hope this book will make that journey easier, and ultimately more rewarding.

There are a great many books that discuss legal reasoning, legal writing, legal research, appellate advocacy, and other lawyering skills. This should come as no surprise, as the legal academy has rightfully (and finally!) focused much more fully on these fundamental aspects of lawyering in recent years. Over the past two decades many people within the legal academy have worked very hard to ensure that your legal education is more comprehensive and well-rounded. The profession has responded to these efforts, and your education is therefore better than it would have been a generation ago.

So many good books have been written in these areas, in fact, that it may seem strange that another is being added to this already crowded field. This volume is meant as an adjunct to the more detailed treatments of legal analysis and communication that you may be assigned. Like other books in the "*Mastering...*" series, this book is designed to give the reader (whether a novice law student, or a more advanced user), a sense of the landscape of contemporary scholarship and theories on the topic. While not an exhaustive review of all the literature on legal analysis and communication, what follows is a discussion of the major theories and conceptual constructs that one will encounter in a careful study of these vitally important aspects of what it means to be a lawyer in the United States.

Several things should be mentioned here at the outset. First, you will note throughout this book that I use certain terms that may seem a little stilted and abstract. For example, I refer to the legal system in the U.S. as a "discourse community," and an intellectual "domain." I also use the terms "novice" and "expert" fairly extensively. This terminology is not meant to confuse you, or to unnecessarily complicate the discussion (although it may, admittedly, have that effect). Instead, I am attempting to do two things by using this terminology: 1) draw upon recent scholarship about how the legal system in the U.S. works, and 2) utilize more advanced notions of how students learn important concepts in new domains. Stefan H. Krieger, *Domain Knowledge and the Teaching of Creative Legal Problem Solving*, 11 CLINICAL L. REV. 149 (2004).

It is now widely accepted that the legal system in the United States is a distinct "discourse community." JILL J. RAMSFIELD, THE LAW AS ARCHITECTURE: BUILDING LEGAL DOCUMENTS 16-20 (2000). So, when I suggest-as I do throughout the book-that our legal system is a "domain" that utilizes and shapes the analytical and communication skills of its members according to a shared understanding of the individuals initiated into that system, I am drawing upon a more complicated and textured notion of what our conception of the law entails. This more complicated notion of the U.S. legal system will undoubtedly shape your educational experience, no matter where you attend law school. Similarly, when I say that learning and developing certain skills will assist you in moving from "novice" to "expert," that assessment is based on the extensive research that has been conducted by scholars in the profession aimed at better serving the needs of students and the profession. Robin A. Boyle, *Employing Active Learning Techniques and Metacognition in Law School: Shifting Energy from Professor to Student*, 81 U. DET. MERCY L. REV. 1 (2003). Your studies will truly be a journey of discovery that will lead from your introductory notions of how the law operates, to a more textured and complicated understanding that is similar to others who work and practice in the legal system.

The second thing to note is that an attempt has been made to accommodate (if not fully synthesize) competing theories regarding the topics discussed. In some cases the theories within a topic (paradigms in legal writing, for instance) are just different ways of expressing the same idea. On other topics (for example, theories of jurisprudence), the ideas expressed are not necessarily mutually exclusive. I have tried to be as comprehensive in my discussion of the topics discussed as I can, given the constraints of this volume. I have not made an attempt, however, to be neutral in my treatment of the various ideas discussed. Some of the theories found in the literature are better than others. Where appropriate, I have discussed the relative merits of the ideas explored. While this is clearly not meant to be a work in critical theory, some normative assessment cannot be helped.

Next, as I mentioned above this work should not be viewed as a substitute for any of the skills oriented books that are on the market. This is not a "how-to" book that simplifies or obviates the need for detailed treatments of legal reasoning, writing or advocacy. Rather, this work should be viewed as a compliment to these works. I attempt to explain, and perhaps provide context for, the theoretical constructs that one will find as they use other books on legal analysis and communication. This is not a desk reference or style manual, however. This book is intended to be a learning tool for students (novice and expert) of these topics. This volume should be used as an aide to further understand (and perhaps clarify) the concepts and ideas that one will confront in their study and practice of legal analysis and communication skills.

Finally, the reader will note that I have used somewhat complex philosophical concepts in certain places throughout the text. This use is based on two things: my background, and my belief that one of the principal deficiencies with many of the legal analysis and skills course books out there is that they do not fully explain the foundations of many key concepts they use. I try to explain, where relevant, the theories behind key ideas that are used in the field. I am convinced that this sort of conceptual genealogy will help those who want to (or need to) understand where these ideas spring from. This, in turn, will provide a broader context for key concepts. This is not a philosophical treatise, however. This volume is not designed to be a work in high theory. *Mastering Legal Analysis and Communication* is what I would like to think of as a work in practical jurisprudence, accessible to novices yet helpful to more advanced students of the topics considered. As such, the discussion of the topics and theories contained here are what Jean Baudrillard might call mere simulacra: simple and superficial representations of the true, fleshed out notions that are more fully developed in other places. JEAN BAUDRILLARD, SIMULACRA AND SIMULATION (1995). I have made an attempt to provide copious references for those who wish to delve deeper into the philosophical heart of these ideas. I have also attempted to provide adequate references to the literature on the topics discussed, both in the text and in the bibliography. I have tried, though, to curb my own enthusiasm for these discussions so as to not derail the purposes I outlined above. I hope I have struck the proper balance.

Mastering Legal Analysis and Communication

Chapter 1

Human Reasoning and Legal Analysis

Roadmap to Reasoning and Legal Analysis

- Law school is a unique educational environment designed to initiate you into the profession.

- Law is a social institution that is taught differently in the U.S. than elsewhere in the world.

- In the U.S. common law system, law is an interpretive enterprise.

- Participants in the legal system form a discourse community in which this interpretive enterprise is carried out.

- Modern legal education in the U.S. is composed of a variety of pedagogical approaches designed to help you become a member of the discourse community.

- Your professors will have different pedagogical dispositions (unrelated to the topics they teach). Your task is to be flexible enough to respond to the expectations of each professor you have.

- Legal analysis and communication refers to a set of abilities that you will develop in different ways in all the classes you have in law school.

I. Introduction

Law is a set of concepts and institutions that employ basic human intellectual abilities. How we think, the forms of cognition and analysis we use in everyday life, form the basis for our capabilities to conceptualize, understand and employ legal concepts. Basic forms of human reasoning, logic and intuition form the core of legal analysis and communication. In short, thinking about law is not the providence of the few who understand something special about the universe. Law is a human enterprise that anyone can understand and participate in. Legal analysis and communication is possible by anyone. Law is the ultimate democratic institution. In fact, U.S. Circuit Court Judge Richard Posner has argued that the entire foundation of the democratic enterprise is contingent on this notion. RICHARD A. POSNER, LAW, PRAGMATISM, AND DEMOCRACY (2003).

This being said, thinking about the law and analyzing legal problems will necessitate that you employ your inchoate abilities of reason, logic and intuition in particular ways. Law school is designed to assist you in forming your raw intellectual abilities in such a way that you can quickly and competently think about legal issues and concepts, and communicate your reasoning to others. This is often called "thinking like a lawyer." We all have the potential to know the law well and understand the varieties of legal concepts, but law school forces us to take that potential and mold it into a finely honed set of tools that can be applied to legal questions in ways other actors in the legal system will recognize and accept.

The purpose of this chapter is to orient you to the world you entered when you decided to undertake the study of law. I briefly discuss the nature of law in our system of jurisprudence in order to give some context for why legal educators have chosen the pedagogical approaches they employ. Then I discuss the structure of legal study in the U.S., focusing principally on the lessons that specific pedagogical approaches are designed to instill. Too often, these lessons are left unstated or are only vaguely hinted at by law school professors. This leaves many law students confused (and sometimes even angry) over the object of classroom discourse or other exercises. Finally, I briefly discuss the relationship between thinking about the law and analyzing legal problems, and communicating with others about the results of this thinking and analysis in a professional setting. This relationship is complex, and is often the source of some conflict within the legal academy itself. As such, it is extremely important for anyone who wishes to understand law and the practice of law in the U.S. to grasp the relationship between legal analysis and legal communication. The background that this chapter provides should better equip you to embark upon your studies.

II. The Nature of Law in the U.S.: Some Basic Ideas

Humans have developed, implemented and debated law of some type in every culture around the world. What constitutes law in different cultures is varied and contingent. Anthropologists, sociologists and legal theorists debate the nature and extent of law as a social institution. The specifics of these debates are fascinating, and well worth the time of anyone who has an interest in them. They need not detain us here, however. The only really important thing that we need understand about these debates is that law, regardless of the society we are discussing, is an overlapping set of social institutions that depend upon adherence, acceptance and acknowledgment for legitimacy. Different societies have vastly differing sets of social institutions which comprise their respective legal systems. These institutions often involve many aspects of peoples' lives: economic, moral, political, religious, etc.

Western legal systems are generally quite formalist in nature. This means that the overlapping social institutions that form what people in the West call law tend to be formal establishments that are charged with certain powers and obligations. These establishments are invariably defined in formal ways as well. When we think of how governments are formed, and the existence of different branches, cabinets or departments within the government we can see what this formal organizational structure entails. In fact, this conceptual framework is often so deeply embedded in our thinking that we have a hard time understanding what "formalism" is in the context of structuring legal systems. Many students have difficulty grasping the fact that the sorts of formal legal structures that we see in Western nation-states are not universal categories, but are simply contingent artifacts of a shared cultural and social history that has derived legitimacy from such formal structures.

Even within the Western political and historical tradition, there are differences of approach concerning the nature of law. One dominant approach is to view law as a confined and limited institution within society that is designed to serve specific social functions that other social institutions (family, military, religious, etc.) do not serve. Each institution, in this approach, has a delimited function. These functions are generally exclusive to the domains charged with handling them. The relationships between the institutions and their functions is extremely formal, meaning that normativity is determined by the efficacy of the actions within the system. In this view, law (as a social institution) is not connected to any particular moral apparatus. The role of law, and the actors in the legal system, is to address a delimited set of social concerns that other institutions (and the actors within those institutions) are ill-equipped or incapable of handling. This approach is known as positivism. In legal positivism, the formalism of law carries over to the conception of what constitutes "law." Legal positivists tend to believe that formal legislative action, most often in the form of statutes and codes, is the paradigm example of "law." BRIAN BIX, JURISPRUDENCE: THEORY AND CONTEXT 33–53 (3d ed. 2004); ANTHONY D'AMATO, ED., ANALYTIC JURISPRUDENCE ANTHOLOGY Ch. 2 (1996). Positivist conceptions about law suggest that there is very little interpretavism involved in legal reasoning. Adherents of pure positivism believe that texts which carry legal meaning are discrete and directly determinative. BRIAN BIX, JURISPRUDENCE: THEORY AND CONTEXT 42–43 (3d ed. 2004). That is to say, positivists often argue that the "law," as found in statutes and codes, is almost always clear and easy to understand on its face. *Id.* Under this positivist thesis, lawyers and judges need not interpret the law, they only apply it. *Id.* Many Western European nation-states (and other nation-states who derive their legal systems from Western European models) are based on this sort of positive law conception, especially those nation-states that derive their legal heritage from Roman (and later, Napoleonic) legal thought. This is sometimes called the "civil law" tradition.

The way in which law is conceived in the United States is slightly different than that espoused by this form of positivism (although there are adherents of positivism in the U.S., some of whom may in fact teach at your law school). The U.S. legal system is a common law system. This means that while some of our laws are indeed positive in nature (statutes, codes, administrative rules, and so on), most of what we think of as law in the U.S. is derived from basic legal principles that are enunciated by some actors in the legal system-principally judges. Thus the conception of law that serves as the foundation for our legal system allows for more informal influence than is present in positivist systems of law. Our common law system acknowledges the role of positive law sources, but gives considerable room for the shifting opinions of legal experts in the interpretation of basic legal principles and standards. Many important legal theorists in our tradition have celebrated the ideal that judges can influence the development of law as a social institution.

This alternative conception of law has two important implications for the novice. First, the common law system has had a direct impact on how law is taught in the United States. The "case method" of instruction is a direct consequence of our common law conception of law. Second, our common law legal system, which gives a great deal of interpretative power to judges (and other legal actors), allows for a certain amount of indeterminacy in legal analysis. That is to say, because we see law as largely an interpretative enterprise we generally acknowledge that there is some indeterminacy in virtually every legal issue. *Id.* at 177–187. Whereas positivists suggest that legal texts can clearly (and easily) answer legal issues that arise, legal actors in the common law tradition generally presume that legal issues can be answered in a variety of different ways. *Id.* These different answers flow from the contingencies built into a system which gives human actors (lawyers, judges, juries) power to craft their own interpretations of how legal problems ought to be dealt with. *Id.* These interpretations, in turn, are often influenced by non-legal factors (economics, morality, politics, religious views, etc.). *Id.* at 34; Stephen R. Perry, *Interpre-*

tation and Methodology in Legal Theory, in A. Marmour, ed., Law and Interpretation 97–135 (1995).

Beginning students of our common law system often struggle with the idea that there are often no universally accepted "right answers" to the legal questions that they confront in their studies. They struggle with the contingencies in the system, and with the indeterminacy of legal analysis. The common law often looks like a morass that is impossible to master. This is not a new feeling. Legal theorists in the U.S. during the nineteenth century attempted to develop law as a science that could more easily be categorized and turned in to a taxonomy that would minimize the indeterminacy within the system. Brian Bix, Jurisprudence: Theory and Context 35 (3d ed. 2004). The attempt to develop a "science of law" failed, however, as the nature of law in our common law system is not amenable to the rigid and formal strictures that such a categorization and taxonomy would entail. The eminent American legal theorist, and former U.S. Supreme Court Justice, Oliver Wendell Holmes, Jr. explained it this way:

> The life of the law has not been logic; it has been experience. The felt necessities of the time, the prevalent moral and political theories, intentions of public policy, avowed or unconscious, even the prejudices which judges share with their fellow men, have had a great deal more to do than the syllogism in determining the rules by which men should be governed. The law embodies the story of the nation's development through many centuries, and it cannot be dealt with as if it contained only the axioms and corollaries of a book of mathematics. In order to know what it is, we must know what it has been and what it tends to be. We must assuredly consult history and existing theories of legislation.

Oliver Wendell Holmes, Jr., The Common Law 1 (Dover 1991). It is now generally accepted that law in our common law system is more art than science, and that legal analysis more closely resembles aesthetic judgment than scientific method. See, Stanley Fish, *Anti-Professionalism*, in Doing What Comes Naturally: Change, Rhetoric, and the Practice of Theory in Literary and Legal Studies (1992). As a result, many of the analytical, and later communication, skills that novices learn as they take up the law necessitate that they relinquish the desire for "right answers" and accept that their quest is really for supportable judgments within the frame of reference of the discourse community of law in the U.S. common law system. Professor James Elkins has said:

> The story of legal education is the story of how one learns legal discourse, and how the world and its problems can be seen through the prism of linguistic categories and rhetorical strategies known to law. Seeing the world in this way is relatively easy, and with encouragement and time (always a problem) the student begins to learn the skill of legal discourse.

James R. Elkins, *Thinking Like a Lawyer: Second Thoughts*, 47 Mercer L. Rev. 511, 520 (1996).

This is an important move on the part of those interested in learning about law in the U.S. Once one accepts that the goal is to develop and support legal judgments within a discourse community, the nature of legal analysis and communication becomes easier to understand, learn and employ. Kate Ronald, *On the Outside Looking In: Students' Analyses of Professional Discourse Communities*, 7 Rhetoric Rev. 139 (1988). Discourse theory suggests that within specific kinds of communities (professional groups for instance), the way in which the members communicate is dependent upon their being indoctrinated into the standards of thinking and communicating within that community. Brook K. Baker, *Language Acculturation Process and the Resistance to In"doctrine"ation in the Legal Skills Curriculum and Beyond: A Commentary on Mertz's Critical Anthropology of the Socratic, Doctrinal Classroom*, 34 John Marshall L. Rev. 131 (2000). Further, once the indoctrination has taken place, the analysis and communication becomes richer because of the shared associations of group members. The association brings about a whole host of shared experiences that give deeper and more complex meaning to ideas and words than those outside the discourse community would recognize or understand.

When you entered law school, you "enter[ed] a discourse community and [will] gradually acquire expertise in [this] new domain." Kurt M. Saunders & Linda Levine, *Learning to Think Like a Lawyer*, 29 U.S.F.L. Rev. 121, 122–23 (1994). In order for you to gain this requisite familiarity with this system, you must mold your cognitive abilities in such a way that you can understand and use the "specialized vocabulary and theoretical constructs" that others in the legal system utilize. Gail A. Jaquish & James Ware, *Adopting an Educator Habit of Mind: Modifying What it Means to "Think Like a Lawyer,"* 45 Stan. L. Rev. 1713, 1716 (1993). Professor Jill Ramsfield explains that law is a distinct discourse community because the profession has:

1) A broadly agreed upon set of common goals;
2) Mechanisms of intercommunication among its members;
3) Ways to use these mechanisms to provide information and feedback;

4) A register that uses particular genres to further its aims and a specific lexis, syntax, and phraseology; and

5) A threshold level of members with appropriate expertise.

JILL J. RAMSFIELD, THE LAW AS ARCHITECTURE: BUILDING LEGAL DOCUMENTS 17 (2000). Before you can utilize this distinct mode of discourse effectively, you must master its basic elements thoroughly. Complex thinking within the domain is contingent on having the appropriate expertise. *Id.*

This is not to suggest that law (or any other discourse community) is designed to be a closed or secret system that can only be accessed by initiates in to the rites of the community. As Richard Neumann puts it:

> [T]his kind of knowledge is, after all, one of the characteristics of a profession. To a lay person, the knowledge, the knowledge seems magical, but to the professional it is part of the state of being, so ingrained that the professional cannot imagine life without it.

Richard K. Neumann, *Donald Schon, The Reflective Practitioner, and the Comparative Failure of Legal Education*, 6 CLINICAL L. REV. 401, 408 (2000). Advocates of discourse theory simply maintain, and at one very important level it is difficult to fault their thesis, that once one is in a discourse community their understanding and communication with others in that same discourse community take on richer and more complex forms. What students often experience as they undertake the study of law in the U.S. is a sort of disorientation that is directly associated with their lack of familiarity with legal discourse. James Boyd White has said about the first year of law school:

> From the student's point of view, this year is exciting, often transforming. Pushed by their circumstances and by themselves as perhaps they have never been pushed before, they find resources they did not know they had and discover themselves undergoing a profound change: from bright young students to bright young lawyers ready to go to work in the world.

James Boyd White, *Doctrine in a Vacuum: Reflections on What a Law School Ought (and Ought Not) To Be*, 36 J. LEGAL EDUC. 155, 158 (1986). The language, analysis and communication skills associated with being a member of the legal discourse community are not difficult to grasp, and ultimately master, but until a student does manage to grasp the shared meanings and perspectives of other actors within the discourse community, she will inevitably be adrift in a tumultuous sea.

There remains a great deal to be said about the nature of law in the U.S. legal system, but this short introduction should serve to highlight several important aspects of that system. In particular, I have tried to show how law is not some universal a priori concept that all people accept in identical terms. Law is contingent and specific to particular cultures. In our culture, law is certainly a formal social institution (although not as formalist as positivists would argue). Even though this is the case, our common law heritage allows room for a good deal of indeterminacy in law. As such, members of the legal discourse community need to see that analyzing and communicating about legal issues and problems is an interpretive act. Once these are grasped, perhaps law — as we who are in the discourse community understand it — may not be so mysterious and intractable. Being aware of these aspects will help anyone who is interested in understanding the nature of law and legal analysis in the U.S. Let us now turn more directly to the nature of legal education in the United States. This should give us a better sense of how the pedagogical methods widely employed relate to the legal discourse community.

III. The Structure of Legal Study in the U.S.

Legal education in the United States is different than virtually anything you have experienced before. The way law schools design and implement their curricula are usually very rigid, and the courses that you will have to take are taught in ways that seem alien and confusing. These aspects of legal education give law students around the country a great deal of angst. When this angst is added to the highly competitive environment that exists within many law schools, serious problems can arise. See, Lawrence S. Krieger, *The Inseparability of Professionalism and Personal Satisfaction: Perspectives on Values, Integrity and Happiness*, 11 CLINICAL L. REV. 425, 426 (2005). Like it or not, however, virtually all law schools throughout the United States tend to introduce novices to the profession in strikingly similar fashion. This is due, in part, to the accreditation process law schools must undergo with the American Bar Association [ABA]. There are also historical and pedagogical reasons for the way law schools structure their programs, and for why law school professors teach their classes in the manner they do. In this section I will briefly discuss some of the more obvious — and consequently, perhaps, more important — issues about classes in law school, the people who teach those classes, and the pedagogical methods used in different class settings. As I suggested above, there is a historical and cultural element to this discussion. I will not dwell on these aspects, though, as there are a number of excellent resources on the history of legal education in the United States available in any law library. Some basic historical information is necessary, however, simply to situate the current state of affairs in American legal education. The main point of this section is to de-mystify law school educational practice. This should serve to reduce stress, and make your task of learning the lessons your law school professors want you to learn easier.

Law schools throughout the United States break their curricula down in several different ways. First you will notice that your courses are named after different doctrinal areas within the law: civil procedure, constitutional law, contracts, criminal law, evidence, property, sales, torts, and so on. You will also notice that there are courses that focus on the tasks of lawyering and pro-fessionalism (sometimes called "legal skills" courses): alternative dispute res-olution, client interviewing and counseling, legal analysis, legal research, legal writing, etc. In the upper level curriculum you may see courses (often called seminars) that seem more abstract: comparative law, gender and the law, ju-risprudence, and legal history are common examples. Finally, most law schools offer some form of practice-based courses that focus on live client work (usu-ally called clinics). These divisions may seem baffling and difficult to discern. Given that they are represented, in some form or fashion, in virtually every law school in the U.S. we should explore them in more depth.

Early on in the United States novice lawyers learned their craft through an apprenticeship model. Later, however, universities in the U.S. took an active role in preparing students for law practice. Once law schools became wide-spread among U.S. universities, the method of instruction changed from an ap-prenticeship model to something very similar to the structure seen today. Mark L. Jones, *Fundamental Dimensions of Law and Legal Education: An Historical Framework—A History of U.S. Legal Education Phase I: From the Founding of the Republic Until the 1860s*, 39 John Marshall L. Rev. 1041 (2006). Christo-pher Columbus Langdel, the dean at Harvard Law School in 1870, imple-mented the "case method" of instruction, and divided the curriculum into so-called "doctrinal areas." Arthur T. Vanderbilt, II, An Introduction to the Study of Law 20, 52, 53–54 (1979).

Legal education is carried out quite differently in other countries. In most civil law countries law is taught through a series of lectures, and students are expected to memorize discrete facts about the legal concepts contained in the codes and statutes that comprise the legal apparatus. This model bears more resemblance to how undergraduate education in the U.S. is usually taught.

Currently in the U.S. system of legal education, law school classes are bro-ken down into areas of doctrinal coverage. Students are expected to learn some-thing about the prevailing doctrines or concepts within these areas of coverage.

These courses are called "doctrinal classes" by many within the legal academy. You may hear some of your professors use this terminology. For many years, law school instruction consisted mainly of several semesters of doctrinal classes. Popular movies about the experience of law students in the U.S. usually show this aspect of legal education. Most of the courses that you and every other law student in the U.S. will take probably fall into this category. A few important things need to be said about these courses: 1) the doctrinal areas designated for study are arbitrary; 2) the courses covering these doctrinal areas are not meant to be comprehensive treatments of these areas; and 3) the designation of these courses as "doctrinal" is highly questionable and somewhat controversial.

First, the class titles (contracts, evidence, property, etc.) represent doctrinal areas of concern that are—to some extent—arbitrary and artificial. What this means is that "contracts" is not truly a well-defined and independent body of law. While there are doctrines and concepts that have grown over time within the study of contracts (consideration, promissory estopple, and so on), these concepts are not necessarily independent intellectual ideas. They exist within the context of a law school course in contracts in the United States. For example, before the advent of the case method of study, "contracts" as an independent subject area did not exist. Since the implementation of that method, however, generations of law students in the U.S. have struggled to understand contract doctrines.

Over time students see that the divisions are meaningless. You will learn, for instance, that the lines between contracts and torts begin to blur at some point. You will also see that real world legal problems and issues often contain elements of many different doctrinal areas. Often extracting these different doctrinal elements is impossible, or at the very least impractical. A family law attorney, for example, may have to employ knowledge about constitutional law, contracts, criminal law, evidence, and property on a case she is handling. The attorney will likely not see these as different aspects (or doctrinal concerns) of the case, but will likely see the case in a more holistic manner, drawing all of these elements together.

Second, many students are surprised, and even alarmed, to learn that they are not expected or required to learn everything about the doctrinal areas they study. Very often your professor will chose to cover only certain parts of the book they have required you to buy for your classes. Most students will never draft a contract in their "contracts" class, and many may never even look at a contract as part of that class. "Contracts" in most law schools is a first year class designed to introduce legal analysis and thinking, and not prepare you and your peers to practice contracts law. Nor are such classes really designed to prepare you to take (and pass!) the bar examination. In short, these classes are structured to help you learn to "think like a lawyer." The course designations are more a matter of historical anomaly and practice than anything else. Law schools are bastions of tradition, and law school professors are notorious for sticking with what they know. Since your law school professors were successful at learning about the law and how to think "like a lawyer" by studying the doctrines associated with these arbitrary divisions, they are invariably more comfortable employing them in their classes. This is largely why law schools retain the curricular structures they have.

Finally, the designation of certain classes as "doctrinal" in nature gives those classes a mystique and status that is probably not warranted. Because legal education in the U.S. has been dominated by these sorts of classes for 130 years, one might get the impression that these doctrines and doctrinal designations are really "the law." This impression would relegate any course that is not designed to cover a doctrinal area (legal skills, seminar, and clinical courses) as having secondary importance in your studies. Such an impression is both misleading and dangerous, however. In the modern legal academy, the analytical, communication, practical and technical skills that you need to master in order to move from novice to master in your profession are taught across the curriculum. In the 1990s, legal educators from across the country came together to explore the elements of a complete and comprehensive legal education. They produced what has come to be known as the "McCrate Report." ABA Section of Legal Educ. and Admission to the Bar, Legal Education and Professional Development — An Educational Continuum (1992). What they found was that a proper legal education consists of an array of competencies that do not clearly fall into the categories of clinical, doctrinal, skills, and theory. *Id.* Instead, a thorough and useful legal education will consist of courses which help you develop your analytical and communicative abilities in a dynamic and multifaceted way to cover all these attributes. *Id.* A recent report by the Carnegie Foundation for the Advancement of Teaching has reasserted this view. William M. Sullivan, et al., Educating Lawyers: Preparation for the Profession of Law (2007).

What this means for you is that in any particular class, you will have to hone your abilities in several different ways. In a so-called "doctrinal" class you will have to learn doctrinal theory, but you will also have to learn how to think quickly on your feet, and to write concisely yet comprehensively under time pressure on your exam. In a so-called "skills" course — legal writing perhaps — you will have to develop your technical skills of writing, but you will also have to learn how to think more deeply about a particular area of the law and how the doctrines (perhaps several — contracts, torts and property together, for instance) are employed in the context of complex legal problem solving. The effect of all this is that you should be conscious of what each course demands of you, and not what category (clinic, doctrine, skills, etc.) the course fits in. What is more important, really, is the method of pedagogy employed. Mary Beth Beazley, a law professor at the Ohio State University, has recently suggested that a better division of law school courses would be between "casebook" and "non-casebook" courses. Mary Beth Beazley, *Better Writing, Better Thinking: Using Legal Writing Pedagogy in the "Casebook" Classroom (Without Grading Papers)*, 10 Legal Writing 23 (2004).

This division, which I think makes a lot of sense (from a student's perspective), focuses on the method of instruction that your professor uses. In many classes, casebooks are used. In these classes, you will usually read and brief cases. During class, your professor will call on you or one of your peers to recite the case or cases to be discussed during a particular class period. The professor will then ask you questions about the case, and the doctrines that the case is supposed to illustrate. This is sometimes called the "Socratic method." Anyone who has seen the movie *The Paper Chase* will be familiar with this form of pedagogy. In "non-casebook" courses, students will typically be given a legal problem that they will have to analyze, research and write about. They may even have to negotiate with other students or deliver an oral argument to a panel of judges concerning this problem. It is important to note, however, that doctrines, skills and theories are being developed and honed in both styles of pedagogy. In a very real sense, these different styles are simply separate paths to the same goal: competency as a professional in the complex domain of law.

The lines between clinical, doctrinal, skills and seminar courses — much like the lines between different doctrinal areas — are blurring in many law schools. Many professors who teach courses that have traditionally been thought of as doctrinal courses (sales, commercial paper and secured transactions are examples) are employing the problem method. Additionally, other professors who teach traditional skills courses (legal analysis or legal methods, and legal writing for example) utilize more theoretical or doctrinal styles of pedagogy. Do not get confused by this. Remember what I said in the last section: focus on what your professor wants from you. Do not focus on what the class is called or what you have heard or read about particular classes (or seen in the movies). React to the tasks your professor gives you, and adapt to the needs of any given situation.

It is safe to say that every class you will take in law school is designed to prepare you to think through legal problems, analyze those legal problems, bring specific bodies of legal doctrine to bear upon those problems, and communicate your thoughts about those problems to someone else within the discourse community. If you view your task in this way, you can successfully navigate any class, whether the course is in alternative dispute resolution, appellate advocacy, business organizations, civil litigation, contracts, death penalty appeals, estates and trusts, international law, legal research and writing, negotiations, real estate law, or zoning and land use. Your law school experience will be varied and dynamic. The best lesson you can learn, especially early on, is to be flexible and adaptable. Sometimes this will mean you need to read and digest lots of cases and be ready to talk about them in class. Other times this will mean that you will have to read a few cases more closely, analyze them, and write your analysis so that someone else can review it. Still other times you will have to role play negotiations or oral arguments. No matter the setting, however, these tasks are all designed to help you move from novice to master in the profession. One thing that will aide you in situating these professional tools in proper perspective is understanding the relationship between the analytical aspects of lawyering and the way they can be properly communicated to others in the domain. This is the topic to which we now turn.

IV. Thinking and Doing:
The Relationship between Legal Analysis and Legal Communication

As you develop the tools you will need to move from novice to master in the domain of the law, you will likely be exposed to different dispositions by the professors you work with (and perhaps even within your peer group of students). This is also true of lawyers and judges who work in the legal system. Some will have a more theoretical or abstract approach to understanding and discussing the law. Others may want to know what will help them accomplish their goals (or the goals of their future clients) most quickly. Still others may have a mix of these dispositions when they are working through and discussing legal problems. The purpose of this last section is to explain that while it may appear that different classes or professors approach the material in completely different ways (see the "Differences" section below), these differences are quite often artificial. The distinction between thinking about the law and articulating that thinking in written or oral form is misleading. These processes — "thinking like a lawyer" and employing oral or written skills — are inextricably linked. Any attempt to isolate them is artificial, and in my view, detrimental to your understanding of how to truly "work like a lawyer."

You may have discerned in what you have read thus far that there is an analytical tension between the different pedagogies that are used in modern law schools in the United States. Some classes seem very theoretical, while others seem to have a more practical bent to them. Some law schools highlight one or the other of these dispositions. Some schools are more theoretical in their curricular design and the way the professors approach the materials, while other schools tend to arrange more skills oriented training for their students. In fact, these differences have led many schools to try and distinguish themselves from other law schools by the curricular choices and pedagogical approaches employed.

In effect, this is one way law schools market the education they provide to prospective law students, and to members of the bench and bar who will (hopefully!) employ their graduates. Some schools, for example, highlight their alternative dispute resolution [ADR] programs. Others take great pride in their clinical programs. Still others are known for the quality of their legal writing programs. Alternatively, some law schools have chosen not to devote the resources necessary to develop such programs, but have instead focused on employing noted authorities in traditional theoretical areas of the law. Nonetheless, virtually every law school in the U.S. will have this "theory vs. practice" split appear in some way. This should not worry you. Nor should you get too caught up in the details of how or why your law school might do things a little differently than other law schools. What you do need to do, however, is endeavor to be conscious about the way in which you can exercise and develop your analytical tools in a variety of different settings. Lawyers are professional problem solvers. To be an effective member of the profession you will need to think clearly and precisely, and to be able to make that thinking manifest (in some tangible form) for others to use. These are not different skills, but separate aspects of the same skill.

Let us explore this idea a little further. It deserves more discussion because there is this enduring perception that theory and practice really are separate. Philosophers have argued about this for some time, but the way this debate has shaped legal education in the U.S. is of more immediate concern for you. Why is there this notion that how you think about something is separate from how you discuss or argue (orally or in written form) about it? Some have suggested that this difference stems from the cultural and historical elevation of abstract thought. See, Jürgen Habermas, Theory and Practice (1973). Proponents of this idea suggest that practical thinking has historically been devalued in our culture (and especially our professions). *Id.* This is a hierarchical rank ordering of human knowledge. *Id.* In this view, some knowledge is more important than other knowledge. *Id.* In the context of law school education in the U.S., this dichotomy has certainly been evident. Theoretical approaches to legal reasoning and analysis have ruled the traditional doctrinal curriculum. The practical side of "lawyering," and the classes associated with the skills of lawyering, are relatively new additions to the law school curriculum. In truth, however, the dichotomy between the theoretical and the practical is a false one. See, Byron D. Cooper, *The Integration of Theory, Doctrine, and Practice in Legal Education*, 1 J. ALWD 51 (2001). Whatever its historical or cultural antecedents, viewing theory as distinct from practice is dangerous and misguided.

This means that as you go through school, and even as you enter the profession after law school, you should refrain from the impulse to categorize things according to this false and misleading dichotomy. To be good at your chosen profession, you will need to be flexible enough to analyze, understand, and utilize many different perspectives. Some of them might be more theoretical or abstract than others. Some may seem to have more practical application. It is important to remind yourself, however, that all problems legal professionals face have theoretical or abstract components as well as practical aspects. Focusing too closely on one or the other of these is misguided and potentially detrimental to your understanding. Lawyers or judges who only want to think about and discuss abstract theoretical perspectives on public policy risk having their heads in the clouds and missing something important about how these policies might be put into effect. On the other hand, a lawyer or judge who is always focused simply on the best or most efficient way of dealing with a problem runs the risk of misunderstanding the theoretical foundations of an important legal concept that will affect the application of that concept.

As a result, at the very beginning of your studies you should prepare yourself to develop, exercise, and hone an array of analytical tools during the course of your studies. Do not shirk from some problems or discussions because they are "theoretical," and do not scoff at some tasks because they are "practical skills." As a novice this distinction may even be difficult to make at first. Rest assured, however, you will be exposed to the biases of others during the course of your studies; judges, practicing lawyers, professors, students, and others will all give you unsolicited advice about the theory and practice of law. Like many things, take this as it comes but keep it in perspective. You should soon see that any problem you are presented as a part of your studies will evidence both theoretical and practical aspects. As a result, you need to think about how to address these problems not in isolation, but in a holistic way.

Perhaps some illustrations will assist you here. Most of your classes in law school (certainly in the first year) will be of the traditional casebook variety. You will be asked to read many cases, brief those cases, and be prepared to discuss them with your professor and other students in class. Over the course of a semester, you will read a great many cases in your torts class, for instance. You will brief those cases, and probably discuss them with members of your study group. Perhaps you will be called upon in class to recite a case. Some view this process as an abstract or philosophical way of teaching you legal reasoning, that has little real world practical effect on you as a prospective practicing attorney. But is it really abstract or impractical? Probably not. When we highlight some features of this process that were not mentioned the process looks different. For example, when you brief cases you are practicing close reading of judicial opinions. You are also writing your briefs out (or, as is more likely these days, typing them on your computer). This helps you develop the skill of writing concisely and extracting the most vital concepts from the materials you are given. Finally, you will invariably construct what is called an outline for each of your classes toward the end of the semester. This will require you to categorize, digest, and understand concepts (all "theoretical" skills), but it will also require you to articulate, organize, and write a complex document that has considerable "practical" value to you as you study for and take your final exams.

Now let us look at what has traditionally been classified as a pure "skills" course: your class in legal writing. In a legal writing, or legal research and writing, course students are usually given a fact pattern and asked to extract the legal issue or issues from the fact pattern. They are then asked to research the issue and find relevant cases, statutes and secondary sources. Often such problems will require students to find, read, and understand anywhere from two to a dozen cases, and perhaps a statutory section or two. Once these are found, the students are directed to write a memo or other legal document about the fact pattern they were given. In some settings the students are asked to write a document predicting what the likely outcome of the hypothetical case will be. In other settings students must draft a brief or memorandum of law to persuade someone that their view is the correct one. The professor teaching the course will then review and critique this work-product, frequently meeting individually with the student to discuss their work.

When this narrative is told in this way, such a class looks like a purely practical enterprise. But if we again highlight the aspects of this process that were not mentioned above we can see this class differently. The process of formulating legal issues is necessarily analytical (theoretical), as is the process of determining which cases are relevant (through analogical reasoning), and assessing how to explain and illustrate them in light of the problem. Before any writing can be done, a great deal of analysis must be carried out. In a sense, the "practical" aspects of a legal writing course are inextricably interdependent with the "theoretical" aspects of analyzing the law and legal precedents. So, legal writing courses are not writing courses in the sense one might assume. These courses do not focus on composition skills and grammar. Instead, virtually every legal writing course offered in an American law school is designed to help students use the analytical skills they have been developing in their case-book courses, and to produce a work-product that can be used by someone in the context of legal problem solving. The name of such classes, then, is misleading. These courses are not "legal writing," but are really legal analysis courses with a writing component.

All this is important so that you can see that you will be called upon to develop and utilize a variety of tools as you work through your classes. Some courses may ask you to gain a somewhat superficial knowledge of a whole host of related doctrines within a subject area (contracts, torts, property, etc.), and write an exam at the end of the term. Other courses might ask you to become much more familiar with a smaller group of cases and statutes, but to delve deeper in your understanding in order to write a predictive or persuasive document that could be used in litigation or litigation planning. Either way, your analytical tools will be honed and developed. Interestingly, some professors who teach traditional casebook courses are implementing "practical skills" aspects by using case files, and asking students to do document drafting or dispute resolution exercises as part of their classes. I have always done so in my contracts classes. I am not alone in this, as professors all across the country have experimented with these pedagogical options. You may have the experience of doing such exercises in some of your casebook classes. At the same time, more and more "skills professors" are utilizing high level theory (discourse theory, metaphor theory, narrative theory, rhetorical analysis, and so on) in their courses.

The key to navigating through this morass is being as flexible as you can be, and adapting to the needs of the situation. Getting hung up on whether a problem or idea is just "theory," or worrying about if a problem in one of your classes will have any "practical" use for you is a waste of your time. Remember that all of your classes are designed to help you move from novice in the legal domain to expert. Experts use their skills in their work. They do not make a distinction between (or a big deal about) theory and practice. Such a distinction is meaningless for the expert. All these skills — analyzing the law, discussing that analysis, orally delivering that analysis, and writing about that analysis — are part of the same process of understanding. Your goal is understanding law in the context of the U.S. legal system. Accordingly, you will need to fuse all these aspects together to move from novice to expert.

Differences
Professors Teaching Different Sections of the Same Class

One of the things that students often discuss, and stress about, is the differences between the way their classes are taught, and the way other sections of the same class—or more properly, what they hear from other students about the way other sections—are taught. These discussions often contain elements of two different things: perceived differences between the way classes are taught and real differences between the way classes are taught. The first class of things is sheer mythology akin to urban legend. Every school has many such mythologies, often passing from year to year by section. These mythologies, frequently detailing extreme differences in scope of material covered, acceptable classroom etiquette, and expectations about student work products (exams, papers, memos, etc.), very rarely have any verifiable basis in reality. They are simply products of the stress of a community of individuals attempting to accomplish goals under difficult circumstances. In such conditions, gossip and innuendo thrive. Fear of not being treated fairly also surfaces, especially in the context of highly competitive environments like law school. As a result, what constitutes most discussions about the perceived variances between different sections of the same class in law school should be seen as what they are: products of people blowing off steam in stressful circumstances.

There are often, however, some real differences between the way separate sections of the same class are taught by different professors. Sometimes, a professor will even teach the same class differently in other semesters. This should cause no alarm amongst students. There are very often good reasons why professors construct their classes differently than their colleagues (or differently in other semesters). All humans possess a variety of strengths and abilities. You will likely have noticed that some of your peers are better at some tasks than you are, and that perhaps your strengths lie in other areas. Your professors are no different than you in this regard. Professors bring diverse and varied backgrounds to their classes. How they work through material with you and your classmates is formed by the strengths, weaknesses, educational and work background, pedagogical philosophy, and so on of the particular professor you have. You will learn that as you work through your career in the profession this is true of your colleagues as well. It is important to note that these differences do not really have the effect that many students perceive.

These verifiable differences reveal more about the strategy that your professor has chosen to help you gain the analytical and technical expertise that the class is designed to convey. There are many paths to the same goal. If your professor in your legal research and writing [LRW] class approaches topics in a different way than another professor at the same school (or another school for that matter), there is almost invariably a set of good reasons why the different approach is being used. These reasons will rarely be made explicit (another factor that feeds the mythologies discussed above), but they are there. Your legal writing professor might be a crack whiz at legal citation (maybe she was on law review as a law student and spent hours learning proper citation method to edit submissions), or she may have been a professional editor in a previous career (which might make her emphasize line editing of grammar). Alternatively, your professor might have designed your course with particular goals in mind (for example, one colleague of mine wants students to practice analogical reasoning extensively in his legal writing class), while other professors in the same program might have slightly different goals. Sometimes these differences will happen within a narrow window. For example, in very highly structured legal research and writing programs there is often a common course description, course book, and syllabus across all sections. Frequently even assignments will be used in all sections of the program. At other schools, there is more autonomy on the part of the professors, and more variance between professors who teach different sections of the same class.

No matter what situation you find yourself in, you should do several things. First, trust in your institution and your individual professor. Law school faculties and administrators spend a tremendous amount of time and effort making curricular choices, constructing program policies, and structuring class syllabi and assignments. These choices are expressions of many years of experience, and a tremendous amount of deliberation and discussion both inside the law school you attend and throughout legal education in the United States. Next, you should learn (or remind yourself of) one of the most important lessons about this profession: know your audience and act accordingly. If your professor asks you to construct a memo using a certain process or format, remember that it is your professor who will judge that work-product. It is fruitless to decide that you like the way the professor in another section asks students to discuss cases in a memorandum of law or brief. You are not in that section! As you will learn in practice later on, the same lesson holds true whether you are writing documents for different partners at your firm or different judges in your jurisdiction. Everyone has their own preferences concerning how they want things done (within a specified continuum of course), and those in positions of authority have control over how you accomplish the tasks you are given. The law school classroom is no different. Finally, when in doubt you should discuss the issue with your professor. Invariably your professor will be happy to discuss why the curriculum is designed the way it is, why the class is structured in the manner it is structured, and so on. Just because certain pedagogical choices are not made explicit in your materials or class syllabus does not mean that your professor would not be more than happy to discuss these choices with you. This is especially the case if you explore these choices from an educational perspective (as opposed to a challenge of the professor's authority).

Like many other differences you see in your legal education, this one has little or no effect on your educational experience and what you derive from it. If you trust your professors and your school, keep aware of your audience and act accordingly, and engage in a healthy and productive dialogue with your professor you will learn a lot and accomplish the goals set out for you in your classes. These are good things to keep in mind in all of your classes, but they are especially helpful in the context of writing and other skills related courses in law school. They will also serve you well as you move through your career.

V. Conclusion

When you decided to study law, you entered a unique discourse community that is structured by the history and culture of law practice in the United States. Law in the United States is not a distinct and independently existing entity, but is a social institution that is designed to solve problems in our society. The development of this institution over time has influenced the way students who want to study and be a part of this problem solving process are educated. What you are experiencing, then, is a culmination of a historical and cultural conception of how professionals in the domain of law should be initiated to the domain in the United States. Changes have occurred in U.S. legal education over time. But these changes happen slowly. The way you are being educated today is very similar, with some minor changes, to the way your professors were educated. This process of education is an analytical process, to be sure, but it is also a process of inculturation and initiation to the expectations of others within the system.

Some of these historical and cultural views about law are misleading. The dichotomy between theory and practice is one of these. This situation is changing, however. With the changes in the modern U.S. law school curriculum, the distinction between theory and practice is disappearing because law school administrators, professors, and students are seeing both the educational process in law school and the practice of law in the profession in a more holistic way. Virtually every law school in the U.S. offers an array of courses to help students acquire, develop, and hone a set of analytical tools to make them better problem solvers in the legal domain. Sometimes these courses focus more centrally on theoretical conceptions of law and society. Other times these courses are more closely associated with lawyering practice. But this is a continuum. All courses in the modern law school curriculum are designed to prepare students to be precise and thorough analytical problem solvers. Your job, as a novice in this system, is to try and get as much as you can from every educational opportunity you have in law school. You may not see the immediate utility of something that occurs in many of your classes, but give yourself over to the process your professors have chosen for you. Many students find that the exercises, lessons, and readings that most confused them in law school pay the biggest dividends later on. Like so many things in life, the importance of lessons you learn in law school often do not register with you until long after you have learned them.

Checkpoints

- Remember to view your legal education as an entrée to the profession.

- Keep in mind that the way you learn about the law is formed by the history of our specific culture and history, and that other legal systems operate differently.

- As you work through your courses, examine the ways in which various actors within the system (clients, judges, lawyers, etc.) interpret legal problems differently.

- Determine what it means to be a member of the legal discourse community.

- In each of your classes, discern what the pedagogical approach of your professor is, and what she will expect of you in order to succeed in her class.

- View legal analysis and communication as a comprehensive set of abilities that you will continue to develop throughout your career.

Chapter 2

Paradigms and the Process of Legal Analysis

Roadmap to Using Paradigms in the Process of Legal Analysis

- There are a variety of different conceptual paradigms that you will be taught in law school that will help you learn various tasks that will aid your studies.

- These paradigms are designed to help you emulate more advanced analytical and communicative abilities, even though you are still a novice.

- Analytical paradigms are so useful because legal education is a process-oriented enterprise.

- Using paradigms will quickly and effectively allow you to master the basics. Once this happens, *then* you can utilize your creativity.

- There are no short-cuts. Developing your analytical abilities by following paradigms requires you to engage in the process authentically.

- While there are a variety of paradigms that you will learn and master in law school most share significant similarities, and all are designed to develop your ability to act as others in the legal profession act.

- A gauge of your competency is your ability to utilize the basic paradigms, but adapt them as needed in new or unfamiliar circumstances.

I. Making Analytical Skills Manifest in the Domain of the Law

As we saw in the last chapter, there is a fundamentally important connection between thinking and doing in the profession of law. While it might be eminently interesting to some of us to ponder the law as an abstract domain of human inquiry, I am willing to bet that hardly any of you or your classmates are in this situation. Most people, in fact, go to law school because they see it as a practical career choice. Some even view it as a way to enter a noble and useful profession. These are certainly credible ways of thinking about the study of law. As a result, thinking about the law — or "thinking like a lawyer" — is of little use unless those thoughts can be made manifest. That is to say, legal thinking is only really useful if it can be conveyed to others who can benefit from those thoughts. This illustrates once again the vital connection between theory and practice that I raised in Chapter One.

Your professors in law school will attempt to guide you as you develop your analytical abilities. This is principally done through the use of somewhat rigid analytical structures. These structures are often called paradigms of reasoning. Do not be afraid of this word. A paradigm is simply a structural pattern or model that you will be taught and expected to follow. What this means is that in all of your classes, your professors will force you to structure your thoughts in certain ways. These structures — or analytical paradigms — help you in several ways. First and foremost, these structures will help you prepare for your classes and the assignments you will be given in those classes. These paradigms will also ease your transition from being a novice in the law to becoming an expert. Finally, these analytical paradigms will give you some guidance about how you should structure your thoughts in ways that will conform to the expectations of others in the domain. In effect, by understanding and using these analytical paradigms, you can be better prepared for your classes, move from novice to expert fairly quickly, and conform to the standards of the discourse community of the legal profession. This is why these paradigmatic structures are utilized so extensively in modern U.S. legal education.

In this chapter we will explore these analytical paradigms, examining the different contexts that you will be exposed to in which you must use these structures. We will also look at the various structures that are used, and what they are designed to teach you. Most of these paradigms have substantial similarities, so we will discuss these similarities and explore why the differences exist and what you should do when confronted with these differences. Finally, and perhaps most importantly, we will examine how you can and should use these structural paradigms in law school, and in the different contexts you might experience within the profession.

Before we move on, however, I would like to briefly discuss a perception that students frequently have concerning the use of analytical paradigms in their classes and their work. Many students often complain that being forced to mold their thinking in ways that conform to an analytical paradigm is stifling and oppressive. Others say that using such paradigms robs them of their creativity, and makes everyone think in the same way. It is understandable how you or your peers may have such feelings. There is some basis for this concern. In fact, there is a desire amongst many (perhaps most) of your professors to bring you and your classmates within a predictable range of analysis within the scope of the subject you are studying. This desire is not designed to stifle your creativity, though. Instead, it is driven by the expectation that anyone who attends and graduates from a law school in the U.S. will be able to analyze and discuss (orally and in writing) identifiable legal problems in similar ways.

Think of the use of these paradigms as a way to ensure that everyone within the system is "on the same page" when we examine, analyze and discuss legal problems. LINDA EDWARDS, LEGAL WRITING: PROCESS, ANALYSIS AND ORGANIZATION 1–11 (4th ed. 2006). There is plenty of room for creativity within the predictable range of analytical structures. Once you become an expert, you will see these opportunities to be creative and innovative. As a novice, however, it is important for you to see that understanding, using, and conforming to these paradigms is an important step in your development. In fact, one of the lessons (invariably unstated) that your professors are trying to impress upon you is that following directions and conforming to the expectations of those who have power over your work is extremely important in the legal discourse community. In law school, the people with power over you are your professors. Once you leave law school, however, you will have to conform to the expectations of your employers, your clients, and other actors in the legal system like judges and legislators. Accordingly, being able to embrace and utilize structures provided for you is very important. Fighting these structures will make your journey from novice to expert more difficult than it needs to be, and will delay your development.

Let us now turn to how you might be introduced to these analytical paradigms and how you will be expected to use them in law school. Remember that this is a vital step in your journey to becoming a lawyer. These are not just lessons that are only useful in one context (preparing for class, for instance). Instead, the analytical patterns that will be developed as you force yourself to follow and use these paradigms will have wide application throughout your career. In fact, it is probably not going too far to say that if you develop these skills well you will be prepared to analyze and address legal problems in any context that you will confront in the future.

II. Structuring Your Analysis in Different Contexts

You and your classmates obviously have significant raw intellectual abilities. These abilities enabled you to get into law school after all. In fact, the admissions committee at your law school almost assuredly assessed your ability to think clearly, logically, and rationally by looking at your educational performance in college, your performance on a standardized test, and the comments of your referees about your suitability for law study. Having these raw inchoate abilities allows you to develop the sorts of analytical and practical skills that lawyers need to have in order to be successful. But do not be fooled into thinking that just because you are quite smart, that law and legal process will be easy to figure out. The U.S. legal system is a complicated, multilayered social system. The modern law school curriculum is designed to help smart, capable students mold their considerable mental abilities in ways that will help them become expert members of the profession who can work within this complex system. See, "McCrate Report." ABA SECTION OF LEGAL EDUC. AND ADMISSION TO THE BAR, LEGAL EDUCATION AND PROFESSIONAL DEVELOPMENT — AN EDUCATIONAL CONTINUUM (1992). The principal way this is accomplished is to implement a process-oriented method of thinking. *Id.* What this means is that law school is designed to help you learn a process that will assist you in thinking through legal problems. *Id.*

The importance of process-oriented reasoning is that it gives you a context for utilizing your analytical abilities. Essentially, the process you will learn (if it can be said that there is **one** process that you will learn) involves making mental calculations about what will effectively address the legal problems you face. In truth, it is likely that you will have to learn a set of overlapping yet slightly different processes. Be aware, though, that each of your professors may have a different process for similar tasks, and that different settings may require different processes as well. This applies whether you are thinking about cases you have read and briefed in casebook classes, problems you have been assigned to research and communicate about in non-casebook classes, or actual real world legal work that you are undertaking in clinical or employment settings. We will discuss process-oriented learning more in depth later on, but it is important here to understand that it is this orientation that leads your professors to use paradigms in their teaching, or more properly, to ask you to use them in your work in their classes. So what do we mean when we say that you will use analytical paradigms in your classes?

Simply put, a paradigm of legal reasoning is a formula that you can use in analyzing, understanding, and addressing a legal problem. A formula like this is a way for you, as a novice, to have some mechanism at your disposal that will assist you to systematically confront and deal with problems that would be baffling and mystifying (perhaps even overwhelming) if you had to face them without such a tool. A paradigm is a way for you to begin when you undertake a new task. It is also a method for you to work your way through a legal problem in a manner that will both propel your work and help ensure that you are thinking about and addressing such a problem in a way that is more or less like other actors in the legal system would think about and address it. A paradigm is both a starting point and a structural guide for your work. In other words, the use of a paradigm is a way to ensure that you analyze and work on legal problems like experts would.

One way of thinking about this is to think of how baseball players practice certain tasks in a highly formalized (almost ritualized) way. When new players are learning how to play baseball they will learn the widely accepted ways to carry out a skill — fielding a ground ball for instance — and will practice that action over and over. If sports analogies are not your thing, try thinking about how a novice musician practices scales on her instrument over and over. These formal exercises are not just idle practice. They both involve engaging in a formalized, almost hyper-formalized, repetition of structured action in order to build a foundation for more advanced action. There are no short-cuts. One cannot possibly hope to play baseball for the New York Yankees unless the foundation learned as a novice is solid and thorough, unless the muscle memory of taking grounder after grounder is there. Similarly, it would be impossible for someone to play violin for the Cleveland Symphony unless she has spent hundreds, perhaps thousands, of hours honing the elementary actions that a novice musician practices time and again.

Once these foundations are in place, and one becomes a professional baseball player or world-class musician, they will of course stray somewhat from the hyper-formal and stylized iterations of their novice training. This straying is related to two things: the fact that the move from novice to expert gives them the confidence and skill to adapt the foundation they put in place to account for more advanced situations, and the reality that experts frequently take on a personal style and flair within their domains. Derek Jeter and Yo Yo Ma are the artists they are because they have spent the time and effort required to learn the basics. Only after this expenditure of time and effort could they develop into creative and awesome experts.

You will likely have noticed several things about this analogy. First, I have purposefully emphasized the idea that the basic training one receives within their domain is a foundation for later development to expert status within that domain. This is certainly true of the use of paradigms in legal analysis and communication. Secondly, it seems clear that these sorts of foundations are built through hyper-formal and stylized actions. This is also clearly the case with the use of analytical paradigms in law. Even though this is the case, however, you probably noticed that I acknowledge the fact that experts frequently do not closely follow the formal and stylized actions they learned as novices. It is not as though they abandon this training, but they move beyond it to more advanced action that incorporates the novice foundation with more expert skill. Here again, you will see that the foundations you learn in law school will be adapted and developed into more advanced (and perhaps more subtle) skills. Finally, you probably noticed that I characterized the actions of experts within their domains in artistic terms. Derek Jeter and Yo Yo Ma are surely artists in their respective fields. Similarly, you will meet lawyers who have developed their analytical and practical skills to the point that they appear to be engaged in an aesthetic endeavor and not just technical skills. This last point is very important. Students often think that the hyper-formal and stylized paradigms that they must master and practice inhibit their ability to be creative and develop an individual style. They neglect to see, however, that such creativity and flair is only possible when they have done the hard work of perfecting the basics.

Now that we know a little about analytical paradigms and their purpose, let us look at some of the contexts you are likely to face which will require you to use these structures. Initially, the easy answer may be that as a novice you will use some paradigmatic structure in every aspect of your studies and work. Remember, paradigms keep you from groping around blindly when you confront a new situation. As a result, having a model or structure that you can rely on is very helpful. For example, consider the process of briefing a case. When you entered law school one of the first things you were likely taught was how to read and brief cases for your casebook classes. When you brief cases you follow a paradigm. It is unlikely that your professor explained it in this way, but nonetheless the process of learning how to read cases, extract information from those cases, and construct a case brief you can take to class is clearly an example of using an analytical paradigm. In this very simple lesson (often this takes place in an orientation or introduction to law course before your regular classes begin) you were taught how to analyze, structure and utilize legal information by employing a simple paradigmatic structure.

So you see, there is nothing mystical about this. Paradigms are not some abstract ideas meant to torture you or waste your time. You should embrace the use of analytical paradigms. They have been developed over time by experts in the domain (professors) to assist you with your learning and understanding. Using the analytical paradigm of briefing cases is a great help to you as you enter the domain of the law. Without it, it would be nearly impossible to crack the surface of the discourse community and participate in any meaningful way. You would literally be lost in class without them. By following the advice you were given about how to read cases and construct case briefs, you will be able to get much more information from your casebook classes. In turn, your understanding of the legal concepts will be much richer because of this increased ability to extract and analyze.

A more obvious example of paradigmatic reasoning will likely be found in your legal writing (or legal research and writing) course. All of the major course books for these type of classes employ some sort of paradigmatic structure to help you mold your reasoning about the problems you will address in these classes, and show you models of how to construct a document (or documents) in which you can discuss and apply that reasoning. Writing and other "skills" classes (like trial and appellate advocacy, and alternative dispute resolution) have traditionally employed analytical paradigms to help students see how they should structure their thoughts and actions. Because your professors in these classes are so open and obvious about the use of such paradigms, and because the books you will use explicitly discuss, illustrate, and explain the analytical paradigms used, many students think that these classes are the only environments that require them to learn and use paradigms. This is just not the case, however. This mistake is frequently related to the fact that in casebook courses the materials for the class consists of "law" in the form of cases, commentary and statutes found in the casebook. In non-casebook courses, however, the substance of the course materials is focused on thinking and acting in ways lawyers think and act. This is simply a different pedagogical mechanism, one designed to explain, teach, and help you practice structural models that will assist you in your learning and work.

There are other contexts in which you will be expected to learn and use paradigmatic structures. For instance, when you construct an outline for your classes before exams, you will likely be told how you might structure the material from the semester in an ordered and rational way. Outlining a casebook course according to the doctrines learned in that course is an analytical and paradigmatic structure, albeit one you may learn more about from other students (usually students who have taken the class already) than you will from your professors. Likewise, when you write your exams for your casebook classes you will very likely benefit from an analytical paradigm. Free writing an exam with no structure or point is a painful experience (for both you and your professor!). But if you employ a simple paradigm (the one most frequently used is IRAC, which we will discuss more fully below) as your write your exam, you will be able to address the questions more quickly, efficiently, and fully than if you just "vomited" words on the page with no rhyme or reason. Finally, you will invariably have to do some form of oral presentation during law school — frequently in the context of your legal writing or appellate advocacy classes. These presentations are called "oral arguments," and you will be expected to model your behavior in certain ways. This modeling is frequently taught by using an analytical paradigm, which is often illustrated by showing you examples of other people engaged in the practice of oral argument.

While we will discuss the use (and abuse) of analytical paradigms in some depth later in this chapter, one thing deserves to be said here at the outset. Virtually all of the contexts mentioned above in which you will be taught and expected to use an analytical paradigm will require you to engage in a great deal of hard work and concerted effort. It is only through such work and effort that the use of the paradigms presented by your professors will lead you from novice to expert. While using paradigms helps ease the process and makes your work more efficient, you must still do a lot of hard work. In other words, there is no substitute for the work and effort you will expend. It is the repetition and effect that using and following the paradigm will yield which is the payoff. In other words, using the paradigm is not an end in itself. Using these analytical structures is a means to your better understanding and action in the discourse community.

While you might find it possible to cut some corners by purchasing prepared briefs and outlines, doing so will undermine the usefulness of the exercise of learning and using the analytical paradigms your professors put forth. By not briefing cases and relying on those prepared by commercial services you are detracting from your analytical development. Similarly, if you utilize course outlines prepared by someone else—this holds as true for outlines prepared by other students as it does for commercially prepared outlines—you are undermining your intellectual growth. You will almost assuredly hear this from all of your professors. They are not advising you against buying commercial materials because they have anything against the companies that produce those materials, or because they fear that such materials will undermine the lessons they teach in class. Instead, members of the legal academy tend to disfavor such materials because they detract from your development by keeping you from engaging in necessary and useful actions meant to teach you the structures you need as a member of the profession. In short, using these prepared materials prolongs your move from novice to expert in the domain.

There was no shortcut for Derek Jeter or Yo Yo Ma. They had to spend hours and hours fielding ground balls and practicing scales on the cello. Likewise, you will have to spend a great deal of effort using and following the analytical paradigms your professors present. You should brief all your cases, prepare your own outlines, scrupulously follow the analytical structures your writing and advocacy professors present, and so on. By doing so you are laying a vital foundation, a foundation that cannot be built through short-cuts. You will often not see the benefit of continued adherence to these formal models and structures, but rest assured that the benefit is there. Your professors understand this, so give yourself over to the process. They have your best interests in mind. They want you to progress quickly and competently as members of the profession. By understanding and following these analytical paradigms this will happen.

Now that we understand a little about the use of analytical paradigms in legal education, and the contexts in which you will likely be able to employ them, we should look at some of these formal structures. This brief introduction should give you a better idea of how these paradigms operate as educational tools. It should also help you situate these models within the context of your classes. Though this short introduction is not a substitute for the lessons your professors will teach you about using analytical paradigms, it should help you understand why they are doing so and how you can benefit from using them.

III. What Paradigms Will I Have to Learn (and Why So Many)?

Almost from the first day of law school, your professors have been organizing the lessons you have been taught according to analytical paradigms. You probably did not realize it but they have been, and you have unconsciously been conforming your work to those paradigms. So what are these analytical structures, how are they used in the process of your education, and why are they not explicitly stated as course objectives? The answers to all of these questions are wrapped up in the development of the history of legal education in the United States. Suffice it to say here that as a novice you will be expected by those who are experts in the domain to travel through a certain educational passage before you can join the profession as a full-fledged member. This may sound like an indoctrination or initiation. In some ways it is this, indeed. Even though the analytical paradigms you will be expected to master and use are often unstated you will have to grasp them if you hope to be successful.

In this section I will briefly outline some of the simple paradigms that you will be exposed to early in your law school career. This discussion is not meant to serve as a substitute for the more detailed discussions that you may find on these paradigms elsewhere but is instead designed to point out to you the use of certain paradigmatic structures and how they can be helpful to you in your studies. We will explore basic paradigms related to reading and briefing cases, outlining course materials as an exam review, analyzing and discussing problems in an exam setting (IRAC), structuring and writing your analysis in legal writing documents, and preparing and delivering oral arguments. You will see that modeling your work and studies according to the paradigms used in your classes by your professors will assist you in rapidly becoming better at each of these tasks. As a result, giving yourself over to the process, as I mentioned above, will pay big dividends.

A. Case Reading and Briefing

Perhaps the most important skill you learned, or will learn, early on in your law school career is the ability to read, understand, and discuss the many cases you will cover in your casebook courses. It might not be immediately clear that there is a process to reading these cases and a paradigm related to how you structure your reading, but there is. Ruth Ann McKinney, Reading Like a Lawyer: Time-Saving Strategies for Reading Law Like an Expert (2005); Sarah E. Redfield, Thinking Like a Lawyer: An educator's Guide to Legal Analysis and Research Ch. 2 (2002). In order to do well in your classes you must read the cases you find in your casebooks in a certain way. You must also rework those cases into a form that is useful for you, a form that will prepare you before class, aide your understanding of the discussion that occurs during class, and assist you in debriefing after class (either alone or with your study group). This form is called a case brief. This is an analytical paradigm because it consists of structuring your thoughts along certain lines that will place you and your classmates on the same page (hopefully!) as your professor.

When you began your studies, you no doubt were told that you need to understand several things about the cases you read. First, when you read a case you must identify the facts as they were presented to the court. In the cases you read there are several kinds of facts: background facts, emotionally relevant facts, legally relevant facts, and procedural facts. Linda Edwards, Legal Writing: Process, Analysis and Organization 175 (4th ed. 2006). Next, you will have to determine the legal issue (or issues) the case presents. This can be somewhat tricky for the novice, but it is important to understand what the legal issue is because the way the issue is formed determines — in large part — what the outcome of the case will be. John Dewey, *Logical Method and the Law*, 10 Cornell L.Q. 17 (1924). Legal issues are determined within each doctrinal area of the law. This means that there are legal issues that are specific to contracts, torts, property, and so on. You will learn these distinctions as you gain expertise within the domain.

Let us pause a moment here, because these first two steps in the paradigm of reading cases and building a case brief are very important. The relationship between facts (particularly legally relevant facts) and the legal issue or issues is absolutely vital to your understanding. Legal issues are not abstract questions of law. Instead, they are complex relationships between legal concepts as used in practice and factual scenarios presented to the court. A legal issue, then, is formed and shaped by the facts presented. The importance of this will become more obvious later on when we discuss analogical (and counter-ana-logical) reasoning. For now, it is important that you understand the symbi-otic relationship between legally relevant facts and legal issues.

As you read through cases you will also have to extract the holding or hold-ings in the case. The holding is the answer to the issue presented in the case. It can be a short answer (yes or no), or a more detailed answer which incor-porates the same sort of legally relevant facts that the issue relied on. Either way, the holding is the actual outcome the court ordered in the case. From this holding, you can then develop a rule (or rules) that captures the essence of the legal concept the case is meant to stand for. In a sense, the rule is simply the holding made a little more general. The rule, once it is made more general, can then be applied to future cases or fact scenarios. We will discuss rule for-mulation more fully in Chapter Four.

All of these things — facts, issue(s), holding(s), and rule(s) — are impor-tant pieces of information to extract from the cases you read and, consequently, comprise important parts of the briefs you construct. The most important part of your reading and briefing of any case, however, is the court's reasons for deciding the case in the way it was decided. There is some debate about whether a court's opinion represents the actual reasoning employed (or whether it can possibly be this). John Dewey, *Logical Method and the Law*, 10 CORNELL L.Q. 17 (1924); and David T. ButleRitchie, *"Objectively Speaking," There Is No Such Thing in the Law!*, 5 DISABILITY MEDICINE 68 (2005). This is called the court's reasoning, or sometimes the rationale. This is the "why" behind the court's holding. Understanding and being able to articulate this reasoning is important for a couple of reasons: first, you will definitely have to know this for your class discussion. Professors are forever asking "why" when you dis-cuss holdings and rules. They want to know whether you can understand and articulate why the case was decided in the manner it was decided. Secondly, this reasoning forms the heart of our system of *stare decisis*. Actors in our com-mon law system rely on the reasons stated for the decisions in past cases to help form the reasoning they will employ in present or future cases (this is what Professor Reginald Oh has called a past-present-future relationship). Without understanding the reasons behind why a case was decided the way it was decided, you cannot really grasp the common law. It is the accretion of these reasons as they develop over time that comprises our legal system.

These five aspects of the cases you read — 1) facts, 2) issue(s), 3) holding(s), 4) rule(s), and 5) the reasoning behind the decision — form the core of your analysis and briefing of materials you will cover in your casebook classes. You may be asked or advised to include other information (case citation, judges involved in the decision, statutes implicated, and so on), and there will be some variance between how each of your professors wants you to present these aspects, but you will need to be able to effectively and quickly extract these forms of information from the cases you read. The structure of the case briefs that you construct, then, will more or less follow this basic format.

When you learned to read and brief cases, you likely were not told that this structure (facts, issue, holding, rule, reasoning) was a paradigm to help you make sense of what is going on in the cases you read. To the extent that you were told anything, it is more likely that these things were explained as the "parts of the case," as if they are independent and obvious aspects of the case that anyone can see. After reading a few cases, however, you probably realized that you have to work to extract these aspects from the cases. Sometimes this work is somewhat easy (if the case is simple, or is written well and clearly), but most of the time it is a struggle to dig this information out. It is precisely this difficulty that led to the development of this paradigm of reading and briefing cases. The way we read, brief, and discuss cases in casebook courses is nothing other than an analytical paradigm, a structural model, that assists us in understanding and placing in context the information the cases contain. Without such a tool our classes would be much more difficult, not to mention the impossibility of preparing for class. The use of this paradigm, then, makes your class preparation, participation, and review much more fruitful. Much the same can be said about the preparation of outlines in advance of taking examinations in your casebook courses.

Simple Case Briefing Paradigm
- Facts
- Issue(s)
- Holding(s)
- Rule(s)
- Reasoning and Rationale

B. Outlining Casebook Doctrines As Preparation for Examinations

As you near the end of each semester, you will undoubtedly begin to compile and organize the information that you have covered throughout the term in each of your casebook classes. The traditional way to arrange this material is to construct a course outline that comprehensively condenses yet organizes the concepts or doctrines you have learned about and discussed. If you construct your outline well, it can be an indispensable study aid (and perhaps the only one you will need). These documents are designed to assist you in preparing for the examinations you will take in your casebook classes. As such, they have a limited life span. Nevertheless, the work and effort you put into the drafting of such a document will surely pay off. Like reading and briefing cases, there is a model that you can follow that will help you better organize and more efficiently use your course outlines as study aides.

Outlines are useful because while you draft them you are both reviewing the materials you covered, and organizing your thoughts about how the concepts and doctrines fit together. When you work on your outline you will reread and review the cases you briefed, and recall the discussions you had in class and during your study group meetings. Not all of this information will be worked into your outline—otherwise each of your outlines would be as long as, probably longer than, your casebooks—but you will be making strategic choices about what information to include and what to leave out. As you work through this selection process, you are reinforcing your understanding of the concepts. If you know something well the review is quick, but if you are struggling with a doctrine or idea you will spend more time on it. Perhaps you will consult a hornbook or other outside secondary source to augment your understanding. By creating an outline, you will more systematically cover and review the material you are expected to learn in each of your classes.

There is more to outlining than just reviewing the materials from your class, however. In fact, maybe the most important reason to construct a course outline for each class is that doing so will help you organize the doctrines and concepts in your mind. Traditional outline structures force you to categorize concepts into headings and subheadings. Doing this will make you think about the doctrines in each of your classes, the concepts and cases associated with those doctrines, and assess the best way to categorize them in a rational and useful way. This sort of structural thinking is strategic. You are making a mental assessment about which concepts and doctrines are related and how. You do not make these assessments in a vacuum, but in the context of your particular class, with your particular professor in mind, and concerning the specific materials covered and discussions you and others in your class have engaged in.

So what kind of information is included in a typical law school outline? First and foremost, the major doctrinal concepts within the particular class you are outlining must be represented. For example, in your contracts class you would have headings for "consideration," "offer," "acceptance," and so on.

Often, this basic barebones outline structure can be gleaned from the table of contents in your casebook. Next, you would include the rules you have derived from the cases and statutes you have read throughout the term. These are sometimes called the "black letter rules." In addition to the rules, you will sometimes include some basic information about the cases you have read, or at least some of the cases (particularly the seminal or famous ones). Here again you are well advised to be somewhat careful, because including a "mini-brief" on each case will make your outline extremely long and cumbersome. In making the decision on whether to include or exclude some information on a particular case you are once again engaged in the sort of review process I mentioned above. Beyond the concepts, rules and "mini-briefs," you will also want to include some information about the reasons behind many of these concepts and rules—i.e., the reasoning or rationale that support major doctrinal concepts—as well as any policy considerations that have a bearing on the rules. As I suggested in the section on case briefs above, knowing this information is extremely important. Finally, you will want to include particular information about your professor's views and any important details that came out of class or study group sessions.

Once you have done all this, you have created a very useful yet very personal document. The choices you make about what to include, what to exclude, what to focus on, what to gloss over, and what you and your professor deem to be important and unimportant are all specific to your circumstances and knowledge. This is why it is so important to draft these documents yourself. Beyond the benefit you will gain from systematically reviewing and categorizing the materials, you will benefit even more from the act of creating the document itself. Certain parts of your understanding are stimulated by the process of creation. What needs (or gets) stimulated depends on your understanding of the concepts, your ability to follow the discussions in class, and any outside reading you have done on the subject. Borrowing someone else's outlines, or buying commercial outlines short circuits this process. There will be variations between the document you create and the documents that other students in your class create. This is not a problem, though, as long as each of you carries on the process authentically.

This last point is really important. Remember, this is a process. You are following an analytical paradigm when you outline your casebook courses. By structuring your understanding about each of your classes and categorizing the doctrines and concepts in a formal and graphic model of how these doctrines and concepts relate to each other, you are gaining insight that you would not get from simply reading and reviewing the course materials. By utilizing the outline paradigm, you are advancing your knowledge and understanding in an efficient and organized way. While your outline will look different than those of your peers, and certainly different from commercial outlines, there will be some similarities. It is the differences, however, which will propel your understanding to new levels. As a result, a well crafted outline is indispensable as you prepare for your examinations. Similarly, knowing how to organize your thoughts and display the knowledge you have accumulated throughout the semester on the examination itself is crucial. This brings us to the next important analytical paradigm that you will need to master.

Sample Outline Paradigm

I.   Main Topic or Issue
    A.   Principal Doctrines
    B.   Rules (with elements or factors)
       1.   Case Examples
       2.   Class Hypotheticals
    C.   Additional Information from Class
       or Other Sources
II. Main Topic or Issue
    A.   Principal Doctrines
    B.   Rules (with elements or factors)
       1.   Case Examples
       2.   Class Hypotheticals
    C.   Additional Information from Class
       or Other Sources

C. Using IRAC on Your Law School Examinations

Taking law school exams is a difficult and stressful thing. Most law school exams consist of essay questions, and often 100% of your course grade will depend on the way you perform on the final. You will have worked hard throughout the semester, reading and briefing cases, attending and participating in class, sitting through study group sessions, and drafting a comprehensive outline. All of this hard work is necessary, but performing well on your exams requires more. You can work very hard—perhaps harder than you have in any other educational environment—during the semester, and feel that you are very well prepared as you sit down for a final examination, but still not be satisfied with the grade you earn in the class. This can happen because you did not show the professor the knowledge you possess in your exam answer(s).

Very often, this is because you did not structure your answers to the questions on the examination in a way that would have allowed the professor to see what you know. In other words, many students do not earn points they might otherwise have earned on law school exams because the structure of their answers did not lend itself to showing what they actually know about the law in a clear and easy to understand way. As a result, you can increase your chances for success by using an analytical paradigm to help you structure your exam answers.

The most widely used and taught paradigm or structure for writing exam answers is: IRAC. This acronym stands for Issue, Rule(s), Analysis/Application, and Conclusion. HERBERT N. RAMY, SUCCEEDING IN LAW SCHOOL 114 (2006). This basic structure will assist you as you think about and plan out your examination answers. You may have noticed that this basic structure bears some resemblance to the elements of the case briefing paradigm we discussed above. This is no accident. On most law school essay exams you will be given a fact pattern, or several fact patterns, sometimes very long, that you must read and analyze. You will then have to do several things, including spotting issues, discussing the legal rules that apply to those issues, discussing how these rules relate to the fact pattern and applying them to the facts, and finally giving some sort of conclusion that answers the question. You should easily be able to see that these steps follow closely the IRAC paradigm. In effect, the things you will have to do to completely and clearly address the questions on your exams can be orderly accomplished if you remember this simple acronym and use it when you are writing your essay exam answers. Let us briefly look at each of the steps in this analytical structure.

First, issue spotting on your exams is absolutely vital. When you read the fact patterns on your essay examinations, you should actively annotate the exam question and take notes in the margins. Read the question two or three times to be sure you see everything that is embedded within the fact pattern. Once this is done, and you are sure you have seen everything that is there, you should make a short list of all the legal issues that you see. You do not need to make a long outline. Just make a short list, the kind of list you would make when you go to the grocery store. Just like a grocery list helps you get all the items you need at the store quickly and efficiently, this list of issues will assist you by helping you structure your exam answer. Once you have this list of issues, you might notice that some things you saw in the exam question are actually sub-issues of more general issues. You can place these sub-issues in the proper place as you mentally begin to plan your answer. Once you have decided on the basic structure of your answer, you can then begin to fit the other parts of the paradigm within that structure. It is important to note, though, that this first step—issue spotting and ordering—sets the whole process in motion.

Once you have identified and listed (at least in outline form) the issue or issues the exam question presents, you will have to list and briefly explain the
legal rules that relate to those issues. These rules were initially presented in the
cases and other materials in your casebooks, then reworked and restated in
the briefs you prepared for and discussed in class, and finally condensed in the
outline you drafted before exams. Most professors do not require that you list
the rule or rules exactly, giving precise citations to the case or cases they come
from (in fact, I have never known any professor who requires this). Instead, you
will be expected to know the legal concepts represented by the rules you covered in class and be able to link those concepts to the issue or issues you spotted in the question and the facts given in the fact pattern. In other words, you
must be able to discuss how the legal doctrines relate to the issues and facts.
Very often, if you have done the work throughout the semester and prepared
a good outline, this step will be easier than you might assume. Once you have
spotted an issue, your mind will quickly associate that issue to the rule or rules
you discussed in class concerning the issue. These first two steps are, however,
the easy part of writing essay exams in law school.

The next step in the paradigm is to analyze the facts from the fact pattern
given and apply those facts to the rules. What this means is that you must retell
the story that the fact pattern tells, but restructure it in such a way that the
legal issues implicated and the rules governing those issues mold the story into
an answer to the problem(s) posed. The reason this is so difficult is because your
professor will be looking for a few important things. First, your professor will
expect you to be able to clearly and rationally explain why the hypothetical
case you have been given should be decided or dealt with in a particular way.
In other words, you will have to show your professor that you can explain why,
giving detailed reasons, the hypothetical should turn out the way you conclude. Second, your professor will expect that you can relate this first step (rationally and clearly explaining your analysis) to the reasoning that was put
forth in the relevant cases you read and discussed in class. In effect, your analysis and application here should bear some relationship to the kinds of things
the judges said in the rationale of the cases related to the legal issue. Finally,
your professor will be looking to see how comprehensive you are as you analyze and apply the facts. If you can work in all the facts as elements or factors
of the applicable rule, and explain the logic and policies behind why the rules
should govern in a certain way, you will be in great shape.

After doing all this, you will need to adopt some conclusion or conclusions
that will answer the actual question(s) posed by the exam (this is sometimes
referred to as "the call of the question"). Interestingly, this is almost always the
least important part of the process. This is true for two reasons. First, once

you have gone through the steps before it the conclusion often follows almost mechanically. Second, many law school exams are written in such a way that there is no clear "correct" conclusion. That is to say, most exam questions in law school allow for competing conclusions. Most points on law school essay examinations are earned in the issue spotting, rule identification, and analysis/application steps. Nonetheless, you should always be sure to conclude by giving your opinion as to how the hypothetical case should be decided, paying close attention to the call of the question.

While this section is not a complete primer on how to prepare for an take an essay examination in law school, you should be able to see how utilizing the IRAC paradigm will make your task of reading, understanding, and addressing essay questions much easier and more systematic. Without such a tool at your disposal, you could easily find yourself flailing around blindly in a state of confusion and (growing) agitation as you try to figure out how to answer complex essay questions. Having this structure will aid your thinking, make your work more efficient and timely (time constraints are always a problem on law school examinations), and give you a comfort level that would not be there if you did not have such a paradigm at your disposal. This last point is very important. Going in to your exams you should feel confident if you have done all the work you are expected to do. This confidence can really be an asset, especially if you add it to the comfort of knowing that you can easily and effectively structure your essay exam answers by following the IRAC paradigm. You may have to modify the paradigm slightly to accommodate certain questions, but this basic structure should serve you well as you address questions on examinations in your casebook courses.

Perhaps we should take just a brief moment and assess the paradigms we have discussed thus far. First, we examined the paradigm of reading and briefing cases. Next we explored the paradigm associated with outlining your casebook courses. Finally, we looked at how the IRAC paradigm can assist you in answering your law school essay exams. This is the stuff of your daily routine in law school. Interestingly, all of these paradigms teach you skills that will be utilized in your legal research and writing classes (and other similar skills based courses). In these classes, you will have to research legal concepts, read cases and statutes, organize a body of legal authority, and structure your thoughts into a written document or documents. As you might guess, these skills will also be aided by the use of an analytical paradigm. This is what we will turn to next.

> **Sample Exam Writing Paradigm**
> - Issue(s)
> - Rule(s)
> - Analysis and Application
> - Conclusion(s)

D. Paradigms in Legal Writing Documents

The one part of your legal education where your professors will undoubtedly explicitly discuss and teach you about analytical paradigms is in your legal writing and advocacy courses. All of the major course books on legal writing utilize some form of analytical paradigm to assist you in structuring both your thinking about the legal problems you will work on and the drafting of one or more documents to address those problems. Depending on the text your professor uses, the paradigm might be called by one of a number of different acronyms: CRAC, CREAC, and CRUPAC are common examples, but you may also see alternatives such as CRPAW, FORAC, and TREAT. Whatever paradigm your professor chooses to teach you, however, it is designed to help you organize both your thoughts and your written work more efficiently and effectively. By following the paradigm your professor teaches you, you will be able to rapidly and comprehensively address the problems you work on in ways that approximate the reasoning and work-products of legal experts.

For the purposes of the rest of this discussion we will use the CREAC paradigm, in part because this is the paradigm I am most familiar with (as I use it in my classes), but also because it seems that this might be the most widely used paradigm by legal writing professors in the U.S. The acronym CREAC stands for: Conclusion; Rule; rule Explanation; rule Application; and Conclusion. Linda Edwards, Legal Writing: Process, Analysis and Organization Chs. 4–6. (4th ed. 2006); and David Romantz and Kathleen Elliot Vinson, Legal Analysis: The Fundamental Skill 90–96 (1998). It should be immediately apparent to you that this is intimately related to the simplistic IRAC paradigm we discussed above. Some legal writing texts still use IRAC as their basic model, but this has become uncommon. CREAC is, in fact, a more robust version of IRAC that allows you the opportunity to delve more deeply into (and consequently write more thoroughly about) the relationship between the rules derived from the legal authorities and the facts from the problem you are working on. This more developed paradigm is useful when you have more complex problems to address, when you are expected to provide more thorough and comprehensive analysis, and when time constraints are not as pressing. Where the IRAC paradigm is very useful in an exam setting, the more developed and detailed CREAC paradigm is preferable when you must be more complete and detailed in your analysis and writing. Let us look at the different parts of this paradigm.

1. Conclusion

Legal analysis and communication differs from the sort of academic analysis and writing you may be used to, most noticeably in that lawyers traditionally assert their conclusion or conclusions right at the outset. There are some complex cognitive reasons for this, but we need not prolong our discussion here with these. Suffice it to say that members of the legal discourse community front-load both their analysis and their professional communications (oral and written) with the conclusions they are predicting or advocating. Stating the conclusion clearly and succinctly right at the outset will help structure the analysis, and make the communication of that analysis easier to follow. Actors in the domain (lawyers and judges) are busy and will expect to see your conclusions clearly stated at the very beginning of your analysis. Thus, virtually all analytical paradigms in this context begin with a statement of the conclusion.

2. Rules

After the conclusion is stated, you need to explicitly document and list the rule or rules that you will rely on in your analysis. This is a bold and direct statement of the rule or rules. If the rule you are relying on is a simple or straightforward and easy to apply legal concept, it may be a sentence or two with associated citations to the authority. Often this is not a single sentence, however. It can often be a paragraph or more of related rules and sub-rules. In this case, this is really a rule section of your analysis and communication. In complex situations, you will have to weave together rules from several different sources (statutes, cases, administrative decisions, etc.). This is called a synthesis. We will discuss rule development in much more detail in Chapter Four, but at this point it is important for you to note that within the context of this paradigm, the rule section is the place where you list the relevant legal authority and attribute that authority to its appropriate sources.

3. rule Explanation

The next step in this analytical paradigm is to explain, or "prove" the rules. RICHARD K. NEUMANN, JR., LEGAL REASONING AND WRITING: STRUCTURE,

STRATEGY, AND STYLE, 248 (3d ed. 1998). What this means is that you will be developing the concepts from the authorities in more depth. In this section of the paradigm, you are educating yourself and the reader about the way the rules work, and how they should be viewed in the context of like or similar circumstances. This is where a great deal of your analytical work will be directed. It is here that you must develop the intricacies of the legal concepts, fleshing out the bare-bones rules. Often you will discuss the cases the rules come from and outline why the rules operate they way they do in the context of specific factual situations. Here you will also discuss and develop the reasoning behind the decisions you have identified as relevant. Essentially, you are explaining why the rules make sense. You need to explain the logic and policies behind the rules. You will also explain why contrary authority should not apply in your case.

Because of what you need to accomplish in this section of the paradigm, the rule explanation section is probably the most important part of this analytical paradigm. If this is not carried out properly, your analysis will be incomplete. Anything that relies on your analysis—like your oral or written work—will seriously suffer from this deficiency. Very often, then, this section will be the longest and most in-depth portion of your analysis and discussion. You should remember that this section of the paradigm is focused on developing the law. Do not taint it by discussing the facts of the problem you are working on. That comes in the next step, the rule analysis and application.

4. rule Analysis/Application

After you have developed and fleshed out the details of the rules and explained how they operate, you will then turn to discussing the legal problem you are addressing. This is where you review the facts of the legal problem you have been presented, analyze those facts in light of the rules you have identified, and apply the reasoning from the authorities to the situation at hand. Many students find this to be the easiest part of the process to think about and carry out. This is likely because this step involves facts of their hypothetical case, facts that they and their professor have discussed in an in-depth way throughout the course of working on the problem. This step is also easier because after developing, explaining, and "proving" the rules by discussing the reasoning behind them, the facts of the problem take on a richer texture. In this section of the paradigm, you are answering the question presented by the problem, and explaining why the law applies to your facts in a particular way. Once this is done, the major portion of your task—both analytical and communicative—is accomplished. In fact, these last two sections, rule explanation and rule application, are the heart of this paradigm.

5. Conclusion

After all this hard work is accomplished, you will restate your conclusions. This portion of the paradigm is designed to force you to wrap up your analysis and tie together any loose ends. This will, of course, look a lot like the beginning conclusion you used at the top of the paradigm. It may include some subtle details that would have been confusing to include at the outset, however, details that will make more sense after the analysis has been worked through and explained.

This paradigm is more complicated than those we discussed above, but it allows for a more detailed, comprehensive and thorough analysis of the law. Remember, this is not simply a template for you to follow as you write your legal writing memos and briefs. This is a process to structure your thinking. This analysis can then be shaped into a document, of course, but the important aspects of this are the effect it has on your analysis and understanding. The CREAC paradigm, like the other paradigms used in legal writing and advocacy classes, is meant to be a useful tool in your thinking and your doing. That is what makes all these paradigms so effective—the link they provide between your analytical development and your ability to model your work so that it resembles the work of experts in the domain.

Sample Legal Writing Paradigm

- Conclusion
- Rule(s)
- rule Explanation
- rule Analysis/Application
- Conclusion

Differences

Why is My Professor Teaching me THIS Paradigm?

You may be confused by the fact that there are competing paradigms employed in legal writing and advocacy classes across the country and maybe even at your school. The fact your professor has decided to use one particular analytical paradigm in your class and not one of the alternative paradigms is irrelevant. In some schools all the legal writing and advocacy classes are taught using a single text, and the faculty employ a single organizational paradigm. In other schools, individual professors are encouraged to use whatever text—and the associated paradigm—they are most comfortable with. As a result, you may be taught a different paradigm than a student in another school is being taught. You may even be learning a different paradigm than the one your classmates in different sections are being taught. Do not get tied up over this. The fact is that most of the paradigms are conceptually related, and no matter which organizational structure you are learning you will be honing the same sorts of analytical skills.

Your professor has chosen the text they use and the paradigm that text utilizes for several reasons. First is the pedagogical choice of determining what organizational structure will be most beneficial to you at your particular point of development. Second, your professors are individuals who have varying perspectives on what is most effective as a teaching tool given their strengths and weaknesses. Finally, your professors are heavily influenced by their educational histories and experiences. If they learned legal analysis and communication through the implementation of a particular paradigm, they are much more likely to be comfortable using that paradigm in their classes. Similarly, if your professor is engaged in scholarship related to how analytical paradigms can assist members of the profession in analyzing and communicating about complex legal problems—perhaps even writing their own texts or articles in which they explore alternative paradigmatic formats—they will invariably integrate these into their teaching. In the end, you will benefit from your professor's perspective no matter what paradigm they teach you and regardless of the reason they choose it.

Like many other situations you will face as a member of the profession, your ability to adapt to the demands placed upon you by your professor is an important skill to master. If you are asked to use a different organizational paradigm in your other classes, perhaps even other writing or advocacy classes, it does not mean that the lessons you are learning now will be worthless. Instead, you should consciously attempt to conceptually link—in your own mind—the ideas and structures represented by the different paradigms. This will make your work in your classes, and perhaps more importantly the tasks you will undertake when you begin working as a member of the profession, more comprehensive and thorough.

The people you work for when you leave law school will use, and expect you to use, different paradigms. Each person you work with will have their own preferences. These are often related to what paradigm they were taught, or the one they find more useful for their specific purposes. Being adaptable will permit you to integrate the new or modified paradigm into your knowledge base, thus increasing your analytical skills.

Over time, you will adopt your own preferences. Again, this may be heavily influenced by and closely related to the paradigm you used in some or all of your classes in law school. You will also begin to notice that you will modify and adapt the basic paradigms you used in order to accommodate particular situations. This is a very good sign. It means, in effect, that you are moving beyond the basic formalistic and formulaic use of a paradigm structure to more nuanced and subtle analytical and organizational structures. This is another sure sign that you are moving from novice to expert in the law!

E. Structuring and Preparing for Oral Argument

The last analytical paradigm that we will discuss here involves the preparation for and delivery of oral arguments. This may seem like an odd topic to cover in a chapter on using paradigms in legal analysis, because oral argument seems like a decidedly different skill than the others we have discussed. In fact, there are elements of giving oral arguments that make them different than reading and briefing cases, outlining your classes, writing your exams, and drafting complex legal documents. First, you will have to rely more on your ability to persuade by speaking about the law in an open, often public, setting. Secondly, there is a bit of theater involved in delivering oral arguments. What this means is that the form (and formality) of your performance is important. Finally, delivering an oral argument is a more immediate and explicit interaction between you and those judging your argument. This is almost a dialogue between you and the bench (it should, in fact, have the feel of an intellectual dialogue). These differences should not be overstated, however. While you may focus heavily (perhaps almost exclusively) on these differences when you think about giving your oral argument—something many students in law school dread—doing so will distract you from seeing the analytical nature of this activity. But if you put these differences in context, you can see that there is an analytical paradigm involved in both preparing for and delivering an oral argument.

Looking at this as an analytical exercise, and discerning a paradigm that will enable you to structure and formulate your performance will shift the focus from the things mentioned above (the things that generally make students very nervous, sometimes even panicked, about giving oral arguments). Here again, a paradigm is a useful and convenient way to help you engage in this important activity with more consistency, rationality and confidence. So how do we turn something as daunting as standing before your professors and others from the local legal community into an analytical structure that can be employed whenever you have to give an oral argument? Never fear, there is a process you can employ to help you.

First, look at the steps you will engage in as you prepare for your argument. They are the same sort of steps you would engage in to do the tasks we discussed above. You will research legal concepts, read cases and statutes, formulate the issues and determine the applicable rules, and articulate the reasons why the case should be decided one way or the other using the rationales and public policies you found in previous cases. In fact, quite often you will use the very same materials that you have used in other contexts (writing a memorandum of law or brief, for example) as you prepare for your oral argument. Next, hone down the materials to the precise legal issue or issues that will serve as the basis for your argument. Oral arguments tend to be very short. As a result, there is no way that you can work in the complexity that will be evident in your written work. You should focus on a few lucid and relevant points that are likely to persuade the bench. Accordingly, preparing a very short outline will be helpful. Once you determine the legally relevant issue(s), you can focus the main points of your argument on the appropriate doctrines that lead to your theory of how the case ought to be decided. Finally, you will want to try and anticipate likely questions from the bench. This involves being familiar with alternative theories of the case and preparing answers for why your theory is better than the alternatives. This is not dissimilar to the sorts of analytical structures you used in the writing and construction of your legal documents.

As you can see, preparing for your oral argument will utilize virtually all the analytical skills that you have been mastering in other contexts. By forcing yourself to see this as an analytical process, you can bring your considerable and growing expertise in the areas discussed above to bear on the short oral arguments you will have to give during law school. But what about actually giving the oral argument itself? That is the intimidating and scary part, right? Well, once you have done all this preparation you should be ready to make your arguments and answer any questions the bench may have. Nonetheless, you will likely experience some anxiety (maybe a lot) when you first stand up to deliver your oral argument. Accordingly, doing some simple practical things will assist you in the actual argument.

To begin with, you should have some basic materials that you take with you as you make your way to the podium to deliver your argument. You should have your short outline, which will include some information about the key cases you will discuss or likely be asked about. You should also have both your opening and closing statements roughly sketched out so that you can refer to them in the event you get flustered and freeze up during those portions of your argument. You should not have a script (as nothing is more painful for everyone involved as you reading your argument verbatim), but you should have some text that will prompt you to mention the important points you hope (or hoped) to make. Finally, you should have both your brief and the record at hand in case you or the bench make explicit reference to them during your argument. It may very well be the case that when you give your oral argument you do not have to refer to any of these materials. In fact, very good oral advocates often do not have to refer to their outlines, their prepared text, or their briefs during their arguments. Nonetheless, as a novice you will benefit from having these things available to you.

There is one last thing that needs to be said about oral arguments, something that really does set it aside from the analytical paradigms discussed above. Giving an oral argument in law school, or in front of any court in the U.S., is a very formal endeavor. As a result, there are expectations you will have to conform to concerning the way you dress, the manner of your oral delivery, the way you answer questions, and the demeanor you display during your oral argument. Some settings are much more formal than others. For example, if you participate in the moot court program at your school you will see that moot court competitions require a much more formal and stylized manner of oral argument than your professor will likely expect in your legal writing or appellate advocacy class. This is not unlike the profession, as delivering an oral argument in front of the U.S. Supreme Court is a much more formal occasion than doing so at an intermediate state appellate court. You will undoubtedly be instructed about these expectations by your professors prior to your having to deliver your oral argument. You can also learn a lot about these expectations by watching others—preferably experts—give oral arguments.

The fact that these things (dress, delivery, mannerisms and demeanor) play no role in the earlier paradigms we discussed should not distract you from the fact that you can develop, and should in fact even be taught, another paradigmatic structure that will assist you with these tasks. For example, you can learn how to construct a formal opening statement. You can also learn how to structure the points you want to make during your argument in such a way that you incorporate your points into the questions being asked by the bench. You can also practice certain behaviors so that your argument style conforms to the expectations of the occasion. Do not be fooled, however, into thinking that these things are purely theatrical or performance related skills. Beneath all of these things — preparing adequately, dressing professionally, speaking clearly and concisely, answering questions fully, and delivering your argument with some style — lies analytical structures and understanding that cannot be substituted for any amount of natural stage presence. Just as watching someone read a script during oral argument is painful, watching someone who has some theatrical panache but little legal knowledge is downright agonizing.

The purpose of this section is not to prepare you for oral arguments, either in your classes or in a real world setting. There are better resources for that. Instead, I have tried to show you how this activity, like the others discussed before it, can be reduced to an analytical paradigm that can effectively and somewhat easily assist you — as a novice — to engage in this task in a way that is structured and conforms to the expectations of others in the profession. If you follow the steps mentioned, and model your behavior on those steps, you will rapidly move beyond the novice stage. This is an analytical paradigm and not solely a performance skill because it requires you to mentally plan out and organize complex ideas and concepts in such a way that you can persuade those you will be talking to that your position is the correct one. Viewing this as an analytical paradigm should also help you gain the confidence that you may lack as you think about standing up there in front of people who might scare you, delivering and defending your position.

As you might have noticed, there is a great deal of overlap between the different paradigms we have discussed in this section of the chapter. While each of the contexts we have discussed — class preparation, exam preparation, exam taking, document construction, and oral argument — require you to adapt your mental abilities to certain kinds of tasks, there are threads of commonality that run throughout all these activities. Let us now examine what these are and why they are important.

> **Sample Oral Argument Preparation Paradigm**
> - Focus on the Issue(s) Being Argued
> - (Re)read and (Re)brief the cases
> - Construct a Short Outline (a few main points)
> - Craft Your Opening and Closing Statements
> - Have Important Materials (Briefs, Record, etc.) Close at Hand

IV. Commonalities among Paradigmatic Structures

As you read through the basic paradigmatic structures discussed above, you probably noticed that there is considerable overlap between them. Virtually all of the analytical paradigms that you can use as you engage in the different activities modern law schools demand track back to several core things. These consist of 1) processing information from a variety of sources (statutes, cases, secondary sources, your professor, and class discussions), 2) structuring this information so that you can understand it more clearly, efficiently, and fully, and 3) taking that understanding and organizing it into convenient work-products that will be useful to you and others in the domain. As you will see in the next chapter, these things all relate to the idea of what it means to "think like a lawyer." As such, they are all reinforcing and augmenting your analytical skills and connecting them to your ability to make these skills manifest by talking and writing about the law in professionally useful ways.

As you move beyond the novice stage and gain some level of expertise within the domain, you will begin to see that these paradigms (and the foundation they provide) remain at the core of your conception of what the law is, how it is shaped and understood, and how you go about your work in the profession. You will move beyond these paradigms, certainly, but these structures will always have a formative impact on your analytical conceptualization about the law as a discourse community and how you can organize your thoughts within that discourse community. Just as Derek Jeter and Yo Yo Ma retain the simple lessons they learned when they were picking up their respective crafts, you will retain these basic structures and the core of competency and understanding they represent.

These analytical tools, as simple as they are, are a legacy of your educational journey through law school. My grandmother used to say that "the simple lessons are the best." This may be true. It is certainly true if you understand what the simple lessons are meant to teach, and how simple lessons can provide you with the confidence, skills, and perspective to move on to more complex and nuanced things. When your professors ask you, either explicitly or implicitly, to learn and utilize a conceptual paradigm they are inviting you to begin a journey, but they are also showing you some signposts along the way. Use these lessons in the way they are intended, and you will benefit greatly. So how should they be used? We will turn to this question in the last section of this chapter.

V. Using (and Abusing) Paradigms in Legal Analysis

Part of your journey from novice to expert in the profession is being able to contextualize your knowledge. This means that you must be able to assess the manner in which the analytical and practical skills you gain can best be used to accomplish the tasks you are assigned. This is, in effect, what it means to be a professional problem-solver. Like all tools, the analytical tools we have discussed in this chapter have their proper uses. They can also be misused as well. Part of your responsibility as an adult learner and a new professional in the domain is to determine these uses and misuses.

Some students are reluctant to use the paradigms presented to them because they think they do not need such aids, or that using them is an insult to their intelligence. I have attempted to show in this chapter how utilizing analytical paradigms is not only very useful, it is probably necessary at some level for you to understand certain basic things about law in the U.S., reasoning about law in our system, and working within that system. These structures are part of the educational process and are part of the indoctrination to the domain. These tools and models are part of the fabric of our collective experience. Fighting against them, then, is counter-productive. Accept these analytical paradigms for what they are. Doing so will enrich your education in ways you cannot begin to imagine.

One might get the impression from what I said in the last section that you should blindly and uncritically follow the paradigms your professors introduce. Such an impression would be wrong, however. These analytical tools are the starting point, not an end in themselves. To view the paradigms we have discussed, or any other that you learn or develop on your own, as an end in itself would be to elevate form over function. The forms and structures represented by the various paradigms you will learn throughout your career will serve as a guide, but only as a guide. You cannot simply parrot or mimic these basic analytical forms and assume that you are fulfilling your obligations as a member of the discourse community. Professional competency and intellectual integrity demand that you fill the gaps not covered by basic paradigmatic structures, and work hard to bring to light the full complexity and subtle beauty of fully formed legal analysis and communication. These terms may seem strange and somewhat out of place. They are, in fact, usually reserved for artistic endeavors. In my view, experts within their domains are engaged in artistic production no matter what their domain. Perhaps we can conclude with this analogy. Even though beginning painters will often learn very technical skills, maybe even painting by numbers, they are not truly artists until they move beyond this introductory stage. When you move beyond the stage of using paradigms in a rigid and formulaic way, you will become an expert capable of truly remarkable things.

VI. Conclusion

Analytical paradigms are tools to help you form your mental and practical abilities in ways that will rapidly progress you from novice to expert status in the profession. By employing these paradigms as a novice you will lay a foundation that creates good professional habits. These habits will allow you to evolve into an independent and skilled lawyer and problem-solver. More immediately, however, following these paradigms will give you the basic structures you will need to be successful in law school and in your early employment settings in the profession. These models give you guidance as to how you should structure your thoughts and how to engage in professional behaviors that resemble those of legal experts. As a result, identifying, understanding, and using analytical paradigms is an important, if not absolutely necessary, step in your evolution from neophyte law student to expert lawyer.

You should endeavor to keep these analytical paradigms in context. Use them for the purposes they have been designed and understand both the strengths and weaknesses of each. Follow the guidance of your professor. Adapt the basic structures according to their advice and the situations you confront in your studies and your work. But do not stray too quickly or without a concerted plan. Just because you do not like or understand how to use a paradigm does not mean that you should abandon it. There is great benefit in forcing yourself to follow the basic structure, especially early in your career. Once you have mastered this ability, and you gain the requisite knowledge and expertise that comes along with it, you can begin to leave the nest and take wing.

These structures are designed to help you, not to inhibit your growth. By utilizing these tools, you are exercising analytical and practical abilities that serve an important role in your professional development. But these paradigms must be utilized with other aspects of your mental and practical skills. You must be able to carry out their use while simultaneously employing your raw intellectual capabilities, as well as more advanced analytical skills such as various forms of logic and rhetoric. This chapter has been designed to show you the benefit of several basic paradigmatic structures. In the next chapter we will explore various forms of logic and the basic ideas behind rhetoric, and the relationship of these ideas to legal analysis and communication.

Checkpoints

- Try to determine what paradigms are being employed by your professors. Are there any that you are using that we have not discussed in this chapter?

- Think about the skills and abilities each paradigm you use is meant to teach you. Being conscious of what the lessons are will help you see the connection between the paradigms used and the more advanced abilities you will master.

- Do not forget that legal education is process-oriented.

- Remember that you will have ample opportunity to use your creativity after you have mastered the basics by using the paradigms your professors teach you.

- Be sure to engage in the process of using paradigms authentically. This means that you should not seek, nor use, short-cuts.

- Can you determine the similarities between the various paradigms you have used? What do these similarities tell you about legal analysis and communication?

- Can you adapt the basic paradigms that you have learned to suit your needs in new or novel situations? Does the fact that you have learned these paradigms give you confidence to approach unfamiliar legal problems?

Chapter 3

Logic, Rhetoric and Legal Analysis

Roadmap to Logic, Rhetoric and Legal Analysis

- Logic is an important analytical tool for legal professionals. As such, you should be able to understand formal, informal and pragmatic notions of logic and why they are important.

- Legal analysis is a complex mixture of logic and rhetoric. Understanding legal discourse requires that you be able to both identify and use a variety of logical and rhetorical devices.

- Formal logic is helpful in some legal contexts, but be on guard against the presumption that legal discourse can be condensed to a set of logically formal constants. The common law resists such categorizations.

- Inductive or informal logic is more widely used in the U.S. legal system. In fact, the common law system is an example of an inductive system of reasoning.

- Pragmatic logic refers to a more natural and conceptually useful notion of thinking about problem-solving.

- Rhetoric is a series of discursive practices that allows you to use logic (of any sort), emotion, culture, history and any number of other concerns to craft compelling and useful arguments pertaining to legal problems you confront.

- Any of the abilities or skills we have discussed can be used for either laudable or deplorable purposes. Part of your obligation as a professional in the legal system is to ensure that your use of these abilities and skills conforms to the highest standards of the profession.

I. Law and Logic

Reason is the life of the law; nay,
the common law itself is nothing
else but reason.

Sir Edward Coke

Many people assume that lawyers need to be able to think logically as they do their work. This is why, in part, the Law School Admissions Test [LSAT] focuses on logical reasoning. Logical reasoning is certainly important for anyone working in the legal profession. As is true with most professions, though, the law has its own quirks and peculiarities. Part of your task as you work toward becoming a lawyer is to make your reasoning skills more precise and thorough. Becoming acquainted with the culture of the American legal profession will aide you in this development. As law is largely an intellectual profession, you will be required to mold and reshape your analytical abilities. This is, in large measure, what we mean when we say that you must learn to "think like lawyers." The purpose of this chapter is to help you understand how logical reasoning works and how reasoning logically can help you in law school and as a member of the profession.

While every faculty member that you will encounter in law school has their own definition of exactly what constitutes "thinking like a lawyer," the phrase certainly has something to do with the way in which lawyers reason through problems in an attempt to find possible solutions to those problems. This way of thinking is highly stylized and you will struggle to perfect it throughout your three years of law school (and throughout your entire career). There are some skills that you bring with you which will make this acclimation easier. You have all been exposed to more or less rigorous forms of thinking in the undergraduate classes you took before you came to law school. The informal types of logic that you used as you reasoned through problems in your anthropology, business, computer science, history, philosophy, political science, psychology or zoology classes are inchoate skills that you can draw upon as you undertake your study of the law. Indeed, it is these very skills that you bring with you that will be vital in molding your analytical abilities in a way that will allow you to move from legal neophyte to practicing attorney.

In this chapter, you will be exposed to some basic concepts of logic and rhetoric that you will need to understand in order for you to get as much as possible from the materials you will read and the discussions you will have with your professors and fellow students. If you took logic in college, much (perhaps all) of this will be familiar. Training in formal logic was once believed to be a good background for one who wished to study law. This view had receded over the years, however. Don't worry though, if you did not take logic in college you are not at a disadvantage. The concepts that we will discuss below are relatively straight-forward and easy to grasp. If you read these materials closely you should be able to mold your inchoate logical abilities to help you make sense of this new and fascinating world of study.

II. Logic in Legal Analysis

> I told [John Marshall] it was law logic—
> an artificial system of reasoning,
> exclusively used in the courts of justice,
> but good for nothing anywhere else.

John Quincy Adams

Law school professors debate about whether lawyers actually think differently than do accountants or mathematicians or philosophers. Some maintain that there **is** something distinct about the way in which lawyers think. James Boyd White, *Doctrine in a Vacuum: Reflections on What a Law School Ought (and Ought Not) To Be*, 35 J. LEGAL EDUC. 155, 161 (1986). Others defend the idea that legal thinking utilizes the same logical abilities that astronauts, physicians, or historians use. John O. Mudd, *Thinking Critically About "Thinking Like a Lawyer,"* 33 J. LEGAL EDUC. 704, 705 (1983). While the subtleties of this debate should not detain us here, you will see over the course of your career that there is a stylized sort of thinking that you will be expected to learn in order to discuss the materials in your law classes. This way of thinking will feel artificial and rigid at first. It may even be hard for you to see the utility of learning how to "think like a lawyer." Rest assured, however, this mode of thinking will help you make sense of the sorts of discourse that judges, lawyers and legislators use as they go about their business. You may even find that this stylized and formal mode of analysis has application beyond the law!

There are several skills or tools that go into this conception of "thinking like a lawyer." Much of this new way of thinking is driven by a new lexicon. The terms and phrases that you will read and hear can be baffling. At first, you should always carry your law dictionary with you. Over time, though, you will become more adept at deciphering the terminology. As you learn the language of the law, concepts will become easier to grasp. You will also be aided by the ability to read and retain densely written materials. Good time management is another useful skill that will enable you to focus on your studies. The primary tool that you will need, however, is a rudimentary grasp of logic and rhetoric. As the German philosopher and social critic Friedrich Nietzsche put it, reason, which is the concrete manifestation of logic, is nothing more than a tool to help us accomplish things more effectively and efficiently. Understanding this will help you because thinking logically is a prerequisite to precise reasoning and communication. In the rest of this chapter we will explore different systems of logic and briefly discuss basic rhetoric in order to introduce those systems to you. Since precision is so vital in this profession, let us begin by looking at formal logic.

A. Formal Logic

Logic is the science of arguments. PAUL TIDMAN AND HOWARD KAHANE, LOGIC AND PHILOSOPHY: A MODERN INTRODUCTION Ch. 1 (8th ed. 1999). Many people who decide to go to law school are told by their family and friends that this is a good choice because they like to argue, and they are good at arguing. You may even be one of these people. This is not what we mean when we use the term argument in the context of logic, however. An **argument**, in this sense, is a group of statements which are claimed to support a conclusion which proves something. *Id.* at 1. Arguments are not opinions but are meant to prove a claim. *Id.* The study of logic enables us to see whether arguments offered are good or bad. In this context, good and bad are not meant to convey any ethically normative or moral importance. As you will see in Section IV, however, "good" arguments can be offered for wrong or immoral purposes. As the Anglo-American conception of legal reasoning is built upon arguments about whether one or more laws apply to certain factual situations, a basic understanding of logic is vital to your studies. RUGGERO J. ALDISERT, LOGIC FOR LAWYERS: A GUIDE TO CLEAR LEGAL THINKING Ch. 1(1997).

Arguments are comprised of premises and a conclusion. PAUL TIDMAN AND HOWARD KAHANE, LOGIC AND PHILOSOPHY: A MODERN INTRODUCTION 1 (8th ed. 1999). The **premises** are those statements which are offered in support of the conclusion. *Id.* The **conclusion** is the statement meant to be proved. *Id.* In effect, premises lay out the reasons or evidence which support the conclusion. A basic argument might look like this:

All crimes are violations of the law.
Theft is a crime.
Therefore, theft is a violation of the law.

As you can see, the premises here (the first and second sentences) lead the reader to the conclusion stated in the third sentence. Paul Tidman and Howard Kahane, Logic and Philosophy: A Modern Introduction 1 (8th ed. 1999). In this very simple argument, as in many arguments, the conclusion is hinted at by an indicator word or phrase (here, "therefore"). Other common indicator words and phrases are: accordingly, as a result, consequently, hence, it follows that, thus and whence.

It is important to note that not all statements made in the course of an argument are necessarily premises in the argument. In normal discourse, our arguments are cluttered with extraneous statements which add little — and perhaps even detract from — the conclusions we hope to advance. Steven J. Burton, An Introduction to Law and Legal Reasoning Ch. 5 (2d ed. 1995). We often weave appeals to emotion, opinions, statements of belief, or warnings into our arguments. These things, which are not actual premises in an argument, can sometimes be effectively used rhetorically. We will discuss this further in Section III. While it may seem as though these things are actually offered to bolster our arguments, they are distinct from the arguments themselves. *Id.* You must be clear about what statements actually serve as the premises and conclusion to an argument, and be able to identify the extraneous statements that can get in the way as you try to make sense of what is being said. *Id.*

It should also be noted that premises can be either true or false. Paul Tidman and Howard Kahane, Logic and Philosophy: A Modern Introduction 8–10 (8th ed. 1999). This probably seems like a fairly obvious thing to say, but you should keep it in mind. As we will see, the validity or strength of an argument will depend on the truth or falsity of all the premises to an argument taken collectively. *Id.* You should be careful not to reject any particular conclusion solely on the fact that one (or more) premise(s) may be false, however. *Id.* A valid or strong conclusion may very well follow from several premises (some of which are true, and some of which are false). *Id.* Now that we have gotten these caveats about premises out of the way, we can move on to the different types of arguments that you are likely to see in the cases and other materials you will read. You will also hear your fellow students and your professors put forth arguments in these forms during your discussions both in and out of class.

In logic, there are two distinct types of argument forms: deductive and inductive. *Id.* **Deductive** arguments are those where it is impossible for the premises to be true and the conclusion false. *Id.* Logicians would say that a valid deductive argument is one where the conclusion *necessarily* follows from the premises. *Id.* In other words, if all (or most) of the premises are true then the conclusion *must* follow as a logical necessity. *Id.* at 4–6. The example above is a valid deductive argument, as is the following:

> The interpretation of the laws is the proper and peculiar province of the courts. A constitution is, in fact, and must be regarded by the judges, as a fundamental law. It therefore belongs to them to ascertain its meaning, as well as the meaning of any particular act proceeding from the legislative body.
>
> Alexander Hamilton
> *Federalist Papers*, No. 78

With both of these arguments, if the premises are true then the conclusion **must** follow. *Id.* at 8–13.

The other form of argument that you will frequently see is the inductive argument. *Id.* at 4–6. An **inductive** argument is one where the premises support the conclusion such that if (most of) the premises are true then it would be improbable for the conclusion to be false. *Id.* In other words, in an inductive argument if (most of) the premises are true then it is likely that the conclusion will be true (but it is not absolutely necessary). *Id.* Inductive arguments play on the probability that the premises make the conclusion likely. *Id.* The following is an inductive argument:

> The Simpson incident had shown me that a dog was kept in the stables, and yet, though someone had been in and had fetched out a horse, he had not barked enough to arouse the two lads in the loft. Obviously the midnight visitor was someone whom the dog knew well.
>
> Arthur Conan Doyle
> *Memoirs of Sherlock Holmes*

An inductive argument that has several compelling premises which lead to a high probability that the conclusion will follow is considered a **strong inductive argument**. *Id.* Since inductive arguments are based on probabilities, the more likely it is that a conclusion will follow from a set of premises the stronger the argument is. *Id.* Conversely, the less likely it is that the conclusion will follow from the premises the weaker the argument is. *Id.*

In your study of the law you will see both deductive and inductive arguments, although the latter will be far more common. There was a time when American legal theorists advanced the idea that law is a science similar to geometry or physics, and that the syllogism (a particular type of deductive argument) should be the dominant argument form in legal discourse. Some are still of this opinion. Ruggero J. Aldisert, Logic for Lawyers: A Guide to Clear Legal Thinking (1997). The examples of this sort of thinking invariably used statutes, which are usually written to accommodate the deductive style of reasoning. *Id.* at Ch. 5. Here is an example:

Burglary Statute in State Z

Burglary is defined in state Z as: Breaking and entering the dwelling house of another at night with the intention of committing a felony therein.

Facts

At 2:00 am on August 1, 2000, Robert George entered the home of Ms. Emilia Robinson through an unlocked window and committed grand larceny (a felony) by taking jewelry and other valuables without Ms. Robinson's knowledge or permission.

As you can no doubt see, if you systematically apply the statutory language to the facts of the case deductively it is apparent that George has committed burglary under the statute. In other words, if it is true that George did all the things in the fact pattern above, then he is necessarily in violation of the burglary statute in state Z. Of course, there are some presumptions built in to this conclusion — i.e., 2:00 am is "night" — but this illustration should serve to show the features of a syllogism.

While you will see this use of the deductive argument form in many situations which require the utilization of statutory or code language, you will more commonly see inductive arguments used in legal discourse. Reading several cases in an attempt to determine what the best answer is to a legal problem is likely to be is an exercise in inductive reasoning. The case law method is, in a sense, a perfect example of inductive reasoning. Because the U.S. legal system, like the British system, is a common law system the dominant form of discourse is the analogy. Steven J. Burton, An Introduction to Law and Legal Reasoning 25 (2d ed. 1995). Analogies compare like situations in order to draw conclusions from the available premises. *Id.* at Ch. 2. When you read cases and apply the legal concepts from those cases to other factual situations, you engage in analogical reasoning. *Id.* Analogies are inductive in nature. *Id.* In the context of the common law, the premises are the holdings in previous cases. As you will learn in your other classes, the common law conception of *stare decisis* suggests that judges ought to follow previous decisions in similar cases.

The art of legal discourse — and it is really more an art than a science — is to draw strong analogies from the cases and other materials that legal decision-makers rely on to show how the case you are discussing does or does not fit into the picture you have developed. Logic and rhetoric are tools to help you do just this. We will discuss how these tools can and should be employed. Before you can employ the sorts of informal logic that legal reasoning requires, you should be at least nominally acquainted with the kinds of problems that people experience when they make arguments for or against things. Being able to recognize these problems in your own arguments, and those proposed by others, will enable you to better analyze the materials you will read and the discussions you will have. In this next section, you will be exposed to a short overview of the kinds of faulty arguments you are likely to see. These faulty arguments are called informal fallacies.

B. Informal Fallacies

In your studies you will be exposed to many arguments—both deductive and inductive—which are defective. A defect in an argument is called a **fallacy**. PATRICK HURLEY, A CONCISE INTRODUCTION TO LOGIC 117 (6th ed. 1997). **Formal fallacies** are structural defects in deductive arguments which require a knowledge of symbolic logic. *Id.* I mentioned above, though, that most legal arguments are not formal or symbolic in nature. As a result, this form of fallacy need not distract our attention here. Defects in the content or substance of an argument are called **informal fallacies**. *Id.* at Ch. 3. These are far more common, and you will see myriad examples of these fallacies in the cases contained in the casebooks that you will buy for your classes. You may also see them in the discussions and debates you participate in as part of your legal education. When you begin to debate and write about the assignments you will be given, you should be on guard against committing these fallacies. Recognizing them when they occur in the arguments of others will give you an insight into the strength or weakness of their positions. You will soon come to realize that many arguments that you would have considered persuasive before you came to law school are full of these fallacies!

I have included a list of the most common types of informal fallacies below, with an example of each. See, PATRICK HURLEY, A CONCISE INTRODUCTION TO LOGIC (6th ed. 1997). As you review this list you will begin to see why each fallacy is problematic, and you can probably think of instances when you have (or someone you know has) made arguments which contain one or more of these fallacies.

1. *Appeal to Force:* This fallacy entails a premise that explicitly or implicitly threatens the reader or hearer with some form of harm if the con-

clusion is not accepted. In essence, a weak argument is made stronger through brute or psychological force.

Example:

Secretary to Boss: "I deserve a raise in salary for the coming year. I do good work, and have been here longer than anyone. Also, you know how friendly I am with your wife, and I'm sure you wouldn't want her to find out what's been going on between you and that sexpot client of yours."

2. *Appeal to Pity*: This form of fallacy occurs when the arguer attempts to elicit support for their conclusion by appealing to a sense of pity in the reader or hearer.

Example:

Taxpayer to Judge: "Your Honor, I admit that I declared thirteen children as dependents on my tax return, even though I have only two. If you find me guilty of tax evasion, however, my reputation will be ruined. I'll probably lose my job, my poor wife will not be able to have the operation that she desperately needs, and my kids will starve. Surely you should find me not guilty."

3. *Appeal to the People*: This type of fallacy involves playing on the emotions or sentiments or impulses of a crowd in order to get them to accept a weakly supported conclusion. There are several forms of this fallacy:

> *Bandwagon Arguments*: The arguer hints that if you do not join in you will be left behind.

Example:

Of course you should use Zest™ soap. Why, 90 percent of Americans shower with Zest.™

> *Appeals to Vanity*: Here the arguer attempts to conceal a weak argument by making the reader or hearer feel like they are inadequate if they do not accept the conclusion.

Example:

The Marlboro Man™ represents the ultimate in masculinity. Marlboro™ cigarettes — for those who stand out as real men.

Appeals to Snobbery: Here the arguer attempts to support their argument by playing on the feelings of many who think that they are somehow better than the rest of society.

Example:

A Rolls Royce™ is not for everyone. If you qualify as one of the select few, this distinguished classic may be seen and driven at British Motor Cars, Ltd. (By appointment only please.)

4. *Argument Against the Person:* These are frequently called *ad hominem* arguments. Here, the arguer attempts to discredit the argument of another by attacking the person making it rather than addressing the argument itself.

Example:

Bill Gates has argued at length that Microsoft Corporation does not have a monopoly on computer disc operating systems. But Gates is chief executive officer of Microsoft, and he wants to avoid antitrust action against his company. Therefore, we should ignore Gates's arguments.

5. *Tu Quoque* (You Too!): This sort of argument involves one arguer attacking the credibility of another by reminding him of transgressions that the second person has committed.

Example:

Lobbyist to Senator: "Senator, it makes no sense for you to support this so-called family values legislation which will hurt my client when you yourself have been in an extramarital relationship for years."

6. *Accident (or mistake):* The accident fallacy is committed when the arguer attempts to address a specific case that falls outside the general rule cited.

Example:

Freedom of speech is a constitutionally guaranteed right. Therefore, John Q. Radical should not be arrested for his speech which incited a riot last week.

7. *Straw Person:* One of the most frequently employed fallacies, this faulty argument involves distorting an opponent's argument to make it easier to defeat.

Example:

The student status committee has presented us with an argument favoring alcohol privileges on campus. What do the students want? Is it their intention to stay boozed up from the day they enter as first year students till the day they graduate? Do they expect us to open a bar for them? Or maybe a chain of bars all over campus? Such a proposal is ridiculous!

8. *Missing the Point:* This fallacy is committed when a series of premises only superficially related are used to support an irrelevant (or distantly relevant) conclusion.

Example:

Politician: Crimes of theft and robbery have been increasing at an alarming rate lately. Surely we must become more serious about crime. The conclusion is obvious: we must reinstate the death penalty immediately!

9. *Red Herring:* The red herring fallacy involves diverting the attention of the reader or hearer by changing the subject of the argument to another subtly related (but distinct) subject.

Example:

Environmentalists are continually harping about the dangers of nuclear power. Unfortunately, electricity is dangerous no matter where it comes from. Every year hundreds of people are electrocuted by accident. Since most of these accidents are caused by carelessness, they could be avoided if people would just exercise greater caution. What do these tree-hugger commies know anyway?

10. *Appeal to Unqualified Authority:* In this fallacy, the arguer relies on an authority who is not qualified, not well-recognized in her field or who is biased. Many good arguments are based on qualified authorities, but watch out for arguments which rely on statements of obscure or prejudiced "authorities."

Example:

James W. Johnson, Chairman of R. J. Reynolds Tobacco Company and a leader in the industry for years, testified before congress that tobacco is not an addictive substance and that smoking cigarettes does not produce any addiction. Therefore, we should believe him and conclude that smoking does not in fact lead to any addiction.

11. *Appeal to Ignorance:* When the premises to an argument suggest to the hearer or reader that nothing definitive can be said about an issue one way or another yet the conclusion takes a position, the arguer is guilty of this fallacy.

Example:

Although numerous hikers have reported seeing Big Foot in the forests of the Pacific Northwest, nobody has ever provided conclusive evidence of the creature's existence. Thus, we can only conclude that Big Foot is a myth.

12. *Hasty Generalization:* Hasty generalizations happen when the arguer draws a conclusion from incomplete premises or has a data set that is too small or skewed.

Example:

Judge Pierson has accepted gifts from lawyers who practice in his court, Judge Atherton is biased against plaintiffs, and Judge Stevens hates women. Clearly, the entire American judicial system is in a shambles.

13. *False Cause:* The false cause fallacy is committed when the arguer attempts to make a link between premises and conclusion based on a causal connection which probably does not exist.

Example:

After Florida relaxed its concealed weapons law, the crime rate dropped. It seems clear that allowing people to carry concealed weapons results in a reduction in crime.

14. *Slippery Slope:* Along with the straw person fallacy, the slippery slope type of argument is one of the most common you will see. The slippery slope starts from a small number of verifiable premises, but then moves to conclusions that are thought to be conceptually linked in a way which proves to be faulty.

Example:

Same-sex marriages should never be sanctioned by the state. If these arrangements are sanctioned, they will become an attractive alternative to heterosexual marriage. Married couples will start abandoning their spouses and link up with same-sex partners. Before long, everyone will adopt this lifestyle and no one will have any children. Sanctioning same-sex marriages could lead to the extinction of the human race!

15. *Weak Analogy:* Since lawyers rely so heavily on analogies, you should be particularly on guard against this type of fallacy. Weak analogies occur when the analogy drawn doesn't support the conclusion, or when the analogy only seems to support the conclusion on first blush.

Example:

When an ordinary citizen hears of a crime, he or she should report it to the police. But a defense attorney is a citizen, just like everyone else. Therefore, when a defense attorney learns in confidence that his or her client has committed a crime, he or she should report it to the police.

16. *Begging the Question:* This fallacy is committed when the arguer uses some sort of phraseology to cover up the fact that a principle premise is not supported by the facts. These arguments often can be identified by the fact that they are circular in nature. That is to say, that this sort of fallacy often involves restating the conclusion in another way as support for the conclusion.

Example:

Capital punishment is justified for the crimes of murder and kidnaping because it is quite legitimate and appropriate that someone be put to death for having committed such hateful and inhuman acts.

17. *Suppressed Evidence:* When an arguer ignores some important piece of known evidence in order to mislead the reader or hearer into drawing a faulty conclusion this fallacy is committed.

Example:

The Second Amendment to the Constitution states that the right of the people to keep and bear arms shall not be infringed. But a law controlling handguns would infringe the right to keep and bear arms. Therefore, a law controlling handguns would be unconstitutional.

As you will have no doubt noticed, these flaws are common in our everyday discourse. These sorts of fallacies are rife in our public debates (especially on many news/talk stations). What you will be required to do as part of your legal training is to tighten up the way you think, and be more precise in the way you discuss the situations you encounter both in and out of the classroom. "Thinking like a lawyer" requires you to be more exacting in terms of what you would accept as a persuasive and acceptable argument. This will drive your friends and family crazy as you will probably try to force them to be more exacting as well, but you will begin to see the world in a more precise way. And precision is, after all, extremely important in legal analysis and communication. When you read the newspaper, when you listen to National Public Radio, or watch the news, you will begin to analyze the things you hear and see in a new way. You will (or should) begin to notice that normal discourse—especially the discourse found in the media—is extremely imprecise and logically faulty. Once this begins to happen, you can be satisfied that you are beginning to use the tools we are discussing to their fullest. Do not be confused by what we have covered thus far in this chapter. As I said, you need not be a logician to make the most out of your legal education or to be a good lawyer, and you will normally not be expected to identify and discuss fallacies (formal or informal) in your classes. Instead, you will be expected to think logically, and recognize when others are not doing so. This is, at base, a pragmatic enterprise. Traditional theories of logic attempt to systematize things in a way that legal professionals would not find particularly useful. Viewing human reason as a more pragmatic endeavor, however, more closely approximates the practical reasoning of lawyers and judges. We should now look, then, at how your analytical skills can be employed in a useful and pragmatic way.

C. Pragmatic Logic

Very few people actually engage in a conscious process of logical deduction or inference. Fewer still actually attempt to explicitly plot out or construct arguments that fulfill the requirements of either formal or informal logic (these are called "proofs" by logicians). Instead, invariably most of us work subconsciously as we analyze and develop our notions of how new information should be digested, categorized and used. Lawyers do this all the time. You may have heard someone working in a legal context, or you will almost certainly hear someone at some point in your career, say that they thought through a legal problem "on the fly." What they mean when they say this is not that there is no basis for their analysis and conclusions, but that they did not consciously make the logic explicit (to the extent their analysis and conclusions are logical). Experts in all domains of knowledge frequently do this. This sort of practice is not illegitimate and should not be dismissed out of hand. What these experts are doing is to utilize their reasoning skills, developed within their domain, to quickly and informally process information, assess options, and draw conclusions. In fact, the ability to do this may be the mark of someone who has moved from novice to expert in their domain. In this section, we will explore how this informal process is carried out and utilized, and what the implications are for you as you move from novice to expert.

On initial consideration this idea of analyzing, processing and drawing conclusions "on the fly" may seem strange, and even irresponsible. It would be irresponsible if such a move were carried out by someone who had no knowledge or experience in the domain. It might also be inappropriate or irresponsible if such a move were negligently used to substitute for hard work and professional competency. This is not what I mean at all. The process of reasoning that I am describing here is complex and comprehensive. This reasoning just does not conform to what logicians and philosophers have traditionally developed as formal or informal systems of logic. This notion of human logic resists the attempts of others to apply it to legal reasoning. This is why, in fact, you do not have to be an expert in logic or philosophy in order to be a good lawyer, or to think about the law in insightful and useful ways. In its truest sense, this sort of reasoning is pragmatic. John Dewey, *Logical Method and the Law*, 10 Cornell L.Q., 17 (1924).

One could perhaps make the argument that at a certain level almost all reasoning is pragmatic in the sense that human beings as a species think in certain ways in order to understand, address and deal with situations or problems they confront. John Dewey, Logic: The Theory of Inquiry Ch. 2 (1991). This is as true when we buy groceries as it is when we put a human on the moon. Very rarely do we sit down and construct logical proofs to show us the best — or most logically valid or sound — ways to think about and address these situations and problems. Human beings tend to adapt to and develop concepts, structures, and ideas that work. This determination is invariably made through informal experimental methods. Here again, I am not talking about the formal scientific method that you may be familiar with (which is, by the way, heavily dependent on the sorts of formal and informal logic discussed above). Human beings engage in an informal experimentalism every day, and on almost every problem or concern they think about. The philosopher John Dewey called this "experimental logic." John Dewey, *Logical Method and the Law*, 10 Cornell L.Q. 17, 18 (1924).

Dewey, who has been associated with the American philosophical movement called "pragmatism," believed that discussions of formal and informal logical systems were not as useful as logicians and other philosophers tend to think. According to Dewey, and many who followed him, logic should not be thought of as an abstract enterprise, but as an every day tool utilized by reasoning, problem-solving beings. JOHN DEWEY, LOGIC: THE THEORY OF INQUIRY Ch. 3 (1991). This metaphor — reasoning or experimental logic as a tool to accomplish our mental work — is used by pragmatists like Dewey to effectively illustrate how thinking should be conceived. Instead of a dusty private language that logicians and rationalist philosophers use to "prove" whether an argument is "valid" or "sound," advocates of pragmatic conceptions of reasoning maintain that all humans display a common pattern of reasoning. *Id.* at 105. This pattern is adapted to specific contexts — like professional domains, for example — but is largely based on our inchoate abilities as members of the species. *Id.* at Ch. 2.

Several questions arise in the context of this alternative to traditional logical systems. For example, what characterizes this pragmatic or experimental logic? How would an experimental logic like that advocated by John Dewey help us better understand how we can think more clearly, precisely, and usefully? Finally, and perhaps most importantly in the context of the present discussion, how can understanding and using a pragmatic or experimental logic make you a better law student, and ultimately a better lawyer? A more complete and thorough discussion of Dewey's pragmatic logic is discussed in Chapter Five, but a short discussion here should help you see the attractiveness of such a view; especially in light of the abstract and technical nature of the formal and informal logical systems we looked at above.

According to Dewey, the first step in this experimental or pragmatic reasoning process is the recognition that there is a problem that needs to be solved. JOHN DEWEY, HOW WE THINK Ch. 6 (1991). This recognition kicks our inchoate reasoning abilities into gear. Once we realize that there is a problem that needs to be addressed, we attempt to categorize this problem into known classes of situations in order to give some context to the problem and possible solutions. *Id.* In other words, once we realize there is a problem that we need to address we attempt to classify it with other similar problems we have confronted in the past. This helps us determine the kinds of things that might help us resolve the problem. The next step in this process, after recognition of the problem and the classification of that problem, is the determination of a solution. *Id.* In a way, this is almost a pre-determination of a solution. It is a pre-determination because this solution is perhaps not a final solution. It is only an initial thought of what might work given the problem presented and the classification of that problem into a recognizable and understandable category. *Id.* Once we fix upon this pre-determination of a solution, we then begin to reason more systematically and thoroughly about whether this proposed solution will actually address the problem. At this stage, we will "means test" the pre-determined solution for suitability, often discarding it in favor of more developed and narrowly tailored solutions that address the problem more closely. *Id.* This is a trial and error process that ultimately leads to accepting one of the proposed solutions as the best one given the circumstances. *Id.* It is also this trial and error process that compelled Dewey to call this "experimental reasoning." *Id.* Finally, near the end of this experimental process, we assess the overall effectiveness of our solution. *Id.* If it addresses the problem, the process of reasoning is done. If the solution is not sufficient, we move back and evaluate other possible solutions. *Id.*

This description may sound like another technical or abstract process, but it is really more intuitive than this description makes it sound. If you think about it, this process pretty closely resembles our reasoning on everyday run of the mill problems. Think about sitting at your desk as you read this book. What if the lamp on your desk went out? You would probably intuitively go through a process much like that described above. First you would recognize that there was a problem; the light went out! Then, you would almost immediately conclude that it was caused by one of several things: the light bulb burned out, the electricity failed, the wiring in the lamp shorted out, etc. In essence, you categorize the problem into several of the types of problems you have experienced in like or similar situations before. From this array of options, you would likely choose the most probable (the bulb), and pre-determine this is the most likely cause. You would probably remove the bulb (and if you are like me shake it to see if the filament inside is broken), and perhaps put in a new bulb to see if that rectifies the situation. If it does not, you will quickly go down the list of other possible solutions until one works.

As you can see, this almost exactly follows the process that Dewey describes. The interesting thing is that you do not need to be an expert in any particular kind of logical or philosophical theory to make sense out of this "logic." It is intuitive and natural. It is also applicable in almost any situation, whether you are trying to determine why the cable television is out or how to argue a complex question of law before the State Supreme Court. The only difference between trying to figure out why the light went out or why your cable will not work and an argument before the Supreme Court is that the latter is partially determined by one being exposed to, and trained in, the discourse community of the law.

We will resume this discussion in much more detail in Chapter Five. What is important for you to recognize here is that this form of reasoning is another tool to help you in your analytical development. As Dewey maintains, you have these reasoning abilities already. You were born with them. You can do some things to hone and develop these abilities though. And you will have to adapt them to this new discourse community. In a sense, "thinking like a lawyer" just means using logic—sometimes (perhaps rarely) formal, sometimes (more frequently) informal, and sometimes (most often) experimental—to aid you in your attempt to recognize, address and solve problems. Logic (of whatever sort) is simply an analytical tool you can utilize to assist you in your life and your work. Being more conscious of your own thinking will give you insights into how you can be more effective and efficient at solving problems. This will help you in your life and help you do your job. Different sorts of logical systems are not the only set of analytical tools that you have at your disposal. Focusing too closely or exclusively on the logic employed in analyzing and addressing a problem has its own disadvantages. There are many other analytical tools that you will need in order to move from novice to expert in the domain of the law. A closely related tool that you will also need to develop is a working knowledge of legal rhetoric. It is to this topic that we now turn.

Differences
The Differences Between Formal Logic and Pragmatic Logic

You will have noticed that we have been using the term logic in two different ways. We have referred in this chapter to formal logic and the basic concepts that go with systems employing formal logic. We have also used this in connection with the pragmatic reasoning we just discussed. This should not confuse you. "Logic" simply refers to any system of human reasoning that allows us to display our knowledge.

The traditional philosophical or logical models of human reasoning attempted to formalize logic into a completely closed system. Often, these systems were meant to represent complete and scientific models of reasoning. The history of Western thought is rife with examples of well known philosophers and mathematicians constructing what they hoped to be perfect systems of logic and knowledge. Many times, in fact, these systems of logic were based on mathematical models. It was thought that the only way for human knowledge could be perfected, the only way we could think clearly and precisely, was to make our thinking conform to strict logical systems.

This view had a heavy influence of all areas of human concern. With the development of the scientific method and advances in human knowledge related to the natural world, systems incorporating logical or scientific "laws" into virtually every domain of human concern were common. It was widely assumed that any domain of human concern in which specific knowledge or data is gathered and systematized would benefit from application of strict logical or scientific systems. As we noted above, this led to the development of so-called "scientific sys-tems of law," and to the widespread assumption that formal logic should be the model of good and precise legal thinking.

In the late nineteenth and early twentieth centuries, however, this view began to be questioned. With the development of pragmatism in philosophy and legal realism in legal theory, the idea that legal think-ing can (or should) mirror strict logical systems fell into disrepute. Theorists like John Dewey, Oliver Wendell Holmes, Jr., and Benjamin Cardozo recognized that sound and good legal thinking very often looked nothing like a formal logical proof. They further maintained that attempting to yoke legal reasoning by the "laws" of formal logic is constraining and artificial. Such attempts detract from the practi-cal nature of legal problem-solving. They, and others who held these same convictions, suggested that good and precise legal reasoning is looser and more informal than any system of traditional logic can ac-count for. The alternative — what we have been calling pragmatic logic — was developed to more closely represent the way expert legal thinkers actually think, instead of the way a logician might suggest they ought to think.

This pragmatic view is widely held today in the U.S. legal system. While some, like U.S. Circuit Court Judge Richard Posner, explicitly acknowledge and write about pragmatism and logic, most other lawyers employ pragmatic logic in their day to day activities whether they know it or not. This "logic" is a much more natural and useful way of thinking about legal problems. Though there are surely some in the legal academy who will maintain attempts to bootstrap legal reason-ing into a formal logical paradigm, these attempts are marginal and fruitless. If you understand how to solve problems in the domain in a flexible and dynamic way, you will be employing pragmatic logic.

III. Rhetoric

Legal rhetoric is a mix of logic, emotion, exhortation, and social policy that is designed to persuade the reader or hearer that one position is better than another. Being able to recognize the different kinds of arguments — both good and bad — that we briefly discussed above will greatly aid you in your task as you study the law. You will rarely see clear-cut examples of any of the above types of arguments set out alone, however. Invariably, the arguments offered against or in support of one position or another are buried deep in what I have called legal discourse. Loosely speaking, legal discourse is any discussion—written or oral—about the law and its application. While these types of discussions are often full of arguments, they are usually designed to persuade someone to accept or reject a position. Anthony T. Kronman, *Rhetoric*, 67 U. Cin. L. Rev. 677, 677 (1999). Logic helps in this task, but it is properly subsumed in the context of legal rhetoric. *Id.*

Most of you have probably heard someone dismiss the arguments of another out of hand by saying that they are "just rhetoric." This derogatory use of the term is usually meant to serve as a shorthand way of saying that an argument is not one that should be seriously analyzed because it is not worth the trouble. We will be using rhetoric in a very different way. In the context of legal reasoning, rhetoric is a very important element in the construction of legal discourse. Properly speaking, rhetoric is the application of logic to oral discourse. Legal theorists have expanded this definition to include any form of communication which is meant to persuade the hearer or reader.

Rhetoric, in this expanded legal sense, involves the careful crafting of a series of arguments which purport to develop a legal position. When you read and hear (and later begin to write and discuss) this sort of persuasive rhetoric, you will see that the law draws upon all sorts of cultural, political, and historical referents. These things, added to the language of the law and the common educational experience of lawyers in our legal system, create a tapestry of discourse that will seem baffling at first. Over time, however, you will begin to see patterns in the rhetoric. It should not take long for you to begin to realize that certain ways of presenting legal positions are more persuasive than others. You will see this pattern emerge as you work through your casebooks in contracts, property, and torts.

What is important for you to understand now is that you must analyze the materials you read and the discussions and lectures you hear in a much more exacting and thorough manner than you did prior to coming to law school. Your task, as a law student, will be to test the arguments and positions you will be exposed to in order to see whether they really add up to what the arguer suggests. Judges and lawyers use rhetoric in order to persuade others that their understanding of cases is the correct one. Richard A. Posner, Law, Pragmatism, and Democracy 82–84 (2003). In effect, every opinion written by a judge and every memorandum or brief written by a lawyer is a rhetorical device designed to persuade others that the author is correct. You must always look into these arguments, and subject them to scrutiny. Is there substance to the position offered, and if so does the arguer reason through their position in a way that you (and others) can understand? You need not study formal rhetorical theory (although you might find it interesting and helpful) to make this assessment.

This type of analysis should take place on several different levels. First, you should try to understand what the arguer is trying to prove. What is the purpose of the legal discourse to which you are being exposed? Once you have an idea of what the overall theme or purpose of the discourse is, you should then look closer to analyze the different rhetorical methods which the arguer has employed to "prove" her position. Has she drawn upon your emotions or biases? Has she attempted to develop a line of arguments which depend upon a certain specialized or cultural knowledge? Are there gaps in the arguments? This will give you an insight into the methods of persuasion that the arguer is using. Finally, once you have a better picture of the rhetorical methods employed you should look at the logic of each individual argument which makes up a piece of the larger position. Are there any fallacies embedded within the arguments offered? Does the logic of the argument make sense, or does it seem to fit your pragmatic conception of how the problem might be solved?

Logic and rhetoric are tools in the bag of any well trained lawyer. Over time, you will become comfortable both analyzing the legal discourse of others and constructing your own. This should not be done haphazardly, however. You really cannot "fly by the seat of your pants" when you do this sort of work. You need to be conscientious and thorough. If you are not, something important is likely to slip by you. This ability—along with the other skills we collectively call "thinking like a lawyer"—can only be developed over time. It will take a lot of hard work (and usually a lot of frustration), but it is worth it in the end. Just be sure that your use of these tools is guided by a conscious sense of professionalism and morality. RICHARD A. ZITRIN AND CAROL LANGFORD, THE MORAL COMPASS OF THE AMERICAN LAWYER: TRUTH, JUSTICE, POWER, AND GREED 3–4 (2000). This is so important, in fact, that we will conclude with a few words about the proper use of logic and rhetoric in the context of morality and professionalism.

IV. Using Analytical Tools Responsibly and with Professionalism

Passion and prejudice govern the
world; only under the name of reason.

John Wesley

Before you came to law school, you were undoubtedly exposed to the cultural stereotypes with which lawyers must contend. There are countless lawyer jokes, and it seems as though hardly anyone trusts lawyers very much. RICHARD A. ZITRIN AND CAROL LANGFORD, THE MORAL COMPASS OF THE AMERICAN LAWYER: TRUTH, JUSTICE, POWER, AND GREED pp. 2–4 (2000). Indeed, some of you were probably asked by your family and friends why you would even want to enter the legal profession at all. There are many reasons for this, but certainly one important factor is the propensity of lawyers to use the sort of reasoning skills that they possess (which they began to hone and develop in law school) to get someone who has clearly done something wrong out of trouble, or to confuse an issue so that certain interests prevail. *Id.* at 47. These characterizations are, of course, artificial and subject to one's perspective, but there seems to be a widespread belief that lawyers are involved in this sort of thing all the time. This belief may be factually inaccurate (most lawyers probably do not engage in this sort of behavior), but it happens enough to perpetuate the belief. It is a widely held perception that lawyers in the U.S. are hired guns who will develop whatever argument they need in order to get their client what they want. *Id.* at 189–190. Just as Socrates was accused over two thousand years ago by the people of Athens of "making the weaker argument seem the stronger," lawyers in our society are often seen as using the tools of logic and rhetoric to subvert, rather than serve and preserve the interests of justice.

Every lawyer has the responsibility, both the professional and moral responsibility, to check their work on many different levels. *Id.* at 236. As you will learn in your class on professional responsibility, there are many rules which govern what lawyers can and cannot do. *Id.* There are no rules, however, which require that you use logic and rhetoric in a just and reasonable way. This is left to the discretion of every member of the profession. One of the principle fallacies lawyers make—a fallacy which I did not mention above—is to use the rigors of logical analysis and rhetorical persuasion in morally questionable and professionally irresponsible ways. The sort of behavior which falls into this category is open to debate, but there are undoubtedly many instances which even the untrained eye can discern as being over the line. Making a sound and persuasive argument for an improper purpose is something that reflects poorly on the lawyer who makes such an argument, as well as the profession as a whole. *Id.* at 163–168. Be careful about how you use the tools we have been discussing. Like any tools they can be used powerfully in the right way, but they can be used just as powerfully in the wrong way. You should always subject the arguments you make, and those which you hear others make, to a final analysis based in morality and professionalism. *Id.* at 236. If you do so, you will be living up to the highest standards of the profession.

V. Conclusion

The study of logic and rhetoric can be intimidating to many people. You will benefit tremendously from the understanding and use of these abilities in your new profession, however. I have attempted to show in this chapter that you can use your innate logical and reasoning abilities in your legal studies and in your career. While some rudimentary formal training in logic and rhetoric — the kind you might get here or in some of your law school classes — will help you more quickly understand the patterns of legal discourse (especially the historical patterns), remember that legal reasoning is a practical enterprise. Recognizing the logical or rhetorical moves being made is one ability that you might develop through such training. More important, however, is the ability to reason through legal problems pragmatically. You already have the mental tools available to you to be successful in this. You must simply hone and sharpen your skills of practical reasoning in a way that will enable you to both conceptualize and communicate your reasoning to others. You should not be shy about testing yourself (and others) on the logic involved when you make claims or arguments. You should test both the logic and morality involved in these claims and arguments. This will help you understand both the strength and persuasiveness of your work. Doing this will also make it easier to spot weaknesses in the logic and rhetoric of others. "Thinking like a lawyer" is, in a very real sense, the culmination of these abilities.

Checkpoints

- Do you understand the differences between formal, informal and pragmatic logic? In what situations might each be useful? Which is most useful to legal professionals?

- Can you identify the logical and rhetorical devices that your classmates and your professors use? Can you see such devices in the cases you read? What is your assessment of the relative strengths and weaknesses of these devices when you encounter them?

- When would formal logic be helpful in legal analysis?

- Why is inductive reasoning more prevalent in the U.S. legal system? What does it mean when we say that the common law system is an example of inductive reasoning?

- How does pragmatic logic differ from the other forms of logic that we have discussed? Do you think that pragmatic logic is more practical?

- What is the relationship between rhetoric and legal discourse? Is rhetoric always an element of legal analysis and communication?

- What are the ethical or moral responsibilities of members of the profession regarding their use of logic? Do you agree that every member of the profession must police themselves regarding the proper use of logic and rhetoric? Why or why not?

Chapter 4

Advanced Analytical Tools in Legal Analysis

Roadmap to Advanced Analytical Tools in Legal Analysis

- Rule-based reasoning involves utilizing a variety of interpretative techniques in finding, formulating, and communicating about legal rules.

- Legal rules can be constructed as balancing tests, elements tests, or factors tests. The choice of which will determine the way the rule is formulated, interpreted, and used.

- The dominant analytical model used in legal analysis and communication is the analogy. Analogies, and counter-analogies, involve showing how legal authorities lead to certain outcomes in specific factual situations.

- Synthesizing case law into complex rules will allow you to develop precedents that yield more than the sum of their constituent parts.

- Statutory interpretation involves more than just reading and understanding the words used in the statutes you read. Statutory interpretation is a complicated interpretative enterprise that will require you to determine meaning beyond the test of the statutes you use.

I. Introduction

In the first three chapters we have explored the basic structure and format of legal education in the U.S., several analytical paradigms that will assist you as you enter the legal discourse community, and different forms of logic that are employed in legal reasoning. The progression of these chapters has been designed to assist you on your journey to becoming a full-fledged expert in the U.S. legal system, to help you understand this journey, and to equip you with the sorts of analytical tools you will need along the way. Moving from novice to expert in the law requires more than an understanding of logic and the use of analytical paradigms, however. To complete this journey, you will have to develop more advanced analytical tools that will make your legal analysis and communication more skillful and nuanced. The metaphor of law school as a journey is a useful one. It is used extensively and effectively by Ruta Stropus and Charlotte Taylor. Ruta K. Stropus and Charlotte D. Taylor, Bridging the Gap Between College and Law School (2001). If you keep in mind that you are on a continuing journey into this new discourse community, you will better understand the need for building on the more formal and rigid foundations we discussed earlier. This chapter is designed to help you understand and learn these tools. Below we will examine the processes of rule-based reasoning, analogical (and counter-analogical) reasoning, synthesizing case law, policy reasoning, and statutory construction. Developing these skills in a deeper and more textured way will make your legal analysis much richer, another sure sign that you are gaining expertise in the domain.

You will be introduced to these skills as you enter the domain as a novice. In fact, many of the paradigmatic and logic lessons that we have discussed in previous chapters are rudimentary steps to these more advanced skills. Thinking logically and following analytical models that will assist you in your work and studies are the foundation for being able to engage in these more advanced forms of reasoning. As a result, there is really no conceptual distinction between the rudimentary use of your analytical abilities and the more advanced forms of legal reasoning. Instead, this can more accurately be described as a progression, an evolution of your intellectual abilities. This evolution is formed and shaped by your introduction and growing incorporation into the profession. In other words, when you begin to shape and funnel your thinking abilities so that you actually begin to "think like a lawyer" without being prompted, and without the conscious use of formalized models, your education will pay its biggest dividends. When you actually incorporate these traits into your thinking without consciously thinking about them, you cease to be a novice and become an expert.

The sections of this chapter are intended to help you move from a basic understanding of several analytically important concepts, to a more complex and expert understanding of those concepts. You will hear a great deal in many of your classes about how to use rules and rule-base structures, but here we will examine what this means in a more direct and deliberate way. We will flesh out what it means when your professors say that you need to understand and use legal rules, and associate that understanding and use to the way legal experts work with rules. Similarly, we will delve more deeply and directly into using analogies in legal analysis and communication. Simple analogies and counter-analogies comprise the bulk of your studies in your law school classes. Understanding the details of how analogies work, however, is more complicated than you might imagine. We will also discuss how experts synthesize case law, weaving together a series of cases to develop more comprehensive and robust rules. Then we will examine public policy analysis, a topic many novices struggle with. Finally, we will briefly explore the art of statutory interpretation. Together, understanding and being able to use these advanced analytical skills will be a big step in your intellectual and practical development. Let us begin by looking at rule-based reasoning.

II. Rule-Based Reasoning

Rules form the tapestry of ideas that lawyers work with in the legal system. As Professor Linda Edwards puts it, a "rule of law ... is a statement that explains the test for deciding [a] particular legal issue." Linda Edwards, Legal Writing: Process, Analysis and Organization 17 (4th ed. 2006). When we talk about rules, we are referring to constitutions, statutes, regulations, and ordinances. We also use the term "rule" when we are talking about legal principles derived from case law. Colloquial usage within the profession is somewhat loose. Lawyers often call things "rules" which, strictly speaking, do not carry the force of law. This is a social convention that has bled over to the profession. Any time we have some sort of outward constraint on someone else's behavior, we tend to call this constraint a rule. Games have rules, social institutions have rules, religious denominations have rules, and so on. Just because a rule does not carry the force of law does not mean that such a rule is not important. Nor are rules normally the sorts of things that are discretely and mechanically defined. Rule-based reasoning usually allows for a certain amount of latitude in the way rules are articulated.

Statutes are perhaps the most clear example of rules in our legal system. Statutes that are still in effect are rules that carry the effect of law in a direct and immediate way. These rules direct and control the behavior of those in our society. Traditionally there has been a close conceptual association between these statutory rules and the law. As a result statutes are often used as paradigm examples of what "rules" are in our system. Steven J. Burton, An Introduction to Law and Legal Reasoning 18–23 (2d ed. 1995). Consider one of the examples we looked at in Chapter Three:

> Burglary is defined in state Z as: Breaking and entering the dwelling house of another at night with the intention of committing a felony therein.

This rule is pretty straightforward, and is generally fairly easy to understand. This rule, as enacted by the legislature in state Z, has the force of law, and is designed to keep people from burgling others in state Z (or at least to allow the state to punish those who break this rule). When a set of facts are applied to this rule, we can see how rudimentary logical deduction works in legal analysis:

> At 2:00 a.m. on August 1, 2000, Robert George entered the home of Ms. Emilia Robinson through an unlocked window and committed grand larceny (a felony) by taking jewelry and other valuables without Ms. Robinson's knowledge or permission.

By applying these facts to the rule, we can see that if the state can prove their case Mr. George will in all likelihood be convicted under the statute. Some scholars attempt to use this model as the way rule-based reasoning ought to work in our system.

There is one significant weakness in this position, however. In the U.S. legal system, understanding rules is an interpretative enterprise. You might have noticed in our example that there are several concepts embedded within the burglary statute in state Z that are ambiguous. For example, what does "breaking" mean? What about "entering"? Does one have to own her home before it becomes a "dwelling house," or does that designation attach if she is renting? When is it "night"? As you can see, the answers to these questions will determine greatly George's potential guilt under the statute.

The answers to questions like these are almost never included in the text of our statutes (otherwise, codes would be thousands and thousands of pages longer than they already are). Instead, the basic rules found in statutes are interpreted over time by judges who apply the statutes to the particular cases that come before them. To find the answers to the questions I listed above, then, you would have to research the case law in state Z and see how the judges have defined these terms. If they have not been clearly defined, then you will have to engage in an even more complex interpretive enterprise.

Most rules in the U.S. legal system are not discrete and well-defined like the rules in a Parker Brothers game. The well-known legal scholar Karl Llewelyn described rules in this way:

> We have discovered in our teaching of the law that general propositions are empty. We have discovered that students who come eager to learn the rules and who do learn them, *and who learn nothing more*, will take away the shell and not the substance. We have discovered that rules *alone*, mere forms of words, are worthless. We have learned that the concrete instance, the heaping up of concrete instances, is necessary in order to make any general proposition, be it rule of law

or any other, *mean* anything at all. Without the concrete instances the general proposition is baggage, impedimenta, stuff about the feet. It not only does not help. It hinders.

Karl N. Llewelyn, The Bramble Bush 12 (1951).

As you can see, rules are not simple things. They sometimes carry the force of law, but not always. Often, rules are open to a great deal of interpretation. Steven J. Burton, An Introduction to Law and Legal Reasoning 18–23 (2d ed. 1995). In fact, what lawyers often mean when they use the term "rule" is not a static model of statutory enactment that is clear and needs no interpretation, but is instead an articulation of a legal principle from a judge's opinion. *Id.* Because of this, how rules are viewed and used can change over time. *Id.* Sometimes these opinions consist of judges interpreting statutes. Other times these opinions are simply judges filling the gaps in the law. H.L.A. Hart, The Concept of Law 129–131 (1961).

All of this is a perfectly legitimate and accepted part of our legal system. What it means for you, however, is that you must let go of the idea that rules are simple and easy to use concepts that can be found and applied in a mechanical way. Law in the U.S., and legal practice in our system, is not the mechanical application of discrete rules to specific instances. There are some who cling to such a notion, or at least profess to, but these people are in an extreme minority. If rules were easy to apply in a mechanical way, computers would be better lawyers than humans. Some have even tinkered with the idea of developing artificial intelligence systems to carry out such tasks. Nevertheless, most people who work in the U.S. legal system see that this sort of formalism is, as Llewellyn says, worthless. There just is no simple way to find and use rules. There is no "black letter" rule book for the law (notwithstanding the attempts of many to construct them).

This often creates a bit of an intellectual crisis for novices in the law. I am sure anyone who has taught law students (particularly first year law students) in the U.S. during the last 100 years would love to have a dime for every time they were told by one of their students that they "just want to know the law," or that we should "just tell them the rules." I know I would! As Llewellyn suggests, though, this is a novice mistake. Experts in the domain know that rule-based reasoning is a complex and multifaceted analytical skill. Richard K. Neumann, Jr., Legal Reasoning and Legal Writing: Structure, Strategy, and Style Ch. 2 (4th ed. 2001). It is a skill, in fact, that allows for a great deal of creativity within the domain. *Id.* This creativity comes from the fact that the complex and varied tapestry of legal rules and their articulation allows lawyers and judges to mold and re-articulate rules in ways that work for them. That is to say, experts in the domain use legal rules in creative ways by combining, shaping, and applying them to the circumstances they and their clients face.

If rules were discrete and easy to use, if our system was a formal positivist one, students might find some comfort in that. Experts in the law, however, would not. Such formalist, positivist conceptions of law might be a crutch for novices, but they are a cage for lawyers who want to adapt law to particular instances. RICHARD A. POSNER, LAW, PRAGMATISM, AND DEMOCRACY 19 (2003). Since law is a social institution, one that (at least in the U.S.) is designed to adapt to new circumstances and evolve over time, our conception of rules must be more nuanced and subtle. Throughout our history experts in our system have developed a conception of rules that is flexible and mutable. This view suggests that rules can be molded and changed depending on how they are articulated. Rules are shaped by the words used and how these words are likely to be interpreted. Law is, after all, a discourse community. JILL J. RAMSFIELD, THE LAW AS ARCHITECTURE: BUILDING LEGAL DOCUMENTS 16–20 (2000). Viewing rules in this way is an opportunity for experts in the system to help shape the system, not just act as "apparatchiks" mechanically putting pegs into their proper holes.

Before we discuss the full implications of this tremendous opportunity to utilize our analytical abilities in creative and formative ways, let us pause here and discuss three different types of rule structures. These are important because the structure a rule takes will have considerable impact upon how it will be interpreted and how it can be used. *Id.* Rules can be stated as either "balancing tests," "elements tests," or "factors tests." LINDA EDWARDS, LEGAL WRITING: PROCESS, ANALYSIS AND ORGANIZATION Ch. 2 (4th ed. 2006). There are other possible rule structures (for example, "conjunctive tests," "disjunctive tests," and "simple declarative" rule structures), but for the purposes of our discussion here, these three most common formulations will be suitably instructive. *Id.* at 19–22. The choice to categorize any particular rule as a "balancing test," an "elements test," or a "factors test" rule is often not clear. *Id.* at Ch. 17. In fact, it is often up to the judge or lawyer who is advancing the test to make this determination (providing, of course, an argument for why their interpretation is correct). Nonetheless, you will see many examples of each of these forms. Accordingly, let us look at these different styles of rule formulation.

A. Balancing Tests

There is something seemingly intuitive about balancing tests. Perhaps that is why they are so common in legal reasoning. We often think of things in "either-or" structures. You might find yourself thinking something like this : "Tonight I could study some more for my contracts class, or I could go to the basketball game." This is a simple balancing test. You could restate this as a rule, but it would probably be a waste of time. Your mind just works that way. When you have a lot to do, and there are competing obligations and desires, you will likely engage in a balancing of interests to determine what you should do (and what you will do — these are frequently not the same thing). So, balancing tests should not seem strange to you.

Balancing tests are designed to weigh the interests of one position or interest against another competing position or interest. These tests provide some mechanism to assist legal decision-makers in assessing which of the competing positions or interests should prevail. Consider this example:

> A party must respond to properly propounded interrogatories unless the burden of responding substantially outweighs the questioning party's legitimate need for the information.

Linda Edwards, Legal Writing: Process, Analysis and Organization 20–21 (4th ed. 2006). As you no doubt will notice, this rule sets up a balancing between the "burden of responding" and the competing "legitimate need for the information." This balancing is a judgment call, and will depend on the facts associated with the particular case, but nevertheless this rule provides a fairly clear guideline as to what interests must be compared and contrasted. *Id.*

Balancing tests are very often general in their structure. What this means is that once the competing interests are provided, the general balancing test usually does not give a tremendous amount of guidance as to how the interests should be weighed. When this is true, this gives a great deal of latitude to the legal decision-maker. Sometimes, a balancing test will incorporate another sub-rule to guide the balancing. *Id.* Such sub-rules might be elements tests or factors tests that can give the legal decision-maker some help as to how to make the decision. *Id.* Consider the following additions to the rule we discussed above:

"burden of answering"

- the time and effort necessary to answer;
- the cost of compiling the information;

- any privacy concerns of the objecting party;
- and other circumstances raised by that particular party's situation.

vs.

"legitimate need for the information"

- how important the information would be to the issues of the trial;
- whether the information would be available from some other source or in some other form;
- any other circumstances relating to the party's need for the information.

Id. at 21. You can no doubt see that this additional information (which was derived from other rules that I have called sub-rules because they relate to the more general rule about interrogatories) will give the decision maker much more to go on in deciding how to weigh these competing interests. Do not be fooled, however, there will still be a lot of discretion vested in the decision-maker.

The most important thing to keep in mind is that balancing tests are mechanisms designed to compare some interests against other interests. Recognizing what these competing interests are and how to weigh them is key. If you can determine these things, working with balancing tests is pretty easy because of their intuitive nature. Be sure to assess the sub-rules that will give guidance about how the weighing should be carried out. *Id.* at 20–21. Are some things more important than others? How should the interests be aligned and are there any special considerations that ought to be factored in? Questions like these help you understand the full texture of balancing tests and how they work.

B. Elements Tests

Elements tests are a little more complicated than balancing tests. These sorts of rules gather together related requirements stated in a rule, and organizes them. Richard K. Neumann, Jr., Legal Reasoning and Legal Writing: Structure, Strategy, and Style § 2.1 (4th ed. 2001). Think of elements as a list of required attributes that must be met before the test can be satisfied. The attributes of an elements test are frequently numbered. Taken together these attributes—or elements—comprise the parts of the rule. Let's look at the burglary example we discussed earlier in the chapter:

> Burglary is defined in state Z as: Breaking and entering the dwelling house of another at night with the intention of committing a felony therein.

On its face, this might not look like an elements test. But if you look deeper, you will probably see that in state Z burglary is defined by several attributes or elements. We can rewrite this rule to bring out this elemental structure. Sometimes this reorganizing and rewriting is called diagraming. *Id.*, at 18.

Diagraming a rule has great application. Diagraming rules makes them easier for you to use and apply. *Id.* In the context of elements tests, for example, diagraming these rules will make it easier for you to see what the parts of the rule are, and how there parts operate together. *Id.* The burglary statute from state Z might be diagramed in the following way:

> Burglary is committed in state Z when one (1) breaks and (2) enters (3) the dwelling home (4) of another (5) at night (6) with the intention of committing a felony therein.

Id. We can further clarify and categorize these elements like this:

> Burglary (in state Z):
> 1) breaking;
> 2) entering;
> 3) the dwelling home;
> 4) of another;
> 5) at night;
> 6) with the intention of committing a felony therein.

By engaging in this diagraming process, the rule on burglary in state Z can be reorganized in a way that makes it easier to understand and use.

There are several important things you need to notice about elements tests. First, these rules are not always stated in elemental form. Often they are just written or expressed as a general rule, without the elements being identified. You can see this in the burglary statute we discussed above. Second, in the typical elements test all the elements must be satisfied before the test applies. For example, before one could be convicted of burglary in state Z a jury would have to find that all six of the elements we identified were met. Because of this aspect of these rules, elements tests are sometimes called "categorical rules." David Crump, How to Reason About the Law: An Interdisciplinary Approach to the Foundations of Public Policy 344–348 (2001). Finally, as we saw in Chapter Three, these sorts of tests are the rules that come closest to pure logical deduction in legal reasoning. If all the elements of burglary are proved, then by deduction the statute has been violated. While elements tests are perhaps not as intuitive as balancing tests, the logic involved makes them fairly easy to grasp and use. The last rule form that we will discuss is factors tests.

C. Factors Tests

Factors tests tend to be somewhat more flexible than elements tests. Linda Edwards, Legal Writing: Process, Analysis and Organization 19 (4th ed. 2006). These are sometimes called "guidelines," but that terminology tends to diminish the importance of factors tests. "Guidelines" suggest that these rules are discretionary, but many factors tests are clearly not discretionary (even though the factors themselves may give some discretion to the legal decision-maker). Richard K. Neumann, Jr., Legal Reasoning and Legal Writing: Structure, Strategy, and Style 19 (4th ed. 2001). These tests are usually more detailed than balancing tests, however, and do not operate as a weighing of one interest against another. Instead, factors tests lay out a number of different criteria that need to be considered in making a decision. *Id.* These criteria are literally the factors that go into making the decision. *Id.* Think about the process you engaged in when deciding where to go to law school. You were probably admitted to several schools, and when you were deciding which to attend you likely looked at several factors to help you conclude which would be the best choice for you. For example, you undoubtedly compared tuition cost, location, reputation of the school, and so on. If you tried, you could probably develop a list of the criteria, or factors, that went into your decision. A factors test, then, is simply a list of the factors that should be evaluated in making a decision.

Sometimes these factors tests are called "totality of the circumstances" tests, because the list of criteria or factors are often meant to address all of the relevant concerns that can be brought to bear upon a decision. Strictly speaking, however, there is one difference between a factors test and a totality of the circumstances test. The former usually have the list of factors listed, while the latter do not. In the context of legal reasoning a factors test is a rule that lists the basic legal concept to be employed, along with a list of factors that must be evaluated in light of that basic concept. Let us look at a well known factors test:

> Child custody shall be decided in accordance with the best interests of the child. Factors to consider in deciding the best interests of the child include: the fitness of each parent; the lifestyle of each parent; the relationship between the child and each parent; the placement of the child's siblings, if any; living accommodations; the district lines of the child's school; the proximity of extended family and friends; religious issues; and any other relevant factors that have an impact on the child's best interests.

Linda Edwards, Legal Writing: Process, Analysis and Organization 19 (4th ed. 2006). You can see the basic rule — the "best interests of the child" — right at the beginning. If the rule ended there, legal decision-makers would have some difficulties, as the rule would give virtually no guidance as to how it should be employed. Factors tests are useful because they give guidance about how the general rule ought to be used in different factual situations.

Like an elements test, factors tests can easily be reworked and rewritten to make them somewhat easier to understand and use. They can be diagramed. A diagraming of the "best interests of the child" rule might look something like this:

> Child custody shall determined according to the best interests of the child. Factors to consider in making this determination include:
>
> - the fitness of each parent;
> - the lifestyle of each parent;
> - the relationship between the child and each parent;
> - the placement of the child's siblings, if any;
> - living accommodations;
> - the district lines of the child's school;
> - the proximity of extended family and friends;
> - religious issues; and
> - any other relevant factors that have an impact on the child's best interests.

Id. at 20. This diagraming of the "best interests of the child" test easily illustrates the list of things that a legal decision-maker must take into account when deciding where a child should be placed in a custody dispute. *Id.* Note that in this test there is no real rank ordering of the factors (we did not apply numbers to them), because none are clearly more important than the others. In fact, some may not even apply in particular circumstances.

This last point is important, because factors tests are generally constructed to allow for the factors to be employed with some flexibility. These are tests designed to be flexible enough to accommodate a whole host of factual situations. Factors tests are generally longer than other sorts of tests, because they usually include all (or almost all) the factors that must be evaluated. Factors are included in order to give the legal decision-maker some guidance, but also to keep them from acting in an arbitrary way. *Id.* at 19. Factors tests also differ from balancing tests and elements tests in that they involve a more complex analytical skill. Where balancing tests employ an "either-or" logic, and elements tests employ a form of deductive logic, factors tests require that you juggle many competing and potentially countervailing interests in your mind at the same time. You might think of this as a multi-focal logic. In my view, the closest analytical system that approximates this multi-focal logic is the pragmatic reasoning we discussed briefly in Chapter Three (and will discuss in much more depth in Chapter Five). Because we frequently use our intuitions to craft useful lists of criteria that help us make good decisions, the logic of using factors tests in legal analysis will seem familiar. Weighing factors still permits flexibility and adaptability, but allows many competing concerns to be factored into the analysis of complex problems. DAVID CRUMP, HOW TO REASON ABOUT THE LAW: AN INTERDISCIPLINARY APPROACH TO THE FOUNDATIONS OF PUBLIC POLICY 347–348 (2001).

All of these types of tests (balancing tests, elements tests, and factors tests) are simply ways of articulating rules. Each maintains a different structure, but all are designed to make rules clearer and easier to use. Having clear and easy to use rules is, of course, tremendously helpful, especially in a profession that depends on rules so heavily. But you should note two things here: 1) you must understand these rule structures in order to move from novice to expert in the law; and 2) you should not immediately and uncritically accept the use of any particular rule structure that you confront in your studies or your work. Let us look at these two things in turn.

We have seen that on your journey from novice to expert you will be expected to learn a great many things. Often the lessons you learn will require you to conform your understanding to a series of formal—perhaps even rigid—analytical paradigms. As you will recall, when we discussed the use of analytical paradigms in legal reasoning in Chapter Two I suggested that these structures will enable you to more quickly and thoroughly understand how to think and act like lawyers think and act. The use of formal rule structures is a related analytical skill. Understanding what these rule structures are (and perhaps more importantly, recognizing when they are being used) is an important step in your intellectual development. Since lawyers and judges use these various rule forms in their work, it is vital that you recognize and understand them.

You will also recall, however, that I cautioned you in Chapter Two against turning analytical paradigms into rigid and absolute dogmas that will constrain (not assist) your thinking and creativity. A similar caution should be noted here. Just because you have seen a rule expressed or articulated as one type of test does not mean that such a structure is fixed in stone. Often, the choice as to which structure a rule is articulated as is up for contestation. You may see a legal concept announced as a balancing test in one legal opinion. Another legal opinion may articulate that same legal concept as a factors test. Yet a third might put forth the notion that the legal concept in question is really an elements test. Part of your job (aside from making determinations about the relative precedential value of each of these authorities) is to assess which of these various rule structures is best. Sometimes you will see a clear progression or evolution in the legal concept, with the latest articulation being the clearest and most authoritative construction. Very often, however, there is no clear guide. So what do you do then? This brings us to the last point you should understand about rule-based reasoning.

Working with rules is more of an art than a science. If you keep this in mind, you will see how experts in the law carry out their activities. In the common law system, even under the system of *stare decisis*, there is a tremendous amount of flexibility or "give." What I mean by this is that there is room for disagreement about virtually every legal concept. Smart, well-meaning, and diligent lawyers and judges articulate, understand, and use rules (the same rules) in different ways. This allows for you, as a burgeoning expert in the domain, to contribute to the discourse. Your views about the correct way to articulate or use a particular legal concept matters. You can literally contribute to the substance of the legal work you do.

As a result, when you see a rule you should view this as a beginning, not an end. The rules you find (in administrative opinions, cases, statutes, etc.) almost always allow room for some interpretation and rendering. Again, think of this as a creative or artistic act. If a legal principle has been expressed as a balancing test, but you see it more clearly as a factors test and believe that using it as a factors test is more useful there is no constraint on you doing so. There are constraints, however, on misstating the law. I do not mean to suggest that the interpretative process I am describing is in any way related to misstatements of the law, as that would be a violation of both moral and professional principles. This is especially the case if the way the law has been stated in various authorities is unclear or inconsistent. Sometimes, perhaps rarely, legal rules are stated with great precision and authoritativeness. In these rare situations, you will have to follow the structure of the rule statement closely. In the great preponderance of other circumstances, however, you can utilize your own analytical views about how a legal rule ought to be articulated and used. You must, of course, provide an argument or justification for why your alternative articulation is reasonable and comports with the spirit of the legal principle, but if you can do this you will be engaging in legal discourse in a deep and meaningful way. This is one of the great joys of working in our system. There is room for creativity and finesse. Rule-based reasoning is one of the best opportunities to display these traits while still working within the confines of a complex institutional framework.

III. Analogical (and Counter-Analogical) Reasoning

Analogical reasoning (and its corollary, counter-analogical reasoning) is perhaps the most important and distinguishing feature of our system of jurisprudence. The common law case method and the principle of *stare decisis* necessitate that legal actors in our system use ideas from previous cases in deciding present and future cases. In other words, lawyers and judges are constantly engaged in comparing and contrasting cases as they try to determine how legal problems should be resolved. Favorable comparisons are called analogies, while contrasting comparisons are called counter-analogies (this process is also sometimes called "distinguishing" cases). RICHARD K. NEUMANN, JR., LEGAL REASONING AND LEGAL WRITING: STRUCTURE, STRATEGY, AND STYLE 138 (4th ed. 2001); and LINDA EDWARDS, LEGAL WRITING: PROCESS, ANALYSIS AND ORGANIZATION 105–110 (4th ed. 2006). As a result, the ability to analyze cases, the principles they stand for, and the fact patterns that lead to certain outcomes is vital. This is why many of your classes—especially your casebook classes—force you to engage in these activities, thus developing your analytical abilities in these contexts. Analogical reasoning requires you to do more, however.

Analogical reasoning requires that you take your understanding of the precedents—both the law and the facts from those precedents—and assess how these precedents should relate to legally and factually similar circumstances. STEVEN J. BURTON, AN INTRODUCTION TO LAW AND LEGAL REASONING 27–31 (2d ed. 1995). One scholar has put it this way: "The analogical form contributes significantly to the rationality of legal thought by providing a framework for analysis, identifying starting points for reasoning, and framing a legal issue." *Id.* at 40. As an attorney your job will often be to craft an argument from the tapestry of authorities, explaining why certain authorities should be followed in particular factual situations, and why others should not. This ability builds on the simpler analytical skills we have explored in earlier chapters, but requires you to engage in a more complex intellectual process. This means that the cases you select to serve as precedents and the analogies or counter-analogies you make will depend on several things: the cases must correctly identify and discuss the relevant legal issue(s); you must articulate the rules from those cases in useful ways; and you must discuss the significant factual similarities and differences that make the analogy (or counter-analogy) a good one. LINDA EDWARDS, LEGAL WRITING: PROCESS, ANALYSIS AND ORGANIZATION 105–110 (4th ed. 2006).

Like rule-based reasoning, analogical reasoning should be somewhat familiar to you. Cognitively we are comfortable making analogies and counter-analogies and working them into our arguments. There is something intuitive about this, so intuitive in fact that small children grasp this ability at a very early age. Consider a common situation:

> Jim and Judy decide that their 8-year-old son Bobbie must go to bed at 8:00 p.m. every night. Bobbie is a good boy, and their decision is based mainly on the fact that he is engaged in gymnastics, and practice is before school. Bobbie has several brothers and sisters. His brother Kyle, who is 10 years old, was allowed to stay up until 9:00 p.m. when he was 8 years old. Kyle was involved in band when he was Bobbie's age. Band practice was after school. The younger siblings are not in school yet, and their bedtimes vary depending on their ages.

You can probably anticipate that Bobbie will not be happy with his parents' decision. You will also probably see that Bobbie is very likely to argue that Jim and Judy are being unfair. He will undoubtedly maintain that he should be able to stay awake until 9:00 p.m. because Kyle was allowed to do so when he was 8 years old. This is an analogical argument, and Bobbie does not need to be taught about this argument form for it make sense (to him, and to us). Although this argument may be informal, there is an analytical element to it that cannot be denied. You may have noticed that I said Bobbie would likely argue that his parents were being unfair. This is an important aspect of analogical reasoning. When we make analogies the comparisons made play on the principle that following decisions in like or similar circumstances is the just and proper thing to do. The system of *stare decisis* incorporates a notion of justice by employing analogical reasoning. In other words, analogical reasoning is what provides our common law system with a framework for making just decisions. The legal philosopher H.L.A. Hart put it this way:

> [T]hough "Treat like cases alike and different cases differently" is a central element in the idea of justice, it is by itself incomplete and, until supplemented, cannot afford any determinate guide to conduct.... [U]ntil it is established what resemblances and differences are relevant, "Treat like cases alike" must remain an empty form. To fill it we must know when, for the purposes in hand, cases are to be regarded as alike and what differences are relevant.

H.L.A. HART, THE CONCEPT OF LAW 155 (1961). You can probably guess that I am not urging you to adopt an empty form of reasoning. So how does the intuitive and somewhat rudimentary ability to analogize similar situations evolve into a more developed skill of analogizing and distinguishing multiple cases and authorities together in order to analyze, predict or persuade actors in the legal system, and to do so justly? Let us look at this next.

Professor Steven Burton has said that "[u]nderlying good legal reasoning ... [is] well-accepted rules identifying the authoritative base points, a vocabulary and method encouraging rigorous consideration of both similarities and differences, and a form or expression for framing the issue to be decided." Steven J. Burton, An Introduction to Law and Legal Reasoning 27 (2d ed. 1995). This can be restated into three steps that are involved in analogical legal reasoning:

Steps in Analogical Legal Reasoning

A. Identification of the body of case law and other authority (precedents) that will assist you in the analogy;
B. Discussion and analysis of those precedents to illustrate the connection between the authorities and the legal problem you are addressing, and evaluating the similarities and differences between the precedents and your case; and
C. Discussing and judging what the similarities and differences between the precedents and your case suggest about the outcome of your case.

See, *Id.* at 40. Perhaps it would be helpful to look at each of these steps individually. If you have a hard time following this discussion, don't worry. I will list a short example at the end to illustrate how this all works.

A. Identification of Relevant Precedents

Many of the things you will learn in your law school classes help you learn how you read and understand cases. As a result, you will rapidly become an expert at these skills. You may have more problems gaining this expertise when it comes to identifying a body of relevant authority on your own, however. In your casebook courses the cases are selected for you. In some of your non-casebook courses, though, you may be required to research and evaluate authorities in light of a legal problem you are working on. In the best of all possible scenarios, you will be able to carry out this research in a completely "open universe." This means that your research will entail looking at all possible authorities that are relevant to the legal problem. This is the ideal situation because it prepares you to engage in the sort of actual legal analysis you will need to employ as an expert in the domain.

In a sense (and many people overlook this fact) actually engaging in the research and evaluating the authorities this research yields is an important early step in your legal analysis of the problem. By reading all the relevant authorities and evaluating the connection of those cases, statutes and rules to the legal problem you are working on, you will begin to crystallize in your mind an understanding of how this rich tapestry can be woven together to assist you in crafting an answer to this problem. You will notice that there will be a great many more authorities than you will end up actually using in your analysis, but this is a vital part of the process. Seeing what is out there, evaluating how each authority relates to your theory of the case (does it help or hinder that theory?), and selecting a subset of that body of case law to analyze and discuss in some depth is a process; a process that will yield a complex understanding of how the law on the particular problem you are addressing operates.

One last thing should be said about this step in analogical legal reasoning. You will recall that I said above that analogical reasoning is contextual in nature (in fact, as you might have noticed throughout this text, all legal reasoning is contextual). What this means is that the analysis and selection you will make of the relevant authorities will be driven by the way you have formulated the legal issue or issues that are represented in the problem you are working on. This is, in turn, controlled to a large extent by the position (or client) you represent. What this means is that for the vast majority of legal problems you will work on, in school and in practice, there is no one right way of constructing an analogy between the relevant case law and your problem. Instead, your job will be to develop a body of authority that illustrates and works with your theory of the case.

While there are some general guidelines about how you do this, you will (as an expert) have some latitude in selecting and analyzing authorities. LINDA EDWARDS, LEGAL WRITING: PROCESS, ANALYSIS AND ORGANIZATION 237–240 (4th ed. 2006). In exercising this latitude, you will be engaging in a creative process. This creativity will enable you to use the authorities you choose and discuss as the raw materials for your complex analysis. These authorities are the clay from which you will sculpt a representation of the way the law is situated to your problem. This initial selection, then, is a vital step in your analysis. This is a step that will determine the structure of your analogy (or counter-analogy), but it is also an expression of your notion of how the case ought to be decided. This applies whether you are engaged in a predictive or a persuasive enterprise.

As you can see, this first step of identifying the relevant precedents is more than just a research activity. It is an analytical enterprise that will structure and form the steps that follow. From the rules that you develop in the authorities you choose to use, you will actually front-load your analysis. This means that your identification and selection process will largely determine your analysis and the structure of the analogy or counter-analogy. By selecting well, you can clearly and logically analyze and explain how the case law and other authorities relate to your problem, and offer a solution or outcome to that problem. The inverse is true as well, of course. By selecting badly you can confuse both yourself and your reader by muddying the waters and making the legal issue unclear and impossible to understand. By choosing well, however, you will also make the following steps in developing your analogy easier. In a sense, by engaging in the analytical process of identifying and selecting relevant cases that work with your theory of the case, you are mapping out the analogy between the authorities and your case. This mapping will help you discuss and develop the cases as you make the analogy. This is the second step.

B. Discussion and Analysis of the Precedents

Once you have identified, selected, and mapped out the relevant authorities, you can begin to make the analogy or counter-analogy that your problem will require. This entails analyzing both the legal principles and the factual background of the case law you identified and selected. The intersection of these two things is extremely important. In fact, this is how the system of *stare decisis* works. This is the substance of the principle that Hart was discussing above. Legal rules are bare and empty without the substance that relevant (sometimes called determinative) facts provide. By analyzing and discussing the legal rule from the authorities in light of the facts from the cases selected, you can illustrate how the rule works in operation.

This step requires that you actually discuss and evaluate the cases and other authorities, drawing out the relevant themes that will connect them to the legal problem you are working on. Many stories can be told about the cases you have selected as part of your analogy. The way you discuss and analyze this body of authority will be formative for both your theory of the case and the reader's understanding of that case. Sometimes there will be a seminal case, or one that is so directly on point that you can develop it in some depth. Other times there will be several cases that must be worked together to develop the legal and factual scenario that is most helpful to your theory of the case. This is called a synthesis. We will discuss this in more depth below.

In either of these situations, your objective is to flesh out the authority; to give it some substance and content. Tell the story of how this case (or the synthesis of cases) should be viewed retrospectively, in light of how it (or they) can be used prospectively to address your legal problem. This is much more than simply putting the rule (or all the rules in the case of a synthesis) out there for someone else to see. You need to use the content of the cases — the rules and the stories behind those rules — to sculpt the legal landscape. An expert lawyer or judge will deftly construct a complex mixture of legal rules and facts from precedents that literally leads others in the domain down a path that will end in successful resolution of the problem. Of course, successful resolution would end (we hope) in acceptance that your analysis is correct, and that your position (or your client's) prevails.

This involves highlighting both the similarities between the precedents you have selected and the differences. See, Linda Edwards, Legal Writing: Process, Analysis and Organization 106–112 (4th ed. 2006). As Steven Burton puts it: "[y]ou should, by rigorous analysis of the facts of the cases, proceed to identify the many plausible points of factual similarity and difference." Steven J. Burton, An Introduction to Law and Legal Reasoning 29 (2d ed. 1995). This analysis and discussion will enable you to craft or sculpt the authority into something useful. I do not mean to suggest here that precedent can be distorted or misstated. Those practices violate principles of ethics and professional responsibility. What I am suggesting is that a good lawyer or judge will be able to use the precedents to their advantage by strategically selecting and discussing them. This involves the careful use of the precedents and particular attention to the way the rules and facts of the precedents resonate with the legal issue and facts of your problem.

The mechanics of this can vary somewhat. In any case, however, you will want to delve deeply enough into the precedents to identify the legal issue and determinative facts (of course these will be shaped in light of your problem case), and explains why the precedent was decided the way it was. In other words, you need to illustrate and prove the legal rule in light of its factual context. This will involve you elaborating about why and how the legal principle involved was shaped by the facts present in the case or cases that make up the precedents. This discussion should lay out and discuss the legal and factual similarities as well as the legal and factual differences. The art, at this stage, is that the similarities and differences will not be explicitly discussed as such. They will simply be set out as the parameters of the analysis concerning the precedents.

So, in a short discussion of a single seminal case you will highlight the legal issue involved, the determinative facts that led to the decision, and the reasoning announced by the court that supported their decision. Some of the facts discussed will later flow right into your articulation of the case you are working on. Other facts will not be related to your case. Similarly, certain aspects of the reasoning or rationale will closely resemble arguments in favor of certain outcomes in your case. Other aspects of the rationale will suggest different outcomes. How you discuss the precedent, then, continues to shape the analysis and analogy. The way you discuss the law, facts and rationale of the precedents you selected in step one will fill in the analytical gaps. Roughly, this process corresponds with the rule explanation step that we discussed in the legal writing paradigm in Chapter Two. This is the hard work. If you do it well, however, the next step should be much easier for you to accomplish. With all this done, you can finish your analogy by moving to a discussion of how the precedents should control the outcome of your legal problem.

C. Assessment of What the Precedents Suggest about Your Case

Once you have done the hard part of identifying and mapping out the precedents that will assist you in developing and discussing the analogies or counter-analogies that will support your legal reasoning, you can then construct and put forth your views about how the authority does and should effect your legal problem. Again, these views are inextricably bound up with the context of your problem, the facts of that problem, and the desired outcome. Here you will assess how the precedents will effect the outcome of your case. If you have engaged in the first two steps fully and have constructed your analogies or counter-analogies well, the effect should be clear and easy to understand.

There are two pathways here. First, the analogy could suggest that the legal problem you are working on should be decided like one or more of the precedents. On the other hand, a counter-analogy might suggest that your legal problem be decided differently than the authority. The path you take to resolving whatever legal problem you are working on will depend on your facts, the authorities you find and what they say about the law in the context of particular fact scenarios, and how you have developed these raw materials into a coherent narrative about how the law should control your legal problem.

In effect, when you use analogies and counter-analogies you are suggesting that a certain interpretation of the relevant authority should lead to a particular outcome because that outcome is both reasonable and consistent with precedent. In the common law, these aspects — reasonability and consistency — are hallmarks of *stare decisis*. In other words, by constructing an analogy or counter-analogy well you are both explaining and illustrating how the law works and should be applied in your case.

This last step depends, as I suggested above, on the relationship of your analogies or counter-analogies to an important yet intangible and illusive concept — justice. One of the things that makes analogies work is their relationship to some sense of fairness. We generally adhere to the principle of deciding "like or similar cases alike" because doing so is fair and just. As you are constructing your analogies, then, you must be sure to factor this in. To the extent that your analysis shows how your case should or should not be controlled by the relevant available precedents, this concept of justice will be satisfied. If there is a gap or disconnect between your analogies or counter-analogies and the precedents on point, however, your cause (and your client's) will not be served. You need to show—not just assert—how the precedent leads to the conclusion you suggest. This showing demands that you walk others through the analysis, setting out the parameters of the legal and factual landscape that you have sculpted, and proving to them that your assessment is the correct one.

Taken together, these steps can help you learn to take the intuitive skills you have to both see and use analogies and counter-analogies, and develop them into a more robust and developed skill set. This is another paradigm of sorts, but you need not think of it that way. As you develop your ability to craft and use complex analogies and counter-analogies, you will not follow a formula. Instead, you will often see the connections in your mind as you engage in the reiterative process of finding, reading, understanding, culling and using the available relevant authorities. The most important thing you need to notice is that you must be able to convey these connections to others in the domain so they can see and use them. There will surely be competing accounts of how the precedents stack up in light of particular factual circumstances, but this is what makes the common law system so interesting. Your ability to sculpt a landscape and convey that to others is a skill and an opportunity. Engaging in this process mechanically undermines the artistic aspect of this skill. Now let us turn to some simple examples to illustrate this process a little more concretely.

Examples

Let us examine briefly the simple problem I discussed at the beginning of this section, the one involving Bobbie and Kyle. If you follow an analytical procedure like the one described above, you might see that there was an intuitive sense to Bobbie's position that his parents are being unfair. However, you will also undoubtedly see that there is something more complicated going on that Bobbie did not see. The case of Kyle involved some facts that had an impact on the rule (Kyle was involved in a school activity that required after school practice) which are not present in Bobbie's case. In other words, the analogy is not a good one because of this factual dissimilarity. There is good reason, then, for Jim and Judy to distinguish Bobbie's situation from Kyle's. Even in this simple familial dispute, you can see both the analogies—or, in this case, counter-analogies — and the complexity of using these analytical skills well. Just imagine how hard this can be in complex legal environments.

Consider this legal problem:

> Your client — Jimmy — comes to you complaining that his neighbor — Scott — has destroyed a shed that is situated in your client's back yard. Scott had not cared for a tree on his property for some time. Jimmy recently told Scott that the tree looked like it was ready to fall, and that he should do something about the dangerous tree. The neighbor did not call a professional yard service, but instead cut off some of the branches near the bottom of the tree. This made the tree top heavy. In a storm last night the tree fell over and demolished your client's shed.

You will likely recognize that this is a tort issue, and you may even further recognize it as a negligence cause of action. You are not sure what the likelihood of prevailing on a negligence theory is given these facts, however, so you tell your client that you will have to research the issue. You restrict your research to your state jurisdiction. Your research reveals the following five cases (all from your jurisdiction, all still good law, and all from the highest court in the state):

Case One — Kirk vs. Khan
Khan was cutting down a tree on his property. He did not use safety equipment or appropriate precautions. The tree fell on Kirk's property, damaging Kirk's home. Kirk sued for negligence. The court decided that Khan was liable for the damages to Kirk's home because he did not use safety equipment and he did not take appropriate precautions to protect his neighbor's property from damage.

Case Two — Picard vs. Q
Q was cutting down a tree on his property. Q was using all the safety equipment and precautions that his municipality required. Even so, the tree fell at an odd angle and damaged some shrubs on Picard's property. Picard sued for negligence. The court decided that Q was not liable for negligence because he used the safety equipment his municipality required and took appropriate precautions to protect his neighbor's property. The court also mentioned that the damage to Picard's property was confined to the shrubs, and not to a structure or fixture placed upon the land.

Case Three — Janeway vs. Borg Queen

A large dead tree was located on Borg Queen's property. Several neighbors, but not Janeway, had told Borg Queen that the tree was dangerous and should be cut down. Borg Queen ignored them, saying that she is the "one who is many." During the storm the tree fell and damaged Janeway's home. Janeway sued in negligence. The court held that Borg Queen was liable for the damage to Janeway's house because she was on notice about the dangerous condition, yet did not take any precautions to alleviate the danger. The court also said, in dicta, that even though Borg Queen might have multiple personality disorder she was still liable because she did not plead lack of mental capacity as a defense.

Case Four — Neo vs. Smith

Smith lives next to Neo. Because Smith believes that Neo is a disgusting meat sack, Smith continually torments Neo. Smith throws garbage on Neo's property, and glares at Neo from behind his stylish sunglasses every time Neo is in his own yard. Neo is creeped out by Smith's behavior. One day Smith pushes down a big tree that is on his property, trying to smash Neo as he sits in a hammock reading the newspaper. The tree misses Neo but destroys a shed on Neo's property. Neo sues Smith for several intentional torts and for negligence. The court decided that Smith is liable for the intentional torts, but not for negligence because he intended to cause harm to either Neo or his property.

Case Five — Sisko vs. Gul Dukat

A tree on Gul Dukat's property was damaged in a storm. Gul Dukat hired a professional service to come to his property and fix the tree. The tree service worked on the tree and told Gul Dukat that the tree was in good shape and should live for another 100 years. Two weeks later, and after 3 days of rain, the tree fell on to Sisko's garage, damaging the structure. Sisko sued Gul Dukat for negligence. The court held that Gul Dukat was not liable for negligence because he had engaged the services of a professional yard service to fix the damaged tree. The court felt that Gul Dukat had taken all reasonable steps to protect his neighbors. The court went on to say that if anyone was liable for negligence, it would be the tree service because they were the professionals and they worked on the tree.

You will probably notice several things about these cases. Each has facts that are similar to your case, although not exactly the same. All of the cases are negligence causes of action. Also, all of the cases involve action, or inaction, on the part of the property owner who damaged his neighbor's property. Finally, you will notice that all but one of the cases deal with unintentional damage.

By following the steps outlined above, you could discuss and analyze the cases in light of your fact pattern. You would examine the similarities and differences. By doing so, you would highlight some of the facts and certain aspects of the reasoning from most of the cases. This would enable you to draft an analogy between those cases — or more properly a synthesis of the cases — and your fact pattern. Such an analogy would discuss the similarities of relevant cases, and the differences of those cases. Once this is done, you could support your conclusion by suggesting how the precedents should be followed or distinguished, covering each in turn.

Even though you have not written out such an analogy, you could probably see fairly quickly that Scott will likely be liable to Jimmie in negligence because Scott did not take appropriate precautions in caring for the damaged tree. The important aspect is for you to be able to draw out the parts of the precedents that support such a conclusion. Could you do so? This is a good exercise for you to try.

Analogical legal reasoning is an important yet complicated skill. While there is an intuitive aspect to such reasoning, the formal character of legal analysis and communication require that you be more systematic in the creation and use of analogies. Analogies and counter-analogies allow you to use authorities effectively in your work. By following a procedure like the one outlined above, you can be sure to effectively and comprehensively identify, discuss, analyze, and apply the precedents to any legal problem you are working on, showing how the precedents will affect those problems. Such a procedure will aid you in becoming more adept at employing analogies in many different situations, whether you are engaging in predictive or persuasive legal analysis and communication.

IV. Synthesizing Case Law

The ability to synthesize legal rules from a body of legal authority is another key indicator of one who has attained expert status in the domain of the law. Strictly speaking, there are two types of synthesis you can engage in: rule synthesis and case law synthesis. DAVID ROMANTZ AND KATHLEEN ELLIOT VINson, Legal Analysis: The Fundamental Skill 22–23, 39–43 (1998). A rule synthesis is a crafting of a single rule from several related rules. Linda Edwards, Legal Writing: Process, Analysis and Organization 53–55, 61–63 (4th ed. 2006). Since rules in isolation are not as useful as many think, as we saw above, the more common process of synthesizing involves working together a discussion of several cases into a coherent whole. David Romantz and Kathleen Elliot Vinson, Legal Analysis: The Fundamental Skill 39–40 (1998). This process is designed to show the operation of a series of cases related to a particular legal issue. You do this by highlighting both the facts and the law and explaining how the cases work together. Richard K. Neumann, Jr., Legal Reasoning and Legal Writing: Structure, Strategy, and Style 139 (4th ed. 2001). This sort of synthesis, if done well, reveals something about the law that the individual cases themselves do not yield. *Id.* The final synthesis will equal more than the sum of its parts.

Essentially, a case law synthesis is a binding together of several cases to form (or explain) a complex precedent or set or interdependent precedents. By synthesizing cases together, you can develop a more complex or robust precedent structure. This is useful in two distinct situations:

(1) Where showing the genealogy of precedents is important in understanding how a particular authority will (or should) be applied; or

(2) Where you do not have a single precedent which will support the proposition that you want to advance, but where there are several precedents which taken as a whole will support that proposition.

This is more than just a stringing together of several related cases. You should develop a "thread of continuity" which runs throughout the cases that conceptually ties them all to the proposition you are advancing. In other words, show how you see the cases fitting together to get to the proposition you are putting forth. This "thread" should be immediately evident to your reader to be effective. You should note that in the process of synthesizing cases together, you will not necessarily discuss each and every case cited in any depth. You will often use other methods (parenthetical commentary, for example) to show the connections between the cases.

In order for this synthesis to work, you will need to work through the cases independently on your own to determine what part each case will play in the final proposition. Chart out the parts of the whole concept, and make sure that you have a case or cases which fits and substantiates each part. Sometimes this is best done visually (perhaps you can chart it out on a blackboard), but however you do it you need to make sure that you have enough to support the final idea which you want to advance. Remember not to leave it up to the reader to make the connections. You need to do this for her.

Once you have done this, and you understand how the cases fit together and how they lead to the conclusion you want to advance, turn the whole thing on its head. Put the conclusion first, then list the rules and so on. This will make more sense to the reader as she goes through your discussion. Don't leave the conclusion (i.e., the proposition you want the synthesis to support) until the end of your discussion. Tell the reader what the synthesis is designed to accomplish, then walk her through it.

While the discussion above outlines synthesizing in a written work product, do not lose sight of the fact that this is an analytical exercise. You must think about the cases (rules and facts), analyze them, structure the synthesis, and then construct it. In terms of process, you might think of following these steps:

Steps in Synthesizing Case Law

(1) Decide what concepts you want to extract from the cases (remembering, of course, that it must be substantiated by the cases);

(2) Determine which cases will play a role in the construction of the theme of your synthesis;

(3) Try to figure out the most logical order in which to piece the cases together to get the desired construction; and

(4) Always be conscious of maintaining a thread of continuity throughout the cases and your discussion which will guide the reader to your conclusion (the concept or proposition you are advancing).

This process, like the process discussed above concerning analogical reasoning, is designed to help you emulate expert thinking. This process will allow you to quickly draft case syntheses fairly quickly.

There are some hazards you can encounter along the way, however. For example, many novices believe that just mentioning the relevant cases will be enough for a reader to understand how the cases work together. This is clearly not correct. When you construct a synthesis you must make the structure evident to the reader. Also, novices often assume that the understanding they have gained by engaging in the process of constructing the synthesis will be communicated by laying out the end process in its simplest terms. This is also clearly not correct. You have done the hard work to gain this understanding, but you must explain how the synthesis works before a reader will see the full importance of the synthesis. Perhaps an example will illustrate.

Example of a Case Law Synthesis

Below you will find a short case law synthesis discussing the willful blindness exception to the innocent owner defense in a federal property forfeiture case. You will notice several things. First, the selection begins with the general rule, but then shows the connection of that rule to the sub-rule concerning the exception. Next, you will notice that both cases and a statutory section are woven together. Finally, you will see that cases are treated in a number of different ways. Some are just cited. In some instances the rules are stated from the cases, and in others the case is developed fully with both facts and law being part of the discussion. Can you see the theme of the synthesis? How about the structure? Can you follow this structure? Finally, can you pick out the thread of continuity that draws these cases and the statute together?

> Traditionally, "innocence of the owner of property subject to forfeiture is not a defense" to the forfeiture. *One Blue 1977 AMC Jeep CJ-5*, 783 F.2d 759, 762 (8th Cir. 1986). However, the Supreme Court has carved out a narrow exception to this rule. *See Calero-Toledo v. Pearson Yacht Leasing Co.*, 316 U.S. 663, 680–84 (1974). The Eighth Circuit Court of Appeals has recognized this exception, citing specifically to *Calero-Toledo. One 1976 Cessna Model 210 Aircraft*, 890 F.2d 77 (8th Cir. 1989). In *Cessna*, the Eighth Circuit said that "proof by a preponderance of evidence that the property [in question] was taken from the owner without his consent or that the owner was neither aware of nor involved in the wrongful activity and had done all that he could to prevent the property's misuse, will defeat an action in forfeiture." *Id.*, at 80. In 1988, Congress codified this exception, altering it slightly. See, 21 U.S.C. sec. 881(a)(4)(C). This subsection provides:
>
> > No conveyance shall be forfeited under this paragraph to the extent of an interest of an owner, by reason of any act or omission established by that owner to have been committed or omitted without the knowledge, consent, or willful blindness of the owner.
>
> *Id.* This statutory language, and not the standard identified in *Calero-Toledo*, is at issue in this case. *See One 1989 Jeep Wagoneer*, 976 F.2d 1172, 1175 (8th Cir. 1992). Under the statute, to prevail on an innocent-owner defense, claimants must establish that the acts giving rise to the forfeiture occurred "without [their] knowledge, consent or willful blindness." *Id.*

In *One 1989 Jeep Wagoneer*, the Eighth Circuit defined "willful blindness" by analogizing asset forfeiture to tax fraud:

> [W]illful blindness involves an owner who deliberately closes his eyes to what otherwise would have been obvious and whose acts or omissions show a conscious purpose to avoid knowing the truth.

Id. At 1175.

In *One 1989 Jeep Wagoneer*, the court held that the element of willful blindness places mental state or intent at issue, and in such cases "summary judgment must be granted with caution, as usually such issues raise questions for determination by a factfinder." *Id.* At 1176. The court applied this rule to the facts before it and reversed the trial court's grant of summary judgment, finding that the claimants had provided evidence that they had been monitoring use of the defendant vehicle by their son, whose criminal acts gave rise to the forfeiture. *Id.* In addition, the claimants produced evidence that they had been monitoring their son's daily activities, that their son did not use the defendant vehicle exclusively, and that he also owned a car of his own. *Id.* The court concluded that willful blindness was an issue of fact in the case, which it remanded to the district court for trial on that issue. *Id.*

Synthesizing case law is a difficult art to learn. Even very good lawyers struggle with how to sort through and cull a dense body of case law, extracting the most important authorities and weaving them together to craft an analytical structure that is literally more than the sum of its constituent parts. By working deliberately, however, analyzing as you go, and mapping out the structure you want others to see in your analysis, you can construct a novel and useful articulation of a number of different but related legal concepts that work together in a special way. This is a creative process, but one that demands hard work and reasoned effort. Do not assume that just writing things out will make a synthesis apparent to another member of the profession. You have to show them how it works. Like so many of the analytical and communication skills we have discussed throughout this work, however, this should not be viewed as a burden but as an opportunity. Now let us move on to another difficult yet rewarding analytical skill to master: engaging in policy based reasoning.

V. Policy Based Reasoning

Policy based reasoning refers to the ability to discern the underlying reasons why legal decisions are made. Policy based reasoning helps you and others in the system reach results by "analyzing what answer would be best for the society at large." LINDA EDWARDS, LEGAL WRITING: PROCESS, ANALYSIS AND ORGANIZATION 6 (4th ed. 2006). These are public policies that shape and form legal decision-making. Looked at in this way, policy is the foundation that makes legal decisions legitimate. As Professor Richard Neumann puts it:

> Policy is elicited from precedent that explains the underlying goals that the rules involved are intended to advance.... Not only is policy important in clearing up ambiguities in the law, but judges are guided by policy concerns even in applying law that seems on the surface to be unambiguous. A court needs confidence that a contemplated decision really is consistent with the law's goals. Thus, legal analysis persistently asks what the rules are meant to accomplish, whether the proposed result would accomplish that, and whether the rules and the result would create more problems than they would solve.

RICHARD K. NEUMANN, JR., LEGAL REASONING AND LEGAL WRITING: STRUCTURE, STRATEGY, AND STYLE 139 (4th ed. 2001). Identifying and understanding policy, however, is a very difficult enterprise. Quite often the authorities we draw upon—constitutions, statutes, cases, etc.—do not provide much in the way of a clear statement of the policies they are meant to uphold. Sometimes these authorities are completely silent as to the policies they serve. This is one of the primary reasons that novices have such a difficult time mining the authorities they work with for the policy considerations that support a legal position.

There are several kinds of concerns that comprise what we have been calling public policy. These have been classified by Professor Ellie Margolis. Ellie Margolis, *Closing the Floodgates: Making Persuasive Policy Arguments in Appellate Briefs*, 62 MONTANA L. REV. 59 (2001). She has identified four main types of public policy that affect legal decision-making. These are: 1) policies affecting judicial administration; 2) normative policies; 3) institutional competence policies; and 4) economic policies. *Id.* Judicial administration policies deal with the ability of the court system to work efficiently, effectively, and fairly. *Id.* at 72. The policies behind procedural rules are good examples. Normative policies are those concerns that "promote shared societal values." LINDA EDWARDS, LEGAL WRITING: PROCESS, ANALYSIS AND ORGANIZATION 95 (4th ed. 2006). These policies are general principles that evoke moral or ethical considerations, professional considerations, social concerns, or broad-based justice theories. Ellie Margolis, *Closing the Floodgates: Making Persuasive Policy Arguments in Appellate Briefs*, 62 Montana L. Rev. 59, 74 (2001). Institutional competence policies relate to the idea that our legal and political systems are highly structured, and that within this structure people who occupy certain positions are granted authority to act in particular ways. *Id.* at 77. These policies are not unlike judicial administration policies, but focus more closely on non-judicial actors in the political or social system. The policies behind the separation of powers doctrine would be a good example. Finally, economic policies are designed to "maximize efficient resource allocation, keep economic costs in line with resulting benefits, and maintain a free market." *Id.* at 78–79.

This framework is extremely useful, and should help illustrate to you the sorts of concerns that can be captured by policy based reasoning. There are several things you should keep in mind here, however. First, these general categories might give you guidance but you should be aware that within each category the kinds of things that will qualify as public policy vary widely, and change substantially over time. Second, any particular decision will likely rest on a variety of different policy considerations, sometimes (perhaps often) several from each of these different categories. Also, the considerations from each category frequently compete with each other. For example, sometimes moral concerns (normative policies) are directly in competition with cost-benefit analysis (economic policies). Finally, you should bear in mind that legal decision-makers have the ability to chose from a variety of different approaches in deciding which policies to employ in justifying a decision. Some judges, for example, tend to favor economic policies when making their decisions. Others are more focused on normative concerns. Yet others are not dogmatic in either of these ways, but tend to pick and choose pragmatically from amongst the different policy considerations as they attempt to craft the best solution to the problem being addressed. What you should see from all this is that working with policy is both extremely complex and often very frustrating.

Public policies can emanate from many different places. Frequently actors in the judicial arena will draw upon historical, religious, or cultural texts to find public policy. Moral theories from a wide variety of different philosophical and theological traditions also serve as the basis for many public policies. Widespread public opinion can also form policy. More concretely, legislative history can provide some clue as to why certain statutes were passed. In the context of the common law, judges sometimes (but not often) clearly identify the policy basis for their decisions. All of these perspectives have an impact on policy based reasoning. The main problem is that frequently these perspectives are left unstated, or are only vaguely hinted at. The reason why policy based reasoning is so difficult and frustrating is that there are almost never any clear guides as to where to find it, how to completely understand it, and what appropriate uses for it might be. Of all the things you are expected to learn on your journey to becoming an expert in the domain, policy based reasoning is the most abstract and elusive. Nonetheless, honing your skills in this aspect of legal analysis is a sure indicator of your progression in the profession. By using policy based reasoning you can work to "expand, limit, or create new law." DAVID ROMANTZ AND KATHLEEN ELLIOT VINSON, LEGAL ANALYSIS: THE FUN-DAMENTAL SKILL 78 (1998). As a result, this is a powerful tool for you to have at your disposal.

There really are no good steps to follow in attempting to determine how to identify, understand, or use public policy in your analysis. So what can you do? I have said that working with policy is vital to becoming an expert in the field. So how can you gain this skill of policy based reasoning? When you are working with statutes, read the legislative histories that accompany the relevant sections. Frequently, this will give you some sense as to the purpose of the statute. While not foolproof, knowing the policies that led to the enactment of a statute can help you begin to form policy arguments pertaining to that statute. When you are working with case law as precedent, read closely to see if the judge who wrote the opinion set forth any policy reasons for her decision. Here again, this is not an airtight way to capture the public policy behind a decision, but it is a good start.

If the statutes or cases most relevant to a legal problem you are working on do not have any clearly stated enunciation of the policy rationales for their en-actment or holding, you should still be able to extract some information about the policies behind them. Just because a policy is unstated does not mean that it is not there. Consider this example:

> In 1899 the highest court in the state decided to adopt common law marriage. In its decision, the court held that people who live together, and hold themselves out, as man and wife for a period of seven years, shall have the same rights and obligations as couples who have gone through formal and sanctioned marriage ceremonies recognized by law. As a result of the case, Keith and Beatrice—who have lived to-gether as man and wife for 11 years, and who have five children to-gether—were deemed to be married in the eyes of the law. The opinion did not list any policy reasons for the decision.

You can very likely see that even though the court did not announce the pub-lic policy concerns that were the basis for their decision, there surely are such concerns behind the holding. For example, there are probably religious reasons for this decision. There are also very likely moral considerations that transcend any particular religious tradition involved. Additionally, there are undoubtedly economic reasons for the decision. The social concerns of the society over the institution of the family were probably involved as well. How many reasons can you extract from this short example? Can you articulate them? Would they be useful, say, in making the argument in 2007 that same-sex couples should be afforded the right to marry (or be treated as if they were married)?

As you can no doubt see, policy based reasoning is hard and often requires you to dig deeper than you are accustomed to in analyzing and using authorities. Often it will even require you to go beyond the authorities themselves to draw upon more broad based cultural, religious and social considerations. Perhaps this is why using policy based reasoning in legal analysis is so difficult; to do it well you must be able to reach outside the legal system and engage concerns that are broader and more esoteric than the structured and well-formulated ideas that most lawyers are more comfortable with. This is an important part of the equation. By increasing your knowledge of cultural, religious, and social concerns that go beyond—and may not even have direct relevance to—the U.S. legal system, you will make yourself better equipped to engage in policy based reasoning within the legal system.

VI. Statutory Construction

The ability to read, analyze, and interpret statutes is another very important advanced analytical skill that you will need throughout your career, and it is one that does not get enough attention in law school. Statutory interpretation, in particular, is a vital skill that experts in the domain of the law must possess. More and more of our lives are coming under federal, state, or local regulatory control. As a result, statutes, regulations, and administrative rules are more frequently involved in legal problems you will work on. This skill, like the others discussed in this chapter, is one that will show your progression as a member of the profession. While you will read and understand most aspects of the statutes or codes you are exposed to in some of your classes, the full tapestry of this analytical ability will continue to grow as you work with statutes more closely throughout your career. As you read and work with statutory language, and see how others (primarily judges) do so, you will begin to see the intricacies of this important aspect of legal analysis and communication.

One of the things you will notice about statutory interpretation is that there are different schools of thought, or approaches, as to how statutes ought to be read and applied in legal reasoning. As with policy based reasoning, many actors in the legal system maintain an almost dogmatic approach to this form of legal analysis. What this means is that some judges and lawyers will identify their philosophy of statutory interpretation. They will then read all statutes through the lens created by this philosophical perspective. Others will be more flexible in their use, drawing upon different approaches depending on the circumstances involved. Regardless of the disposition you see in the cases and the commentaries you read, several different philosophical approaches have been identified by scholars studying statutory interpretation and should be useful to you as you work to master this skill.

Professors Linda Jellum and David Hricik have recently identified what they have called "three dominant approaches to statutory interpretation." LINDA D. JELLUM AND DAVID CHARLES HRICIK, MODERN STATUTORY INTERPRETATION: PROBLEMS, THEORIES, AND LAWYERING STRATEGIES 95–101 (2006). These dominant approaches are: 1) textualism; 2) intentionalism; and 3) purposivism. While there are many other approaches that have been identified throughout legal history, these three approaches are, as Professors Jellum and Hricik say, the dominant ways in which actors in the legal system read and apply statutes. Let us look at the approaches that Professors Jellum and Hricik have identified in turn.

A. Textualism

Adherents to the school of textualism attempt to stick as closely as possible to the text of a statute, often saying that they are reading the "plain meaning" of the statute. This is perhaps the simplest (or narrowist) and most straightforward method of statutory interpretation. It involves reading a statute on its face and using only the words the legislature enacted in determining what the statute means. Adherents of this view are called "textualists," and are perhaps the most dogmatic of any of the groups represented by the different schools of interpretation. As Professors Jellum and Hricik put it:

> Textualists view themselves first as agents, not of the legislature, but of the Constitution. They believe that by holding Congress to its words, they ensure that only language actually enacted will be given the force of law and, further, that they will not engage in legislating, which is, they believe, the exclusive province of Congress.

Id. at 95. Textualists believe that interpreting statutes according to their plain meaning is the only legitimate way to approach the enterprise. This position is based on two things: 1) the difficulty in discerning the intent of the legislature (even with legislative history); and 2) the belief that going beyond the bare words of statutes is a violation of the Constitutional principle of the separation of powers. *Id.,* at 96.

Strict textualists are rare. *Id.* More common are people who argue that statutory interpretation should begin with the plain meaning of the words of the statute. In this more moderate view if no ambiguity exists, then the plain meaning should be adhered to. If an ambiguity exists, however, then one of the other approaches can be employed. *Id.*

There are some problems with textualism. First, words in English are often inherently ambiguous. As a result, saying that one can derive the plain meaning is at best misleading, and at worst disingenuous. Also, textualism has been criticized as being overly mechanical and simplistic. *Id.* Finally, some have maintained that this approach is often employed in such a way that it actually thwarts the powers of the legislature instead of preserving it. *Id.* at 97. This criticism relates to the fact that very often when a judge says that a particular word or term means "X," what they really mean is that the word or term means "X" to **them.** There is an inherent subjectivity built into this interpretive process. *Id.* By attempting to objectively identify the plain meaning, the textualist judge is really letting subjectivity in through the back door. See Paul E. McGreal, *Slighting Context: On the Illogic of Ordinary Speech in Statutory Interpretation,* 52 . Kan. L. Rev. 325 (2004).

B. Intentionalism

Intentionalism broadens out the scope of statutory review. Instead of just looking at the text and attempting to discern its meaning, a judge or lawyer employing the intentionalist approach will look beyond the statute in an attempt to discern the intention of the people who drafted and passed the statute. The idea here is that in the process of interpreting a statute more information is better than less. Jellum and Hricik describe the philosophy behind intentionalism this way:

> An intentionalist does not need a reason — like ambiguity or absurdity — to consider sources beyond the text. Intentionalists attempt to discern intent by perusing all available sources, including, principally, legislative history.... Intentionalists believe that in interpreting language it is imperative to be truthful to the intent of the author, and to do so, one must consult extrinsic sources.

Id. at 97. This philosophy turns on the notion that our system actually requires legal decision-makers to go beyond the text in order to be true to the principle of allowing the legislature to legislate. To do so is supporting the constitutional structure of our system.

Nonetheless, there are problems with intentionalism as well. For example, critics point out that legislative histories are notoriously incomplete and open to manipulation by groups that have unfair access to the legislative process (through lobbyists, for example). *Id.* at 98 (citing to *Blanchard v. Bergeron*, 489 U.S. 87, 98–99 (1989)). Also, critics of intentionalism believe that legal decision-makers can pick and choose their extrinsic sources to support their view of how the case should be decided. *Id.*; Antonin Scalia, A Matter of Interpretation 36 (1997). Finally, there is a good deal of controversy related to what sources can be consulted. Some maintain that only legislative history can be looked at. Others suggest that sources beyond the legislative history can be consulted. This is an ongoing controversy within the profession concerning the nature of the legislative process itself; one that deals with the purpose of legislation. This brings us to the last dominant approach.

C. Purposivism

The final prevalent approach to statutory interpretation is called purposivism. Of the three approaches discussed here, purposivism is the broadest form of statutory interpretation. Purposivists argue that legal decision-makers should use whatever materials they have at their disposal to discern the purpose behind the statute. *Id.* at 99. This broad approach, it is argued, allows legal decision-makers to act as the agents of the legislatures by putting into effect the policies behind a statute. According to Jellum and Hricik:

> [P]urposivists do not need a reason—like ambiguity or absurdity— to look to extratextual sources to discern meaning. Instead ... they believe that the interpretive function cannot be completed without considering other sources.... [Purposivism] allows courts to seek meaning from the broadest number of sources to make a more informed decision.

Id. at 100. This is necessary, because (as we saw above) words are often bare and lack content and context. As Karl Llewellyn put it, "If a statute is to make sense, it must be read in light of some assumed purpose. A statute merely declaring a rule, with no purpose or objective, is nonsense." Karl N. Llewellyn, *Remarks on the Theory of Appellate Decision and the Rules or Canons About How Statutes Are to be Construed*, 3 Vand. L. Rev. 395, 400 (1950). In other words, according to purposivists like Llewellyn, all statutes are designed to address certain social concerns. The public policies that affect these social concerns should inform the interpretation of these statutes in order to ensure that the legislative process fulfills its proper purpose. LINDA D. JELLUM AND DAVID CHARLES HRICIK, MODERN STATUTORY INTERPRETATION: PROBLEMS, THEORIES, AND LAWYERING STRATEGIES 100 (2006).

Like the other two approaches, purposivism has its detractors. Some critics complain that by opening up the process of statutory interpretation to vague and ill-defined things such as public policy, legal decision-makers are clearly engaging in legislating from the bench. *Id.* at 100. Others point to the fact that virtually every statute could be supported by a variety of different public policies and that the selection of certain policies over others is an inherently subjective process. *Id.* Finally, some suggest that allowing judges and other legal decision-makers to use public policy and other extrinsic sources to interpret statutes draws them into the political process. *Id.*

While there are other methods of statutory interpretation—some which are subcategories of these three dominant approaches—you can probably see how these three perspectives affect the process of reading, understanding, and using statutes. Beyond the basic approach that one uses in interpreting statutes, there are other interpretive devices that you should be aware of. For example, there are a variety of "canons of interpretation" that legal decision-makers use to determine what statutes mean and how they should be applied. *Id.* at Ch. 7; and Karl N. Llewellyn, *Remarks on the Theory of Appellate Decision and the Rules or Canons About How Statutes Are to be Construed*, 3 VAND. L. REV. 395, 400 (1950). These canons—or basic guidelines to interpretation—have evolved over time, and assist legal decision-makers in addressing statutory issues with some level of consistency and legitimacy. Some canons are textual, meaning that they relate to how the words of a statute ought to be read or applied. LINDA D. JELLUM AND DAVID CHARLES HRICIK, MODERN STATUTORY INTERPRETATION: PROBLEMS, THEORIES, AND LAWYERING STRATEGIES 145 (2006). Other canons can be described as "policy based" as they deal primarily with the policy based reasons that underlie a statutory text.

As you can see, when one intersects the adoption of a philosophical approach to statutory interpretation with the employment of one or more textual and/or policy based canons, statutory interpretation can become an extremely complicated and difficult enterprise. As one commentator has put it, "[s]tatutory interpretation requires some of the most complex mental processing that ordinary human beings are called upon to perform." Morell E. Mullins, Sr., *Tools, Not Rules: The Heuristic Nature of Statutory Interpretation*, 30 J. LEGIS. 1, 5 (2003) (quoted in LINDA D. JELLUM AND DAVID CHARLES HRICIK, MODERN STATUTORY INTERPRETATION: PROBLEMS, THEORIES, AND LAWYERING STRATEGIES 5 (2006)). Like so many of the analytical skills that we have discussed in this chapter, however, this is yet another opportunity for you — as an expert in the domain — to utilize your creative skills to shape and have an impact upon the work that you do. Statutory interpretation is a dynamic and exciting process. Once you move beyond the mechanical process of a simple reading and application of statutory materials, you will see that in our legal system statutes (like cases) allow some room for interpretation and rendering. This is not an illegitimate part of the process. It is simply an expression of the common law system at work. Even Supreme Court Justice Antonin Scalia, perhaps one of the most ardent supporters of textualism, acknowledges this when he says "I play the game like everybody else.... I'm in a system which has accepted rules and legislative history is used.... You read my opinions, I sin with the rest of them." Frank H. Easterbrook, *What does Legislative History Tell Us?*, 66 CHI-KENT L. REV. 441, 442 n.4 (1991) (quoting JUDGES AND LEGISLATORS: TOWARD INSTITUTIONAL COMITY, 174–175 (R. Katzmann ed. 1988)(Justice Scalia's comments during a panel discussion). In fact, this is no sin. Using your analytical abilities in this way shows that you are an expert doing your job effectively and creatively.

VII. Conclusion

We have seen throughout this chapter that there are a great many analytical skills that must be developed in your journey from novice to expert in the legal profession. This journey will entail you moving beyond the simple and mechanistic application of the basic skills we discussed in earlier chapters. You must become adept at using rule-based reasoning, utilizing the full panoply of interpretive and formative devices at your disposal. You will also need to master using analogies and counter-analogies to connect the legal work you do to precedents that you find in the corpus of legal materials available to you. Synthesizing legal precedents into more complex and robust authority is also a key skill that you will develop. This will allow you to develop legal arguments that are more than the sum of their parts. Many of these skills will be aided by a keen appreciation of policy based reasoning. While this sort of reasoning is difficult, the results it will yield is worth the effort. Finally, the complicated skill of interpreting statutory texts will signal your development into a legal expert.

This chapter has been designed to introduce these advanced skills and to give you some context for learning them. This is not a substitute for a fuller and more detailed study of each of these topics. There are very good resources out there for more advanced exploration of these concepts. What I have tried to do here is show you what you need to learn in order to master advanced analytical skills. I have also attempted to show you how learning and using each of these skills is an opportunity to be creative. In truth, each of the analytical abilities I discussed in this chapter is better described as an art than a skill. The latter connotes a technical ability, while the former describes a creative endeavor. When you see experts in the legal system engage in these things, you will see what I mean when I say these are artistic, not technical, abilities. You will likely be in awe when you realize this. Some day, a novice lawyer or law student will have the same view of the way in which you carry out your craft.

Checkpoints

- What do we mean by rule-based reasoning? What are the various interpretive techniques used in finding, formulating and communicating about legal rules?

- You should be comfortable identifying, formulating and using balancing tests, elements tests, and factors tests. You should also be able to understand which form is best considering your needs and the rules you have found and formulated.

- Why do you think the dominant form of legal analysis and communication in our system is the analogy? What does using analogies and counter-analogies enable you to do?

- Remember that synthesizing case law into complex rules allows you to develop rule structures that yield more than the sum of the parts that go into the synthesis.

- What does statutory interpretation involve? What are the various approaches to statutory interpretation, how do they differ, and when is each appropriate?

Chapter 5

Complex Legal Analysis and Communication

Roadmap to Complex Legal Analysis and Communication

- Pragmatic legal reasoning involves using a multi-focal logic to determine what tactics or techniques will be useful in addressing new or novel circumstances. Pragmatic — or experimental logic — is more than just the fixed forms of formal logic. This alternative logic is designed to allow you flexibility and creativity in your work.

- Cognitive or conceptual metaphor theory suggests that humans fundamentally understand the world in terms of the associations between known and unknown concepts. If this is true, our legal analysis and communication can be greatly aided by ensuring that we are using and drawing upon useful and compelling metaphors as we develop our ideas of how cases and other legal problems should be resolved.

- Understanding narrative theory and story-telling techniques is a vital tool in the arsenal of all legal professionals. Compelling narratives and stories draw the reader into the process of constructing meaning. When this sort of relationship is established, your analytical and communication skills are being utilized in their fullest forms.

- The use of rhetoric in legal analysis and communication is perhaps the culmination of all the skills and abilities we have discussed. Rhetorical thinking and communication involves drawing together your powers of logic, persuasion, and credibility to relate to others in the legal system. These relationships will involve, to a greater or lesser degree, all the things you learn throughout your time as a member of the profession.

I. Introduction

Thus far, we have explored a series of related analytical skills that will help you progress from the novice stage to mastering the tasks (analytical and communicative) in which expert lawyers engage. This progression has introduced each of these steps in increments. As a novice, using paradigms of legal reasoning and communication will help you model your work so that it resembles the work of experts in the domain. By honing your logical abilities, you will begin to think more precisely and will be able to see the faults in arguments put forth by yourself and others. And finally, by mastering the sorts of reasoning structures we discussed in Chapter Four you will be able to move from modeling the behaviors of experts in the legal system to becoming an expert yourself. This chapter is designed to help you continue this progression, to introduce you to a series of concepts that can only really be understood and employed once you have mastered the basics.

The topics we will discuss here build on the skills you have mastered thus far, but will require more than just the basics. Your professional journey from novice to expert begins with these analytical abilities, but it does not end there. To move beyond this advanced stage, and continue your intellectual progression, you will have to continue your education on your own. This continued analytical development is, perhaps, the last key sign that you have developed into an expert member of the profession. By taking on ownership of your development, you are striking out on a path of discovery that will lead to unknown places. This chapter is meant to help you understand several advanced analytical ideas that will assist you in charting that path.

The concepts represented in this chapter consist of several high level theories about how to continue to craft the expert skills you will have mastered, by filtering them through more detailed and complex concepts. Do not be put off when I say that these are advanced theoretical skills. Remember the dichotomy between theory and practice is a false one. These conceptual frameworks will enable you to continue to mold and craft your analytical and communication skills. We will begin by looking at pragmatic legal reasoning in much more detail than we did in Chapter Three. In my view, this will set the stage for continuing the progression I mentioned above. By understanding the full implications of experimental logic, you can see how the other advanced analytical and communication skills can be pieced together in a pragmatic way to accommodate the situations you will encounter as an expert in the domain.

Once this is accomplished, we will explore some ideas that are both novel and cutting-edge in legal theory. We will first examine the theory that we think of important ideas—legal and non-legal—through metaphors. This theory, which has been used in many intellectual arenas over the past two decades, has recently been more directly applied to legal analysis and communication. Then we will explore two related ideas—narrative and storytelling—that have also recently gained some currency in the context of advanced legal reasoning and writing. These literary concepts have great application for experts in the legal domain. Finally, we will reexamine the field of rhetoric, delving more deeply into basic rhetorical concepts and their application in legal analysis and communication.

Taken together, these ideas will expand your thinking on what exactly comprises legal analysis and communication. These theories represent a variety of different perspectives on how to think about legal analysis and communication. As a result, the subsections that follow are largely independent of one another. The hope is that by discussing several different aspects of advanced legal analysis and communication you will begin to stretch your analytical muscles a little, that you will be able to push the boundaries of your technical training and take a more creative view of thinking and working within the domain. The more formal and restrictive view that you learned (necessarily) as a novice will open up, allowing you to incorporate the sorts of advanced and interdisciplinary theories we will discuss in this chapter. Having these perspectives as part of your analytical repertoire will further draw upon and give expression to your creativity. These ideas, and others you will learn on your own, will expand your thinking and your abilities as a legal professional. None of these sections will make you an expert in the topics they cover. They should, however, introduce you to some novel and stimulating perspectives that you might want to explore further. Let us start by looking again at pragmatic legal reasoning.

II. More on Pragmatic Legal Reasoning

I suggested above that pragmatic legal reasoning is helpful because it allows you to be flexible in your approach to legal problems. This sort of analysis gives you the perspective and the tools to select most effectively from amongst a variety of reasoning and communication skills as you address complex legal problems. Instead of mechanically selecting and employing the same formal paradigms of reasoning (or logic) whenever you confront a legal problem, thinking pragmatically will enable you to be more flexible and nimble in selecting those skills and strategies that will best assist you in accomplishing your tasks with subtlety and precision. In other words, in order to move beyond the sort of "one size fits all" thinking that law school tends to convey, you will need to develop more mental and practical agility. Understanding and using the kind of "logic" that the philosopher John Dewey developed is a way to gaining this agility.

John Dewey was an American philosopher in the late nineteenth and early twentieth centuries. He wrote on a wide variety of topics, including democracy, education, epistemology (theories of knowledge), legal theory, and moral reasoning. In our discussion, we will be looking at the intersection between his epistemological views and his conception of legal reasoning. Like the other theories we discuss in this chapter, Dewey's legal epistemology has gained some popularity in recent years. This popularity is not just a fad, in my estimation. Pragmatic legal reasoning provides something that other theories of legal reasoning do not. It more closely approximates the actual practice of expert legal reasoning and better explains the way creativity and subjectivity fit into the process. As you might guess from what you have read thus far throughout this work, I am convinced that the existence of creativity and subjectivity within the legal system is not a bad thing. In fact, I would go so far as to say that it is impossible to have a complex institutional system without creativity and subjectivity. Many systems of legal reasoning and jurisprudence attempt to eliminate these aspects, thus constructing a "scientific" system of legal theory. See, BRIAN BIX, JURISPRUDENCE: THEORY AND CONTEXT 35 (3d ed. 2004). This is, in the view of many, an impossibility. *Id.* at 59–60. Complex human reasoning, in any domain, is multifaceted and pragmatic (in the fullest conception of that word). Experts in the legal domain display this trait all the time. So let us look at the theory behind pragmatic legal epistemology.

A. Dewey's Experimental Logic and the Law

In his short essay entitled "Logical Method and Law," John Dewey presented a theory which was designed to give those involved in legal decision-making "a single way of treating cases for certain purposes or consequences in spite of their diversity." John Dewey, *Logical Method and the Law*, 10 CORNELL L.Q. 17, 22 (1924). Dewey explained what he called an experimental logic whose "meaning and worth are subject to inquiry and revision in view of what happens, what the consequences are, when it is used as a method of treatment." *Id.* at 22–23. According to Dewey, when administrative officers, judges, or lawyers are involved in legal reasoning they should trust this experimental logic to guide them to general principles which emerge as "statements of generic ways in which it has been found helpful to treat concrete cases." *Id.* at 22. In other words, by looking at the consequences of legal reasoning in other cases, we can formulate better decisions in the cases we work on.

Dewey believed that the analytical system behind the common law is consequentialist. This means that legal analysis and communication in our system is designed to address the end products, not the process that leads to those ends. At one obvious level this seems correct. For all the fancy talk about universal principles of justice and fairness that other legal theories pronounce, the day to day operation of our legal system seems to turn more on the practical aspects of how we deal with particular cases in specific factual situations. This is as true in transactional work as it is in litigation settings. For Dewey (and other pragmatists as well), human reasoning is a system of trial and error.

We work best, according to this pragmatic theory, when we are flexible enough to try ideas in a fluid and malleable way. By doing so, we are drawing from a wide variety of conceptual schemes, using those that best fit the situations we face. In some circumstances we might find that one particular analytical skill is useful. In another situation we might find that an entirely different skill is most useful (even if the two situations are not dramatically different). For Dewey, and others who think like him, this kind of intellectual dexterity will lead us to the most rational and useful outcomes. Our thinking is best when it accomplishes the goals we have set, when we have addressed the concerns we face, and when we gained some practical consequences from our thinking. After all, this is what our mental abilities are designed to do most directly, right? According to Dewey, using "experimental logic" is the best way to accomplish these things. Before we can assess whether or not Dewey's predictions of the effect of his theory are correct, however, we must first determine the process involved in his articulation of experimental logic.

1. Experimental Logic in the Process of Human Reasoning

Dewey believed that legal reasoning displays what he called the "common structure or pattern of human inquiry." JOHN DEWEY, LOGIC: THE THEORY OF INQUIRY 105 (1991). In fact, he seemed to believe that legal reasoning was a paradigm example of how humans think. According to Dewey, we utilize our reasoning abilities in similar ways no matter in what human endeavor we are engaged. *Id.* The structure of reason is not, as some may assume, fixed and abstract. Dewey parted ways with the rationalist philosophical tradition represented by the well-known philosophers Rene Descartes and Immanuel Kant and adopted a more fluid and practical form of thinking. *Id.* at Ch. 1; See, RICHARD RORTY, CONSEQUENCES OF PRAGMATISM 161 (1982). This more pragmatic form was designed to deal with the practical outcomes of thinking, not the abstract notions of mind or cognition that other epistemologists and logicians had developed. Thinking is good if it works. It works if it accomplishes what it is meant to accomplish. This was the foundation of Dewey's pragmatist project.

This "common structure or pattern of reasoning" involves several steps which yield a shifting pattern of data that humans can use to determine whether a course of action (or thought) will serve as useful or not. JOHN DEWEY, LOGIC: THE THEORY OF INQUIRY 108 (1991). This was Dewey's most obvious disagreement with the rationalist tradition. Theories related to that tradition insist that there are closed, constant and true forms of intuition and logic that the human mind understands. For Dewey, human reasoning is an experimental process of inquiry and reflection. JOHN DEWEY, LOGIC: THE THEORY OF INQUIRY Ch. 6 (1991); JOHN DEWEY, HOW WE THINK Ch. 6 (1991). Instead of looking into the philosophy of mind as the rationalist philosophers had done, Dewey wanted to bring human reason into the light of everyday experience. He says, for instance, that "[t]he search for the pattern of inquiry is ... not one instituted in the dark or at large. It is checked and controlled by knowledge of the kinds of inquiry that have and that have not worked; methods which ... can be so compared as to yield reasoned or rational conclusions." JOHN DEWEY, LOGIC: THE THEORY OF INQUIRY 108 (1991). Human knowledge, then, is ends (or consequences) oriented.

This yields a more contingent and mutable form of reasoning. As the philosopher Richard Rorty puts it, "[t]he natural approach to sentences [which concern the way we reason], Dewey tells us, is not 'Do they get it right?', but more like 'What would it be like to believe that? What would happen if I did? What would I be committing myself to?'" RICHARD RORTY, CONSEQUENCES OF PRAGMATISM 163 (1982). The search, then, is not for universal truths, but for "methods which experience up to the present time shows to be the best methods available for achieving certain results...." JOHN DEWEY, LOGIC: THE THEORY OF INQUIRY 108 (1991). This is a significant departure in the field of epistemology. Where traditional epistemologists sought logical constants, Dewey's quest is more properly characterized as a way to categorize experience in a useful and practical way.

According to Dewey, human reasoning follows several steps through reflection and inquiry. *Id.* at 108–120. He identifies these steps in the process of inquiry as: (I) The Antecedent Conditions of Inquiry: Recognizing the Indeterminate Situation; (II) The Institution of a Problem; (III) The Determination of a Problem-Solution; (IV) Reasoning About the Solution; and (V) The Operational Character of Facts-Meanings in the Resolution of the Problem. *Id.* at 108–116. Dewey gives a more truncated description of this process elsewhere:

> "Upon examination, each instance reveals, more or less clearly, five logically distinct steps: (i) a felt difficulty; (ii) its location and definition; (iii) suggestion of [a] possible solution; (iv) development by reasoning of the bearings of the suggestion; (v) further observation and experiment leading to its acceptance or rejection...."

JOHN DEWEY, HOW WE THINK 72 (1991). You may remember that we discussed these briefly in Chapter Three. If you recall this discussion, you will remember that while this process might seem abstract as it is stated, it is really quite intuitive and easy to grasp. The steps in this process follow quite closely the natural and practical way we tend to think about problems. The fascinating and important aspect of Dewey's philosophy is that he is not asking us to learn a new way of thinking, but is instead attempting to describe the way we **do** think. In other words, he is drawing our attention to what we do analytically and describing how we do it. This is meant to make us think more critically about our analytical habits, which in turn will make us more skilled at using our analysis and more precise in the use of these abilities. Now let us look at how all this is applied to legal reasoning in particular.

2. *Legal Reasoning as an Example of Experimental Logic*

Legal reasoning is just the application of the "common pattern or structure" of human reasoning to a particular intellectual domain. Actors in the legal system employ their analytical abilities using the same pattern of inquiry; they simply do so in the context of addressing legal questions within the discourse community of the U.S. legal system. This contextual application is just another aspect of the pragmatic nature of human reasoning. The cultural and professional expectations of others within the domain help to mold and structure the pattern of inquiry. But the pattern of inquiry remains largely the same.

As a result, reasoning about legal matters—like reasoning about other areas of human intellectual concern such as science and industry—requires people in the domain to begin the process by acknowledging the existence of an indeterminate situation. This should not seem strange. We have seen throughout this work that legal analysis begins when you are initially presented with an indeterminate situation, some "complicated and confused case" which needs to be addressed. John Dewey, *Logical Method and the Law*, 10 CORNELL L.Q. 17, 23 (1924). As we have seen, in our legal system this indeterminacy is a legal problem of some sort—a dispute that needs to be mediated or a transgression which must be addressed. It is the recognition that there is an indeterminate situation, says Dewey, that is the first step in the inquiry. *Id.* There is much more to this initial step than meets the eye, however. In the context of our legal system, even indeterminate situations are shaped (perhaps it is best to say pre-shaped) by the fact that they must be recognized as situations that the legal system can address. This means that this cognitive process is dependent on recognizing a problem as a legal problem, as opposed to a political problem, a scientific problem, a social problem, or a technical problem.

Once an indeterminate situation is recognized as a legal problem, and thus placed within the appropriate field of reference (what I have been calling the proper domain), the process can continue to be employed in the domain.

Within the domain, we do not begin this process of inquiry completely devoid of any and all preconceptions. As Dewey says explicitly, "we generally begin with some vague anticipation of a conclusion (or at least of alternative conclusions), and then we look around for principles and data which will substantiate it or which will enable us to choose between rival conclusions." *Id.* Recall what we said about working with rules and analogical reasoning in Chapter Four. There we said that in the context of legal reasoning the skills are formed by the particular problem we are being faced with, and the stance we have vis-à-vis our relation to that problem. So, the legal problem (indeterminate situation) is important, but so is the role we play in the examination of the problem (advocate, judge, etc.). Let us assume that we are examining a problem from the context of a lawyer representing the interests of her client. This is, after all, the paradigm example of the lawyer's role in the American legal system. According to Dewey:

> [A lawyer] begins with a conclusion which he intends to reach, favorable to his client of course, and then analyzes the facts of the situation to find material out of which to construct a favorable statement of facts, and to form a minor premise. At the same time he goes over recorded cases to find rules of law employed in cases which can be presented as similar, rules which will substantiate a certain way of looking at and interpreting the facts.

Id. The entire system is set up for an advocate to play the role of making determinant that which is not. This process of "making determinant" is not "objective," however, as the possible successful outcomes will all be formed in light of what is best for the client. David T. ButleRitchie, *"Objectively Speaking," There Is No Such Thing in the Law!*, 5 DISABILITY MEDICINE 68 (2005). Some still maintain that objectivity is the aim of law, and that such a thing is possible. BRIAN LEITER, ED., OBJECTIVITY IN LAW AND MORALS (2001). Advocates of pragmatic logic are skeptical, however. The pattern of inquiry described by Dewey is modeled on the more general pattern of human knowledge. JOHN DEWEY, LOGIC: THE THEORY OF INQUIRY 105 (1991). It is not directly analogous to the scientific method, however. John Dewey, *Logical Method and the Law*, 10 CORNELL L.Q. 17, 23 (1924). Remember, legal reasoning is not a science. The consequentialism of this process means that the possible successful outcomes are all tied to who we represent or what role we play in the system.

For lawyers in the Anglo-American tradition there is a heavy element of partisanship built in here. *Id.* The process of reasoning employed by actors in the legal system "is … pre-committed to the establishment of a particular and partisan conclusion.…" *Id.* The vague conclusion that Dewey talks about is largely determined by the outcome which will be most favorable to the particular lawyer's client in the context of the legal problem faced. For judicial decision-makers, though, partisanship is to play no role, at least not officially. Nonetheless, all participants in the process front load their analysis. That is to say, once a legal problem has been conceived and begins to be formed into a determinate legal issue, the immediate first step on the part of anyone engaged in legal reasoning is to light upon a likely conclusion or conclusions that will address the situation. *Id.* Even judges predetermine answers to their inquiries. *Id.* These answers will not be related to the form of advocacy mentioned above (or at least should not be), but will relate more closely to what the judge believes is the correct answer. *Id.*

Largely based on the preconceptions as to probable (or at least possible) outcomes mentioned above, legal decision-makers begin to grapple further with the indeterminacy by framing the legal issue or issues involved into a category that we recognize, and which is at the same time favorable to the vague conclusions originally embraced. *Id.* As Dewey says, the "way in which a problem is conceived decides what specific suggestions are entertained and which are dismissed.…" JOHN DEWEY, LOGIC: THE THEORY OF INQUIRY 112 (1991). The way in which a legal issue is initially drawn, then, very often determines that outcome of the case, as this framing will likely decide which law controls. John Dewey, *Logical Method and the Law*, 10 CORNELL L.Q. 17, 23 (1924). Statutes and cases apply to facts, and the way in which the facts in any given case are arranged (some might say massaged) will determine the statutory provisions and precedents that will apply. *Id.* at 23–26. More often than not the party which prevails is the one that arranged their facts in the most finely tuned fashion, thus availing themselves of the most favorable law. *Id.*

The working through experimental logic which Dewey describes involves a trial and error process that will change depending on the circumstances faced, and even who is engaging in the process of inquiry. As actors in the legal system engage in the process of experimental inquiry, they will explore, assess, and evaluate the data they have at their disposal, using things that work and discarding those that do not. In effect, lawyers and judges consult theories of the case and precedents that relate to their legal problem, assess the connection of those theories and precedents to the proposed outcomes, and evaluate if the theories and precedents will lead to the desired outcome. If they do lead, or are likely to lead, to the desired outcomes, then these analytical tools are used. If they do not, they are rejected in light of better theories of the case or precedents that are more helpful.

Where several intermediate issues must be resolved before the ultimate issue can be addressed adequately, this process of framing issues in recognized categories and applying relevant determinate provisions will take place serially until the ultimate issue is sufficiently resolved. *Id.* Dewey's experimental logic is a progressive inquiry which concludes in a judgement that has "direct existential import." JOHN DEWEY, LOGIC: THE THEORY OF INQUIRY 108, 123 (1991). The rendering of a judicial decision is perhaps the paradigm example of just such a culmination. The deliberations and procedures followed at trial (concerning, for example, what evidence will be admitted, whose version of the applicable law will be adopted, and so on) are the intermediate steps in the progression of partial determinacies. John Dewey, *Logical Method and the Law*, 10 CORNELL L.Q. 17, 23–26 (1924). This process ends, as we might expect, in the case of being disposed of through final judgement. *Id.*

Dewey went into detail about the particular aspects of experimental logic and its application to the sphere of legal reasoning not because he thought it necessary to persuade legal decision-makers to change their reasoning, but because he believed that they already act in this way. But if this is the case, why are we not taught about this process early on in law school? Why do we not discuss pragmatic reasoning explicitly as an aspect of our legal system? Dewey believed that the answers to these questions relates to the fact that legal decision-makers maintain a fiction in order to conceal the process actually used in legal-decision making from the public at large. See, *Id.* This fiction is expressed in the idea that legal decisions must be made according to strictly formal rules of logic which are syllogistic in form. *Id.* at 21. Dewey says, for example, that "the [logic] which has had greatest historic currency and exercised greatest influence on legal decisions, is that of the syllogism." *Id.* He says, further, that this logic "claims to be a logic of fixed forms, rather than of methods of reaching intelligent decisions in concrete situations, or of methods employed in adjusting disputed issues in behalf of the public and enduring interest." *Id.* Dewey was skeptical that this logic could actually form the heart of a highly developed legal system.

The kind of syllogistic logic which Dewey criticizes is advocated by those who wish to attribute formal arguments that necessarily lead to logically "correct" decisions. Dewey discusses Oliver Wendell Holmes, Jr.'s critique of this extensively. Like Dewey, Holmes (and other legal realists) believed that attempts to turn legal reasoning into formal syllogistic logic were both fruitless and dangerously misguided. OLIVER WENDELL HOLMES, JR., THE COMMON LAW (1991); and BRIAN BIX, JURISPRUDENCE: THEORY AND CONTEXT 80–81 (3d ed. 2004). This view of how legal reasoning should work leads to a "mechanical jurisprudence," whereby antecedent legal rules are automatically applied to factual situations in such a way as to determine with absolute logical certainty the proper decision. John Dewey, *Logical Method and the Law*, 10 Cornell L.Q. 17, 21–22 (1924). These are the sorts of arguments we saw in the sections of Chapter Three devoted to formal logic. According to Dewey, however, this sort of syllogistic reasoning in the law is neither possible nor desirable. Dewey does not deny that the spirit of formal (or what is sometimes called Aristotelian) logic is relevant to his theory of experimental logic. It is the formal and strict application of the syllogistic form which Dewey takes issue with. John Dewey, Logic: The Theory of Inquiry Ch. 6 (1991). When legal decision-makers attempt to apply this strictly formal logic to legal decisions, Dewey believed they are engaging in a charade. In Dewey's view, the way the Anglo-American legal system works, with specific reference to its common law heritage, is much closer to the experimental process he champions. John Dewey, *Logical Method and the Law*, 10 Cornell L.Q. 17 (1924). In short, he said, there is a "disparity which exists between actual legal development and the strict requirements of logical theory [based on the syllogism]." *Id.* at 20. But what is the cause of this disparity?

The answer to this question is found in what might be aptly described as the innate human need for security. Dewey equated the desire for logical formality with the aspiration to consistency. *Id.* "The use of prior ready-made and familiar concepts ... give[s] rise to a sense of stability, of guarantee against sudden and arbitrary changes of the rules which determine the consequences which attend acts." *Id.*; John Dewey, Logic: The Theory of Inquiry 134–135 (1991). But Dewey believed this to be a "specious sense of protection," one which is self-perpetuating through habit once established. Dewey, *Logical Method and Law*, 10 Cornell L.Q. 17, 20 (1924). The requirement of explaining formal logical consistency (based on syllogistic reasoning) in legal decision-making, then, is propelled by the intrinsic inertia of habit. But habit alone does not adequately explain the preference for accounts of legal reasoning that privilege formal logical consistency made by most legal theorists in the Anglo-American tradition. *Id.* It is my belief that a further answer lies in the need to maintain the authority of the law as a social institution. Many accounts of legal reasoning attempt to describe the legal system as one that employs formal logic because, it is believed, such accounts would give a sense of objective legitimacy to the system. For Dewey, and for me, this sense is an illusion.

As noted above, it is not that Dewey believed that there is no logic to the way legal decisions are made. He simply believed that there is another type of logic at work. This is a logic of consequences rather than one of antecedents. John Dewey, *Logical Method and the Law*, 10 Cornell L.Q. 17 (1924); and Neil MacCormick, *On Legal Decisions and Their Consequences: From Dewey to Dworkin*, 58 N.Y.U. L. Rev. 242 (1983). Dewey argued for "a logic of prediction of probabilities rather than one of deduction of certainties." John Dewey, *Logical Method and the Law*, 10 Cornell L.Q. 17, 26 (1924). While Dewey himself never actually explicated precisely what the open adoption of a fully consequentialist logic might entail, he did sketch — in broad terms — what he held to be the fundamental tenets of such a view. *Id.* Others have followed up on this attempt in recent years. Neil MacCormick, *On Legal Decisions and Their Consequences, From Dewey to Dworkin*, 58 N.Y.U. L. Rev. 242 (1983).

In an attempt to explain his alternative view Dewey began his essay on "Logical Method of Law" by defining logical theory as "the procedures followed in reaching decisions in those cases in which subsequent experience shows that they were the best which could have been used under the conditions." John Dewey, *Logical Method and the Law*, 10 Cornell L.Q. 17, 17–18 (1924). This seems a troubling place in which to begin this discussion of applying experimental logic to legal reasoning, however. Such a definition appears to allow for the post hoc rationalization of previous decisions based on the excuse that a judicial decision-maker "did the best that she could." Here the issue of consistency mentioned above seems quiet patent. Certainly a legal system needs more precise procedures than this — procedures of general application which maintain a sense of consistency and fairness.

But logical consistency can and does mean more than one thing. Consistency in the Aristotelian sense means the presence of a major and a minor premise (at a minimum), with a conclusion that necessarily follows from these premises. *Id.* at 21. There are other types of consistency, however, like those derived from dialectical logic, or the application of the same principle in like situations. *Id.* I believe that it is this latter form of consistency — the use of "general principles" in similar circumstances — that Dewey advocated. As we saw in our discussion of analogical reasoning in Chapter Four, this is a central feature of the American common law system. In fact, it is what defines the concept of *stare decisis*.

It seems obvious that Dewey recognized the existence of these other types of consistency as he attempted to further delineate the way his experimental logic can be (and is) applied to the law. For example, Dewey said that "[i]t is most important that rules of law should form as coherent generalized logical systems as possible." *Id.* at 19. So consistency in application (as opposed to formal syllogistic consistency) is important. Dewey was not denying that there are situations in which formal logic can be employed in legal reasoning. He did maintain, however, that formal logical consistency should not be the principle goal of the legal system. *Id.* He suggested that "these logical systemizations of law ... with their reduction of a multitude of decisions to a few general principles that are logically consistent ... is clearly in last resort subservient to the economical and effective reaching of decisions in particular cases." *Id.* In other words, formal logic can used to the extent that it is used in the service of sound pragmatic decision-making. In effect, Dewey argued that while consistency is indeed important and formal logic can be useful in legal reasoning, the primary locus of concern for legal decision-makers must be that a proper decision is arrived at in any particular instance regardless of consistency or formal logical coherence.

Another way of looking at this is to say that general legal principles are only useful as tools in attempting to resolve concrete cases. As far as I can tell, these general principles need not necessarily be formally consistent in any syllogistic way. Dewey had denied that Aristotelian logic is the basis for understanding the law. *Id.* at 26. For Dewey, logic is a "means of intellectual survey, analysis, and insight into the factors of the situation to be dealt with. Like other tools they must be modified when they are applied to new conditions and new results have to be achieved." *Id.* Having a fixed and universal sense of logic would be unduly restrictive, since arguments or principles which are logically consistent in the Aristotelian sense cannot change over time. Logical principles—of whatever form—are tools that are never meant to become absolutely static. Such principles must maintain a measure of usefulness in order to justify their continued use. *Id.* To the extent that they are not useful, they should be rejected in the face of principles better equipped to handle the situations we must face and address. Turning legal principles into abstract "systems" or trying to compile a catalogue of "black letter rules" is counter-productive. Doing these things—or attempting to do so—renders law a mechanical abstraction that disconnects it from the social institution it must be. If the principles that legal decision-makers use as tools today do become static, continued adherence to them will widen "the gap between current social conditions and the principles used by the courts." *Id.* The effect of this will be to "breed irritation, disrespect for law, together with virtual alliance between the judiciary and entrenched interests that correspond most nearly to the conditions under which the rules of law were previously laid down." *Id.*

We see in Dewey's theoretical framework several ideas which seem intuitively correct. His notion that legal decision-makers attempt to turn indeterminacies (legal problems) into partial determinacies by framing the issue to fit the problem into a recognized (and favorable) category seems spot on. Similarly, the notion of inquiry leading to ultimate judgement appears to conform with the process we expect from legal reasoning. Overall, it seems that Dewey's account does indeed mirror the sorts of analysis we engage in. In particular, his account clearly tracks the kind of analysis in which expert legal decision-makers engage. I have said several times throughout this book that you do not need to be a philosopher or logician in order to engage in good legal reasoning. Understanding the intricacies of Dewey's account of pragmatic legal reasoning, however, can help you see how to make your thinking more clear and precise. Perhaps looking at the implications of his theory will assist you.

B. Implications for Advanced Legal Analysis and Communication

This notion of pragmatic logic, and the process Dewey identified as the heart of that logic, is simply a representation of how you can systematically engage in legal reasoning designed to yield effective results. Remember, the attractiveness of this theory is that it is designed to be useful, to give us a way for addressing problems within the domain. We think like this naturally — recall the example I used in Chapter 3 about the light bulb — but the increased awareness that knowing about and identifying the parts of the process will give you should help you be more systematic, more deliberate, and more precise in your analytical judgments.

This is a reiterative process, where you conceptualize based on your pre-determinations, find and assess relevant authorities, evaluate whether they get you to the conclusion you anticipated, and determine whether further conceptualization and research is needed. Very often these further steps are needed. This is not, like many theories about legal reasoning, a linear process. It is a recurrent loop that requires you to double back on your initial conceptualizations and research as you move forward. The following figure should give you some idea of what I mean by this:

Figure [A] represents the beginning of the inquiry. At this point you will recognize that a legal problem has been presented. This will usually happen when you are given an assignment or when your client has presented their problem to you. Almost immediately you will do two things: first you will assess whether it is actually a legal problem; and second you will categorize the problem into a recognizable kind of legal problem (contracts, criminal law, family law, etc.) if you determine that it is something the legal system can address. This step is represented by [B] on the figure above.

These first two steps in Dewey's articulation of the pragmatic process of legal reasoning are very important, because they will almost immediately lead to the third step: the (pre)determination of a solution. This is represented as

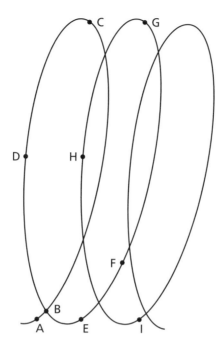

[C] above. This (pre)determination does not end the process, however. If it did, this would be a more or less linear process. Instead, once the (pre)determination is made, you will test this (pre)determination against the available data. This data consists of the authority available to you. In consulting cases and other available authority, you will be assessing whether these resources support or undermine your initial pre-determination. This process of evaluation is represented by [D] above. You will note that [D] is actually a step backwards in the representation. This is because very often when we are engaged in the process of assessing and evaluating data we realize that we must reconceptualize the problem. This is represented in the illustration by the letter [E].

This reconceptualization based on a better understanding of the data leads to a refinement of the issue and further examination of the data ([F]). In turn, another — more informed — determination of a likely conclusion or successful outcome ([G]) is formulated. This new conclusion is then further tested against the authority available ([H]), and evaluated to see whether it will likely lead to the desired outcome ([I]). This process will continue as long as needed until the data is likely to yield the desired outcome. In effect, there can be as many loops as you need in order for the process to play itself out.

You might be able to see how the paradigms and other analytical strategies we discussed in earlier chapters slot into the representation. For example, points [B] and [F] will draw upon your ability to spot and formulate issues. This in turn springs your ability to conceptualize the theory of the case, find relevant authority to address that theory, and formulate a rule or rules that addresses the theory you are working under ([C] and [G]). You might also see how the ability to analogize and counter-analogize is implicated in steps [D] and [H]. Once you are in the loop and have a clearer notion of how things fit together you may synthesize authority, and as you develop your various conclusions you will have to employ policy based reasoning to determine whether your proposed conclusion is likely to be viewed as reasonable and supportable.

Reducing the process of experimental logic to a visual representation like this is somewhat helpful in that it should give you a better sense of how all this fits together. There are drawbacks to using this kind of representation, however. For example, you might be tempted to think that this process is another analytical paradigm that can just be followed. Resist this temptation. Using this pragmatic logic is not like briefing cases or using the paradigm you learned in your legal writing class. The one thing that you must see about using pragmatic logic is that it requires you to be flexible and adaptable. To the extent that something works, use it. If it ceases to be useful, discard it. Remember, this is not a formula. This is an articulation of how we think about problems and how we can use this thinking strategically to get the results we desire. This sort of reasoning is instrumentalist. Our analysis is a tool that should get us the results we desire. To the extent that our thinking reaches that goal, it is productive. If our thinking does not reach that goal, we need to move back and reassess. In effect, this sort of reasoning process will enable you to use all the tools you have learned in law school, all the things we have discussed in earlier chapters, as you work through legal problems. Sometimes you will use one or more of these skills extensively. Other times, you will use a different skill set. Yet other times you may have to employ a version of all the skills you have mastered to address a legal problem. The usefulness of this understanding of legal reasoning is that it allows for this flexibility. In fact, pragmatic logic is designed precisely to account for such flexibility.

III. Cognitive Metaphor Theory

Legal thinking is imaginative thinking. While you may have gotten the impression from your time in law school (and perhaps even, perish the thought, from earlier chapters in this book) that this is not the case, you will have many opportunities to express a tremendous amount of creativity in your work. One of the most effective, and perhaps most profound, is the use of metaphor in your legal analysis and communication. At the outset, this claim may seem puzzling. You probably remember metaphors from your English and composition classes, and you may even occasionally spot the use of metaphors in the things you read in law school (if so, you have probably spotted the many I have used throughout this work). But how do metaphors attain the status I have afforded them? Are metaphors not just literary devices?

This section is not just about using metaphors as literary devices. Instead, the following discussion is designed to introduce you to the idea that as human beings we think about the world in general, and about ideas within specific domains like law, in metaphorical terms. Mark Johnson, *Mind, Metaphor, Law*, 58 MERCER L. REV. 845 (2007). This is a dramatic claim and one which would have wide ranging implications if it is borne out. But what does it mean to say that we think of the world in metaphorical terms? More particularly, what does it mean to say that we think about the law in metaphorical terms? Let us explore this idea further to find out.

A. Cognitive or Conceptual Metaphor Theory

The linguist George Lakoff and the philosopher Mark Johnson have, over the past 25 years, developed a robust theory of how metaphor works in the way humans analyze and make sense of the world. GEORGE LAKOFF & MARK JOHNSON, METAPHORS WE LIVE BY (1980); George Lakoff & Mark Johnson, *The Metaphorical Structure of the Human Conceptual System*, 4 COGNITIVE SCIENCE 195 (1980); George Lakoff & Mark Johnson, *Conceptual Metaphor in Everyday Language*, 77 JOURNAL OF PHILOSOPHY 453 (1980). Over the years their work in this regard has been widely cited in fields as diverse as clinical psychology, cognitive science, linguistics, literary studies, philosophy, and politics. GEORGE LAKOFF & MARK JOHNSON, METAPHORS WE LIVE BY 243 (1980) More recently cognitive metaphor theory has become of interest to legal theorists and scholars. Steven L. Winter, *Re-Embodying Law*, 58 MERCER L. REV. 869 (2007); STEVEN L. WINTER, A CLEARING IN THE FOREST (Chicago 2001). As law is a fundamentally analytical and literary enterprise, this might make sense to you. I hope so.

Advocates of the cognitive theory of metaphor maintain that metaphors are fundamental to the way we understand and experience the world. GEORGE LAKOFF & MARK JOHNSON, METAPHORS WE LIVE BY 4–5 (1980). George Lakoff and Mark Johnson, for example, have said that "our ordinary conceptual system is metaphorical in nature." *Id.* at 4. In essence, the way we think is dependent on metaphor. *Id.* at 6. This has profound implications. If this is correct, then human cognition is determined in no small part by the ability to recognize, understand, and use metaphors. *Id.* at 3-9. This, in turn, suggests that who we are is determined by metaphors. *Id.* In effect, we "live by" metaphors in the truest sense. *Id.* Far from being a mere linguistic device, on this view metaphorical reasoning is a metaphysical principle of the highest order. Jacques Derrida, *White Mythology: Metaphor in the Text of Philosophy*, in MARGINS OF PHILOSOPHY 212 (Alan Bass trans. 1982).

Metaphors are ways of describing or illustrating one concept by equating it to something else. GEORGE LAKOFF & MARK JOHNSON, METAPHORS WE LIVE BY 3 (1980). The relationship between the first concept ("target" in George Lakoff's scheme) and the second concept ("source") is one of ascription. GEORGE LAKOFF, WOMEN, FIRE AND DANGEROUS THINGS: WHAT CATEGORIES REVEAL ABOUT THE MIND 276–278 (1987). In ascribing the characteristics of the source concept upon the target concept, we are conveying meaning about the target concept by playing on one's conceptual understanding of the attributes of the source concept. *Id.* It is this relationship that conveys meaning, not the words that are used. *Id.* In effect, when we are faced with understanding a new or difficult concept, we cognitively seek to relate the unknown idea to something we do know in order to make the new or difficult concept more intelligible. *Id.* Very often, perhaps almost always, this ascriptive relationship is done without consciously thinking about it. GEORGE LAKOFF & MARK JOHNSON, METAPHORS WE LIVE BY 11 (1980).

Some, like Lakoff and Johnson, suggest that this metaphoric aspect of reasoning is cognitive in nature. *Id.* at Chapters 1 & 2. That is to say, advocates of the cognitive theory of metaphor maintain that metaphors are deeply ingrained in the way our brains work. *Id.* According to Lakoff and Johnson and others who follow their views, metaphors make so much sense to us because we are — at base — creatures who understand concepts in metaphorical terms. *Id.* at 3–9. As Lakoff and Johnson put it, "we systematically use inference patterns from one conceptual domain to reason about another conceptual domain." *Id.* at 246. Cognitive — or conceptual — metaphor theory is a systematic aspect of our analytical abilities. *Id.* at 7–9. Lakoff and Johnson suggest that our pervasive use of metaphor in analyzing and describing phenomena flows from the fact that our bodies interface with the world in certain ways. GEORGE LAKOFF & MARK JOHNSON, METAPHORS WE LIVE BY 246 (1980); GEORGE LAKOFF & MARK JOHNSON, PHILOSOPHY IN THE FLESH Ch. 6 (1999). This has been taken so far as to mean that our brains are wired in ways that recognize and utilize metaphorical relationships. GEORGE LAKOFF & MARK JOHNSON, METAPHORS

We Live By 257–259 (1980). These relationships are, in this view, neurological in nature. *Id.*

There are some who disagree with this view, maintaining that metaphors do not have this cognitive structure. Donald Davidson, Inquiries Into Truth and Interpretation 264 (1994). Nonetheless, something rings true in the work of Lakoff and Johnson. According to Steven Winter, and ultimately to Lakoff and Johnson, "[t]hought is not primarily linguistic and propositional, but embodied and imaginative…." Steven L. Winter, A Clearing in the Forest 247 (2001). As Lakoff and Johnson themselves put it, "metaphor is a natural phenomenon. Conceptual metaphor is a natural part of human thought, and linguistic metaphor is a natural part of human language." *Id.* In other words, we cannot extract metaphor from our conceptual schemes. We are metaphorical beings, and everything we do has metaphorical entailments.

We need not go into the specifics of the neuro-biology behind the cognitive or conceptual theory of metaphor here. For purposes of this discussion I will accept the claims of Lakoff, Johnson, and Winter that metaphorical reasoning is a deep cognitive aspect of our analytical processes. The interesting part of this claim is the constitutive nature of metaphor in our analytical frameworks. *Id.* Whether metaphor is a fundamental cognitive aspect of reasoning brought about by neuro-biological, social or phenomenological causes—or some complex mixture of them all—is not really necessary to the application of the theory. George Lakoff & Mark Johnson, Metaphors We Live By 272–273 (1980). Others have done a much better job laying out the cognitive science and philosophy of mind behind the theory of Lakoff and Johnson than I could possibly do. What is useful in the present discussion, however, is that Lakoff, Johnson and Winter appear to be correct in noting that metaphorical reasoning seems to be a fundamental aspect of human reasoning. In other words, the relationship between how we analyze and use concepts and metaphorical reasoning seems to be borne out. It does not appear that metaphor is simply a linguistic device that is used to illustrate complex points. Something deeper is implicated. Understanding why and how this works conceptually or biologically may be interesting but is not a prerequisite to the use or attractiveness of the theory itself.

So what is this cognitive or conceptual theory of metaphor, and how does it operate? Simply put, the ways in which human beings conceive of and make sense of the world is driven by a conceptual system. *Id.* at 3. In essence, we could not make sense of the world and the things that happen in the world without some field of reference. *Id.* at Ch. 1. This field of reference allows us to grapple with phenomena that we confront and make sense of that phenomena in a way that allows us to operate productively. *Id.* at Chs. 1–3. We experience the world in terms of our conceptual field of reference, and literally create our realities by relating phenomena to that field of reference. *Id.* at 67. According to proponents of the cognitive or conceptual theory of metaphor, this conceptual system is metaphorical in nature. *Id.* at 3.

Advocates of the cognitive or conceptual theory of metaphor maintain that human beings always "understand … and experienc[e] one kind of thing in terms of another." *Id.* at 5. This may seem somewhat banal on its face, but for theorists like Lakoff and Johnson the implications are profound. For example, we often conceptualize argumentation between people in terms of violent conflict. *Id.* at Ch. 1. The *argument is war* metaphor is pervasive in our culture and perhaps every culture. *Id.* at Ch. 1. We say things like "your claims are *indefensible,*" "he *attacked* every point in my argument," and "her criticisms were *right on target.*" *Id.* at 4. According to Lakoff and Johnson, these are not simply convenient and artful ways of describing arguments. *Id.* at Ch. 1. They actually form how we think about arguments. *Id.* In other words, we cannot understand the act of arguing without the relationship between arguing and war coming forth in our minds and structuring our conceptual scheme. The terms of the latter (war, the source concept) form our understanding of the former (arguing, the target concept). *Id.* Our understanding is structured according to this pattern. *Id.*

Let's look at this metaphor for a moment to see what exactly Lakoff and Johnson mean. When we make the sort of statements about arguments that I mentioned above we do not literally mean that people engage in actual physical acts of war or violence when they argue (although this has surely been known to happen). Instead, we are employing a cognitive association between the two kinds of activities. This association helps us make sense of the activity. We often plan our arguments by thinking in strategic ways, for example. *Id.* at 4. Or we feel like we have won when our opponent has been vanquished (or driven from the field). *Id.* This existential aspect is important. When we operate conceptually according to these deep cognitive associations, we actually engage the target concept (arguing) in the terms of the source concept (war). *Id.* How we understand arguing, how we do it, and how we explain it, all employ the association with war. *Id.*

According to Lakoff and Johnson, there are a host of common metaphors that help us understand the world. *Id.* at Ch. 2. They have identified structural metaphors, orientational metaphors, ontological metaphors, and a whole host of other common metaphorical concepts that provide fields of reference for our understanding of the world and our place in it. *Id.* The common thread between these sorts of metaphors is that all of them "have entailments through which they highlight and make coherent certain aspects of our experience." *Id.* at 156. Lakoff and Johnson go on to say that metaphors "create realities for us, especially social realities. A metaphor may thus be a guide for future action. Such actions will, of course, fit the metaphor. This will, in turn, reinforce the power of the metaphor to make experience coherent." *Id.* In other words, the use of metaphor enables us to understand but will commonly constrain that understanding as well. Often these constraints will be based in our shared cultural meanings. *Id.* at Ch. 5. As Lakoff and Johnson put it, the "most fundamental values in a culture will be coherent with the metaphorical structure of the most fundamental concepts in the culture." *Id.* at 22. This might explain why the *arguing is war* metaphor has such currency in U.S. culture. *Id.* at 4. Since we understand some things in terms of other things, we are conceptually limited in what we can understand by what we already know (in terms of our root epistemological and cultural understanding). Our limitations are reinscribed. We will continue to understand arguments in terms of violent conflict because this is what we know. *Id.* Conceptualizing arguments in other ways (cooperative ways, for instance) would be difficult because the inscription and reinscription run so deep conceptually and cognitively. *Id.* at Chs. 1–3 & 5.

While much more could be said about the specifics of this theory, enough has been outlined for present purposes. See, Mark Johnson, *Mind, Metaphor, Law*, 58 Mercer L. Rev. 845 (2007). Thus far we have seen that metaphors are fundamental to our understanding, that these metaphors structure how we see the world, provide us with meaning and reference, and serve as a tether to our relationship with phenomena in the world. *Id.* Often these metaphors are based in shared cultural understandings and have both an enabling and limiting effect on our understanding. *Id.* These basic concepts have important implications. In areas like law and politics, for instance, how we relate to one another in the world is set in place by metaphors that cut deep — deep across cultural, economic, historical, and ideological lines. Let us look at how the cognitive theory of metaphor affects the way we analyze and communicate about the law.

B. Implications for Advanced Legal Analysis and Communication

Some notable legal scholars have maintained that metaphors are the bane of legal reasoning. For example, England's Lord Mansfield said that there is "nothing in law so apt to mislead [as] a metaphor." Thomas Ross, *Metaphor and Paradox*, 23 Ga. L. Rev. 1053, 1057 n.9 (1989). Benjamin Cardozo suggested that metaphors in legal analysis and communication had "to be narrowly watched, for starting as devices to liberate thought, they end often by enslaving it." *Berkey v. Third Ave. Ry. Co.*, 155 N.E. 58, 61 (N.Y. 1926). More recently,

Robert Tsai has said that "[l]egal scholars have traditionally understood metaphor as, at worst, a perversion of the law, and at best, as a necessary but temporary place-holder for more fully developed lines of argument." Robert L. Tsai, *Fire, Metaphor, and Constitutional Myth-Making*, 93 GEO. L.J. 181, 186 (2004). These views mirror the long held view that metaphors are mere linguistic devices that are used to trick people into thinking that one thing is like another thing, even when they are not. This comes from the work of Aristotle. Aristotle, The Poetics, in THE RHETORIC AND THE POETICS OF ARISTOTLE, 223, 251 (7457b lines 8–11) (Ingram Bywater trans., Random House 1954).

The fact is, however, that metaphors are an important, and maybe even vital, part of our legal system. As Professor Steven Winter puts it:

> Conventional views of reason—and, particularly, of legal reasoning—emphasize the objective, the literal, and the linear. Such views see metaphor either as a distortion of thought or as an evocation but dangerously imprecise rhetoric. But these conventional views are distorting: the expression of a narrow, rationalist conception of reason that is both inconsistent with the evidence of actual language use and inadequate to the rigors of effective legal reasoning. Metaphor is a central modality of human thought without which we cannot even begin to understand the complex regularities of the products of the human mind.

STEVEN WINTER, A CLEARING IN THE FOREST 43 (2001). As such, the way we actually think of "the law" is dependent on metaphorical constructs. Steven L. Winter, *Re-Embodying Law*, 58 MERCER L. REV. 869, 896 (2007). What this means is that we literally understand both our legal system as a system and many of the formative ideas that operate within that system in metaphorical terms. For example, the common legal concepts "under color of law," "fruit of the poisonous tree," "corporate personhood," and even the "adversary system" are all metaphors that are intimately woven into the fabric of American law. STEVEN WINTER, A CLEARING IN THE FOREST Ch. 7 (2001).

Let's look at one important and widely used metaphor that has substantially shaped the way we understand law. In 1919 Supreme Court Justice Oliver Wendell Holmes, Jr. wrote a dissent in *Abrams v. United States*, a case involving the application of the Espionage Act to five foreign nationals who were convicted of engaging in unlawful acts designed to undermine the U.S. government in time of war. *Abrams v. U.S.*, 250 U.S. 616 (1919). These acts consisted of writing and printing works that were deemed to be "disloyal, scurrilous and [have] abusive language about the form of government of the United States … intended to bring the form of government of the United States into contempt, scorn, contumely, and disrepute ... and ... intended to incite, provoke and encourage resistance to the United States in said war." *Id.* at 616. The defendants challenged these charges, maintaining that the first amendment to the U.S. Constitution permitted them to express their opinions openly, and that the Espionage Act was therefore unconstitutional. *Id.* at 618–619. The majority, in an opinion by Justice Clarke, rejected this argument, saying that the words of the defendants were likely to cause damage to the U.S. government. *Id.* at 623–624. As a result, they held that the Espionage Act was a constitutionally permissible restraint on speech. *Id.*

In his dissent from this opinion, Justice Holmes suggested that this view was dangerous. *Abrams v. U.S.*, 250 U.S. 616, 627 (Holmes, J., dissenting); for an excellent and truly fascinating discussion of this case and the cognitive theory behind the metaphors used, see Steven Winter, A Clearing in the Forest Ch. 10 (2001); see also Linda L. Berger, *What is the Sound of the Corporation Speaking? How the Cognitive Theory of Metaphor Can Help Lawyers Shape the Law*, 2 J. ALWD 169 (2004). In an often quoted selection from his dissent, Holmes coined one of the most famous ideas in American law:

> Persecution for the expression of opinions seems to me perfectly logical. If you have no doubt of your premises or your power and want a certain result with all your heart you naturally express your wishes in law and sweep away all opposition. To allow opposition by speech seems to indicate that you think the speech impotent, as when a man says that he has squared the circle, or that you do not care whole heartedly for the result, or that you doubt either your power or your premises. But when men have realized that time has upset many fighting faiths, they may come to believe even more than they believe the very foundations of their own conduct that the ultimate good desired is better reached by **free trade in ideas**—that the best test of truth is the power of the thought to get itself accepted in the competition of **the market**, and that truth is the only ground upon which their wishes safely can be carried out. That at any rate is the theory of our Constitution. It is an experiment, as all life is an experiment. (Emphasis added)

Abrams v. U.S., 250 U.S. 616, 630 (Holmes, J., dissenting). In this short selection, Justice Holmes developed what has been called "the critical metaphor for the twentieth-century [idealized cognitive model] of the First Amendment: 'the marketplace of ideas.'" Steven Winter, A Clearing in the Forest 271 (2001). This idea would come to dominate the discourse about the free speech aspects of the First Amendment, and would literally change the way lawyers and judges in the U.S. view the principle of free speech. *Lamont v. Postmaster Gen-*

eral, 381 U.S. 301, 308 (1965) (Brennan, J.). There is some dispute as to whether Holmes or Brennan actually coined the central metaphor. Linda L. Berger, *What is the Sound of the Corporation Speaking? How the Cognitive Theory of Metaphor Can Help Lawyers Shape the Law*, 2 J. ALWD 169, 185 (2004). Nonetheless, the metaphor has been a powerful one in the development of our conception of free speech under our constitutional system.

According to Professor Linda Berger, "[a]lthough the metaphor was new, it contained basic conceptual metaphors: the **Mind is a Container** and **Ideas are Objects.** These basic metaphors in turn help generate new and different metaphors when the writer specifies a particular container or object such as **The mind is a machine,** ideas are products." *Id.* at 185–186. (Citing to STEVEN WINTER, A CLEARING IN THE FOREST 271 (2001)). The reason the metaphor worked, and would later have such conceptual influence, was not that it was novel and clever. It worked because it tapped into some internally important concepts that cognitively trip an automatic association. This metaphor and others that carry such important associations for us, literally help us to see legal problems in deeper and more complex ways.

Drawing upon—one might be tempted to say constructing—such metaphors is a very difficult thing to do. MICHAEL R. SMITH, ADVANCED LEGAL WRITING: THEORIES AND STRATEGIES IN PERSUASIVE WRITING Ch. 9 (2002). Yet you might see, even from this short example, that these ideas (remember, they are not literary flights of fancy) can and do shape how we think about law. This is not just confined to actors in the legal discourse community. In fact, the "marketplace of ideas" metaphor, and the entailments it carries, have become a part of our social fabric, it transcends the institution of the law and has had a formative effect on who we are as a society. This is perhaps the clearest example we have seen thus far about how our analytical and communicative abilities can be creatively used to affect law and society. I will end with an incredible quotation from Professor Linda Berger, who explains the connection between cognitive or conceptual metaphor theory and the law. She does about as good a job as anyone could explaining the creative process of legal reasoning and communication:

> For lawyers, the cognitive theory of metaphor promises to make law shaping more imaginative, more human, and more flexible. By explaining that legal reasoning emerges from basic human capacities, the cognitive theory of metaphor makes legal reasoning more comprehensible. Legal concepts are neither "literal, context-free principles" nor "arbitrary or radically subjective social constructions." Instead of discovering objective legal rules or concocting subjective ones, we

derive legal rules within a complex community. The rules are constrained by the community's history, culture, norms, institutions, and practices, but the rules also are flexible and able to evolve in response to changes in human and community conditions.

Linda L. Berger, *What is the Sound of the Corporation Speaking? How the Cognitive Theory of Metaphor Can Help Lawyers Shape the Law*, 2 J. ALWD 169, 178 (2004) (citing to Mark Johnson, *Law Incarnate*, 67 Brooklyn L. Rev. 949 (2002)).

IV. Narrative, Storytelling, and Legal Reasoning

Yes, yes, it's the most comical thing in the world. And we laugh, we laugh, with a will, in the beginning. But it's always the same thing. Yes, it's like the funny story we have heard too often, we still find it funny, but we don't laugh any more.

Samuel Beckett

Narratives compel us. Stories interest us. Perhaps this is why there has been so much interest in the last few decades in what has come to be know as narrative theory. The stories people tell, and how they tell them, drive our realities. In fact, the reality we experience — political, legal, or otherwise — seems to be almost completely formed by the narratives that are presented. Our brains process narratives or stories more easily than they do abstract concepts and rules. Michael R. Smith, Advanced Legal Writing: Theories and Strategies in Persuasive Writing 259 (2002). We learn new things about the world through narratives and stories in the same way we learn through experience. *Id.* at 260. This is as true in the domain of the law as it is in any other. As a result, understanding the power of narrative and storytelling is not just the province of those who study literary theory or literature. All of us respond to and participate in a variety of narratives and stories that comprise our existence. According to the literary theorist Hayden White:

the study of narrative as a form of discourse preeminently suited to mediate between alternative notions of what the moral order should consist of offers the prospect of accounting, at least in part, for changes in what audiences regard as the appropriate modes of discourse as well as the appropriate contents or referents of different modes of representation.

Hayden White, *The Narrativization of Real Events*, in W.J.T. MITCHELL, ED., ON NARRATIVE 250 (1981). Our narratives comport with representations we accept and are guided by. Often these narratives are overlapping. Within each aspect of our lives, and within each domain in society, there are formative narratives. In fact, one of the things that defines a discourse community is the acceptance of a set of common narratives. JILL J. RAMSFIELD, THE LAW AS ARCHITECTURE: BUILDING LEGAL DOCUMENTS 18 (2000).

Lawyers and legal scholars alike have recognized both the power and usefulness of narrative theory and storytelling. Like advocates of metaphor theory, those who argue that narrative and storytelling theories should be employed by lawyers do so because these theoretical perspectives add to the content of legal analysis and communication. Steven L. Winter, *The Cognitive Dimension of the Agon Between Legal Power and Narrative Meaning*, 87 MICH L. REV. 2225 (1989). Using narrative and storytelling techniques are not literary tricks, then, but represent deeper and more contentful ways of conveying substantive meaning. Accordingly, as you move from novice to expert in the legal domain, understanding and utilizing these techniques is extremely important. Philip N. Meyer, *Vignettes from a Narrative Primer*, 12 LEGAL WRITING: THE JOURNAL OF THE LEGAL WRITING INSTITUTE 229 (2006). So let us begin by reviewing some basic ideas about narrative theory and the art of storytelling.

A. Narrative Theory

We all live narratives. We are all protagonists in our own stories. This makes the narrative form extremely familiar to us. In fact, we all engage in the telling and retelling of narratives and stories all the time. Those who write about narrative theory and theories regarding the use of storytelling, however, suggest that we can (and should) be much more deliberate and systematic in our understanding and use of these analytical abilities. MICHAEL R. SMITH, ADVANCED LEGAL WRITING: THEORIES AND STRATEGIES IN PERSUASIVE WRITING (2002). A careful student of narrative theory will recognize that there are several aspects of narratives that need to be understood. These include character, plot, setting, and style. Philip N. Meyer, *Vignettes from a Narrative Primer*, 12 LEGAL WRITING: THE JOURNAL OF THE LEGAL WRITING INSTITUTE 229 (2006). These represent, of course, the different parts of the narrative and storytelling enterprise.

There are more general concepts about narrative and storytelling, however, that must be grasped in order for you to see how these analytical tools contribute to both our understanding of the world and the formation of that understanding. These are meaning, content, and authoritativeness. Each of these things contributes to how we react to narratives and stories as a whole. As a result, these are the aspects of narrative that compel and interest us most immediately and deeply. Let us look at each in turn.

1. Meaning in Narrative

Meaning in narrative refers to the connection a story or narrative establishes between the author and the reader. Narratives and stories that convey meaning in ways that are both easy to grasp and comfortable for the reader are more likely to have a direct impact on the way the reader understands them. According to Steven Winter, narrative:

> engage[s] the audience in the cognitive process by which it regularly makes meaning in its day-to-day world. Because the cognitive process is basically imaginative, the process of making sense of the projected experience of the story will be mimetic of the process by which humans always make meaning. The audience "lives" the story-experience, and is brought personally to engage in the process of constructing meaning out of another's experience.

Steven L. Winter, *The Cognitive Dimension of the Agon Between Legal Power and Narrative Meaning*, 87 Mich L. Rev. 2225, 2277 (1989). It has been suggested that narrative meaning is intimately connected to the experiences of the audience. Michael R. Smith, Advanced Legal Writing: Theories and Strategies in Persuasive Writing 260 (2002). Because we can place ourselves in the shoes of the protagonist in a well-constructed narrative, we can experience the story in a real and immediate way. *Id.* In short we can live the experience, even if it is not an experience we have actually lived before. Steven L. Winter, *The Cognitive Dimension of the Agon Between Legal Power and Narrative Meaning*, 87 Mich L. Rev. 2225, 2276–2277 (1989). Thus, meaning is not conveyed by the content of the words, but is instead constructed by the audience receiving the narrative. Stanley Fish, Is there a Text in This Class? The Authority of Interpretive Communities 28 (1980). According to Stanley Fish:

> *meaning [is] an event*, something that is happening between the words and in the reader's mind, something not visible to the naked eye but which can be made visible (or at least palpable) by the regular introduction of a "searching" question.... [I]t is thus an extension of the ordering operation we perform on experience whenever it is filtered through our temporal-spatial consciousness. In short, it *makes* sense, in exactly the way we make (that is, manufacture) sense of whatever,

if anything, exists outside us; and by making easy sense it tells us that sense can be easily made and that we are capable of easily making it. (Emphasis in original)

Id. at 28–29. So narratives are brought forth by the reader, who provides meaning to the story told. The psychology and philosophy behind this is very complex, but the important point to grasp is that using narratives involves the audience in the analytical process. *Id.* at Ch. 1; Jacques Derrida, *The First Session*, in ACTS OF LITERATURE (Derek Attridge, ed., 1992). When you construct a narrative, you are not ascribing something *to* someone, you are involving them *in* it. This has been called a dialogical process. M.M. BAKHTIN, THE DIALOGIC IMAGINATION: FOUR ESSAYS (Michael Holquist, ed. Texas 1982); and Linda H. Edwards, *The Convergence of Analogical and Dialectical Imaginations in Legal Discourse*, 20 LEGAL STUD. F. 7 (1996).

Meaning, then, is a relationship between author and audience. This relationship depends on the ability to engage the audience in the process of meaning. To the extent that a narrative can be constructed that will compel a reader to make that commitment to engage, it will be successful. If this commitment is not engaged, the narrative is doomed to fail. As a result, all narratives, all stories, must draw the audience into the making of meaning. Good narratives allow readers to see the ease and fruitfulness of making meaning by following the narrative. It literally carries them through the narrative so that they can construe and mediate meaning. As the philosopher Paul Ricoeur put it:

> Following a story, correlatively, is understanding the successive actions, thoughts, and feelings in question insofar as they present a certain directedness. By this I mean that we are pushed ahead by this development and that we reply to its impetus with expectations concerning the outcome and the completion of the entire process. In this sense, the story's conclusion is the pole of attraction of the entire development. But a narrative conclusion can be neither deduced nor predicted. There is no story if our attention is not moved along by a thousand contingencies. This is why a story has to be followed to its conclusion. So rather than being predictable, a conclusion must be acceptable.

Paul Ricoeur, *Narrative Time*, in W.J.T. MITCHELL, ED., ON NARRATIVE 170 (1981). This relationship, this investment, can only happen when the narrative opens up and allows the reader inside the text. This is a relationship that the reader must be drawn into, and this can only happen when the narrative is something *lived* by the reader. Here, being lived means being involved in constructing the process of meaning.

2. Content of Narratives

Narrative content refers to two things: the details that are included in the story, and the timeline upon which these details occur. Hayden White, *The Value of Narrativity*, in W.J.T. MITCHELL, ED., ON NARRATIVE 1–23 (1981). These things, which are sometimes captured together in discussions about plot, are what open up the text and allow the reader to engage in the process of making meaning. Paul Ricoeur, *Narrative Time*, in W.J.T. MITCHELL, ED., ON NARRATIVE 167 (1981). The content, then, is the vehicle for beginning the relationship between the author and the audience, but it is also the continuation of that relationship mediated by the flow of events over a timeline that the audience will permit the author to use. There is a reciprocal relationship between narrative and time. As Paul Ricoeur puts it, "I take temporality to be that structure of existence that reaches language in narrativity and narrativity to be the language structure that has temporality as its ultimate reference." *Id.* at 165. He goes on to relate this to the details or plot of the story by saying:

> The narrative structure that I have chosen as the most relevant for an investigation of the temporal implications of narrativity is that of the "plot." By plot I mean the intelligible whole that governs a succession of events in any story.... A story is *made out of* events to the extent that plot *makes* events *into* a story. The plot, therefore, places us at the crossing point of temporality and narrativity: to be historical, an event must be more than a singular occurrence, a unique happening. It receives its definition from its contribution to the development of a plot. (Emphasis in original)

Id. at 167. The timeline and the details of any narrative are the interfaces for the audiences' participation. But the selection of details is a determination left to the author. The choice as to what details to include (sometimes called plot elements) and which to omit is an important one. This is especially the case when the story being told is not fictional.

When we are telling narratives about real world events, like historical accounts or "factual" recitations in legal documents, we never include all the details or facts. No reader could cope with the white noise of all this material. It would interrupt and confuse the content, and conceal the timeline beneath a mountain of irrelevant minutiae. Hayden White puts this quite well when he says that "every narrative, however seemingly "full," is constructed on the basis of a set of events which might have been included but were left out; and this is true of imaginary as it is of realistic narratives." Hayden White, *The Value of Narrativity*, in W.J.T. MITCHELL, ED., ON NARRATIVE 10 (1981).

So the content of a narrative is controlled as much by what is not said as it is by what is said. If you intersect this with the discussion above on meaning, something interesting begins to emerge. The meaning that a reader constructs is dependent upon the content included, and concomitantly excluded, by the author. So while the reader's part in the narrative is to construct meaning from the narrative (from the details provided by the plot, and by progressing along the timeline of the narrative), the author's contribution is shaping the construction of meaning by crafting the narrative from the available events or facts that could be included.

This is not to suggest manipulation, necessarily, only to acknowledge that the craft of authoring a narrative, telling a story, involves the selection of certain events or elements that will propel the narrative and including them while excluding others in order to engage the reader in the process of making meaning to fill out the content of the narrative or story. As Paul Ricoeur puts it, "[t]o tell and follow a story is already to reflect upon events in order to encompass them in successive wholes." Paul Ricoeur, *Narrative Time*, in W.J.T. MITCHELL, ED., ON NARRATIVE 174 (1981). But these wholes are not "whole" in the truest sense of the word. They are whole in the sense that they comprise the whole narrative, the whole relationship between author and audience. They are not whole in an absolute or "objective" sense. This last point is important because it propels us to the last major important aspect of narratives; authoritativeness. Because a narrative relationship between author and audience is whole in the sense conveyed by Ricoeur, it can be considered to be authoritative. That is to say, the relationship is authoritative because it comprises the whole of the narrative.

3. Authoritativeness of Narratives

The final important aspect of any narrative is the authority that lies behind it. Sometimes this authority is based in the character that tells the narrative. Other times authority stems from the position of the author. Either way, though, a narrative must be backed by some authority before the relationship between author and audience will be cemented. Hayden White says "once we note the presence of the theme of authority ... we perceive the extent to which the truth claims of the narrative and indeed the very right to narrate hinges upon a certain relationship to authority per se." Hayden White, *The Value of Narrativity*, in W.J.T. MITCHELL, ED., ON NARRATIVE 18 (1981). Authoritativeness binds the narrative to the participants: author, audience, and characters.

So, authoritativeness really exists as the culmination of meaning and content. If the content provided by the author leads to the construction of meaning in the audience, a narrative will be authoritative. Another way of putting this is that a working narrative, one that builds the proper relationship between author and audience well, is authentic. This authenticity means that the story will be viewed as authoritative, by the audience and potential audiences.

One interesting aspect of this concept of narrative authority has been discussed in-depth by Hayden White. In evaluating the philosopher G.W.F. Hegel's *Lectures on the Philosophy of History* as a narrative, White discovered that the issue of authoritativeness of narratives — of whatever type — frequently implicates the social institution of the law. He says, for instance:

> once we have been alerted to the intimate relationship that Hegel suggests exists between law, historicality, and narrativity, we cannot but be struck by the frequency with which narrativity, whether of the fictional or the factual sort, presupposes the existence of a legal system against or on behalf of which the typical agents of a narrative account militate. And this raises the suspicion that narrative in general, from the folktale to the novel, from the annals to the fully realized "history," has to do with the topics of law, legality, legitimacy, or, more generally, authority.

Id. at 13. In White's view, not only must narratives be authoritative, they must deal with authority in some way. Authority must be present, eminent in the story. It is this eminence that both feeds and fills out the content. All narratives, in this view, have some relationship to proving some point or other that relates to the exercise of authority. This exercise is, as he says, often legal authority. But even in these situations, there is a deeper eminence: morality. White says:

> if every fully realized story, however we define that familiar but conceptually elusive entity, is a kind of allegory, points to a moral, or endows events, whether real or imaginary, with a significance that they do not possess as a mere sequence, then it seems possible to conclude that every historical narrative has as its latent or manifest purpose the desire to moralize the events of which it treats.

Id. at 13–14. All effective narratives, in White's view, are morality plays. The content and the timeline must engage the audience, and it will do so by pulling upon their moral sentiments (good or bad). Authoritativeness, then, relates to both the stance of the author vis-à-vis the audience, but also, and perhaps more importantly, with the way in which the audience engages the moral quandary of the narrative.

Taken together, these three elements—perhaps it would be correct to call them meta-narrative elements—illustrate a great deal about how and why narrative theory and storytelling have become so influential amongst American academics. Narrative is not just something that relates to movies, novels, and television. Instead, it is something that has a formative effect on how we view the world. There are narratives about the relationship you maintain with your parents. There are narratives about the people you go to school with. There are an endless number of narratives about all manner of things that give your life content and meaning. The question is, who tells those narratives? Who has authority to do so? And when someone does have the authority to tell such a narrative, what should the effect be? These are, at base, moral questions.

As you can see, the elements of content, meaning, and authority weave together in a complex way. In fact, it is probably impossible to completely extract them from one another when talking about narrative. These elements should help us more quickly grasp the way in which narrative works in the context of the legal system, however. Let us now turn to that issue.

B. Implications for Advanced Legal Analysis and Communication

Narrative and storytelling are important aspects of legal analysis and communication. In fact, of the advanced skills that we discuss in this chapter this one is perhaps the easiest to understand. It is also perhaps easy to see why this aspect of reasoning and communication is related to the legal profession. As Professor Linda Edwards has said, "[n]arrative reaches an answer by telling a story whose theme calls forth a particular result. Using storytelling techniques such as characterization, context, description, dialogue, and perspective, narrative appeals to commonly shared notions of justice, mercy, fairness, reasonableness, and empathy." LINDA H. EDWARDS, LEGAL WRITING: PROCESS, ANALYSIS, AND ORGANIZATION 6 (4th ed. 2006). These are all devices that will surely assist you in doing the legal tasks you are assigned and representing the clients you will work with when you leave school. You have probably already learned some basic skills of narrative and storytelling in your legal writing classes. There are certainly many good resources to which you can turn in learning these basic skills. Philip N. Meyer, *Vignettes from a Narrative Primer*, 12 LEGAL WRITING: THE JOURNAL OF THE LEGAL WRITING INSTITUTE 229 (2006); MICHAEL R. SMITH, ADVANCED LEGAL WRITING: THEORIES AND STRATE-

GIES IN PERSUASIVE WRITING Ch. 11 (2002); and Brian J. Foley and Ruth Anne Robbins, *Fiction 101: A Primer for Lawyers on How to Use Fiction Writing Techniques to Write Persuasive Facts Sections*, 32 RUTGERS L.J. 459 (2001).

But as you might have gathered by reading this chapter closely, our discussions of these advanced notions of legal analysis and communication are not designed to give you quick and dirty tactics as to how to use these techniques in your work. In fact, viewing them as techniques at all undermines the basic premise of this chapter; advanced concepts—like storytelling and narrative—are deeper cognitive and analytical perspectives that will change the way you see what it means to be a professional in the discourse community, and allow you to communicate content in a more meaningful and textured way. It is not that learning narrative and storytelling techniques is bad or that using them is cheap. But as you develop as a professional you will see that adopting a perspective that sees the use of narrative and storytelling as a deeper way to engage in the discourse community will open up your work to a new level. In fact, doing so will be a pragmatic way of addressing new and novel strategies in the domain of the law.

Let's look again at the three aspects of narrative theory that we developed above: meaning, content, and authoritativeness. By developing and drawing upon deeper conceptions of narrative, you can infuse the stories you tell with much more content than you may think is possible. Think not just about the facts you have been given, but about the context in which the legal problem you are working on is situated. By selecting the appropriate timeline and working in the most advantageous set of details, you can craft a narrative that will convey much more than a simple factual case. This is true in either predictive or persuasive environments. Remember that the details that are omitted are as important as the ones that are included. As the author of the narrative, you will have both the right and the obligation to engage the audience.

Once this engagement has been established, you will see how meaning—shared meaning—begins to flow from the audience. I do not mean to restate platitudes here. I am not talking about "know your audience." Instead, I am suggesting that you take the discussion about meaning above seriously, and recognize that you are not just the author of any particular narrative. You are initiating a relationship with your audience. This is true if you are writing an office memorandum for your professor or the person you work for during your summer clerkship, a client letter, or a brief to be submitted to the U.S. Supreme Court. You do not totally control your narratives. They are shared with the people you work with and for. This relationship mediates between you as the author and the audience. The legal documents you construct, the oral arguments you make, and the stories you tell as aspects of those professional activities require you to give up some of the control that you might assume you have as the author.

Every story is judged by its overall effect. Some stories are good stories in that they accomplish something, they show us something we did not know before, or explain something in a new and useful way. If you engage in the sort of process we have explored in this section, you will see how this ability can be employed effectively within the discourse community of the law. This will allow you to illustrate how the legal problems you work on intersect profound and deep human concerns, how your narratives can show other actors in the legal system the effect of their actions on the systemic issues of morality and authority. In effect, by developing authentic and authoritative narratives that engage your readers, you can creatively have an impact on the system itself.

One way of doing this is to bring the policy based reasoning we discussed in the last chapter into your narratives. Adding these policy concerns to the content of your narrative will give your readers yet another interface through which to engage the stories you tell. As Professor Linda Edwards puts it:

> Narrative appeals to commonly shared notions of justice, mercy, fairness, reasonableness, and empathy, and the law is not insensitive to those important values. As a matter of fact, those notions underlie much of the more abstract policy rationale in policy-based reasoning. Narrative can serve as a powerful partner with policy-based reasoning, providing a real-life example of the policy that justifies ... rule[s].

LINDA H. EDWARDS, LEGAL WRITING: PROCESS, ANALYSIS, AND ORGANIZATION 7 (4th ed. 2006). This is a wonderful example of how the advanced conceptual skills we have been developing can work with the more basic lawyering skills that you have been learning. It is not as though these are new ideas or concepts for you to learn. Instead, understanding and using narrative and storytelling will take your basic analytical and communicative skills to a higher level, giving you the creative opportunity to use these skills in a more complex and sophisticated way.

When you leave law school, whether it is to work during the summer or when you graduate, pay attention to highly skilled lawyers (you will be able to spot them pretty easily) when they talk about narrative and storytelling. You will see that they do so in an extremely subtle yet complicated way, often taking into account parts of the cases you are working on that you might have completely overlooked or discounted, and making them into a compelling narrative. It is probably safe to say that virtually none of these highly skilled professionals know much, if anything, about the literary and narrative theories of Jacques Derrida, Stanley Fish, Paul Ricoeur, or Hayden White. Nonetheless, they will engage in the dialogical process of narrative construction and engagement in a deeper and more meaningful way. As you learn to master these skills, you will too.

V. Rhetoric

You may remember that we briefly discussed rhetoric at the end of Chapter Three, the chapter on logic and rational (not rationalist) thinking. Perhaps the placement at the end of that chapter was unfortunate. You might have gotten the mistaken impression from that placement that rhetoric is secondary or subordinate to logic (whether formal or pragmatic). This is clearly not the case. In fact, the inclusion of a discussion about rhetoric in a chapter on logical reasoning was designed to suggest that logic and rhetoric are part and parcel of the same sort of analytical abilities. Here we will elaborate more deliberately, and in more depth, on the use of rhetoric in legal analysis and communication. As with the other advanced skills we have explored in this chapter, this discussion should be seen as a beginning, an entrée into a deeper appreciation of complex attributes displayed by expert members of the legal profession. Rhetoric is certainly one of the most important of these attributes.

This association between logic and rhetoric should be kept in mind. Some would suggest that logic (and philosophy) stands in opposition to rhetoric. The ability to think systematically and logically is intimately related to the ability to convey that thought to others in the interest of convincing them that your views are correct. As the French philosopher Roland Barthes put it, "rhetoric must always be read in its structural interplay with its neighbors—grammar, logic, poetics, and philosophy." P.J. CORBETT AND ROBERT J. CONNERS, CLASSICAL RHETORIC FOR THE MODERN STUDENT 1 (4th ed. 1999). In other words, without understanding and using rhetoric, your analysis will never be as effective as it could be. Conversely, becoming a master rhetoritician would be impossible without a thorough understanding of grammar, logic, poetics, and philosophy.

Going back to first principles for a moment, the term rhetoric might be somewhat confusing. As we saw in Chapter Three there are a great many uses of the term, many of which are either wrong or misleading. MICHAEL R. SMITH, ADVANCED LEGAL WRITING: THEORIES AND STRATEGIES IN PERSUASIVE WRITING 77 (2002). In the classical sense, rhetoric referred to "the use of language for persuasive purposes." ARISTOTLE, THE RHETORIC OF ARISTOTLE 7 (1932); MICHAEL R. SMITH, ADVANCED LEGAL WRITING: THEORIES AND STRATEGIES

IN PERSUASIVE WRITING 77 (2002). As we will see below, however, this basic definition is somewhat misleading as well. To say that one uses language to persuade could connote a couple of different things. One could say this meaning that language is used to trick or manipulate another into thinking something is the case when it is, in fact, not the case. This is the foundation for the common misperception that rhetoric is trickery. One could also mean, however, that by using language to persuade, rhetoric is actually an artistic way of illustrating the intricacies of complex thought, a way to open up complicated ideas for others to see and understand. Anthony T. Kronman, *Rhetoric*, 67 U. CIN. L. REV. 677 (1999). Viewed in this way, rhetoric is an indispensable adjunct to sound thinking. This is surely the way Aristotle viewed the topic, as did Roland Barthes and the well known Polish legal theorist Chaim Perelman. Accordingly, we will follow suit here.

A. Classical Rhetoric

Libraries have been filled with discussions about the development and history of rhetoric. You may know that the ancient Greeks developed and used rhetoric — in the manner discussed above — well over two thousand years ago. EDWARD P.J. CORBETT AND ROBERT J. CONNERS, CLASSICAL RHETORIC FOR THE MODERN STUDENT (4th ed. 1999); Michael Frost, *Introduction to Classical Legal Rhetoric: A Lost Heritage*, 8 S. CAL. INTERDISCIPLINARY L.J. 613 (1999); MICHAEL R. SMITH, ADVANCED LEGAL WRITING: THEORIES AND STRATEGIES IN PERSUASIVE WRITING Pt. II (2002). You may also know that the Romans later adopted the study of this art, as did the inheritors of the Greco-Roman tradition in Europe and the Middle East right up through the Middle Ages. EDWARD P.J. CORBETT AND ROBERT J. CONNERS, CLASSICAL RHETORIC FOR THE MODERN STUDENT 15–16 (4th ed. 1999). In fact, rhetoric was a central part of the curriculum of study for educated elites for two thousand years. *Id.*

Classical rhetoric, from the time of Aristotle through the Roman period, was designed to be the means of engaging in distinct discourse communities. Greek and Roman citizens engaged in public debate through rhetorical exchanges. *Id.* To engage in these debates, one had to be schooled in the art of rhetoric. So what did this art consist of? What are the elements of rhetoric that set it apart, and why did they make the study of this art so central to the education of members of these societies? Let us explore these questions.

Briefly stated, classical rhetoric consisted of the study of *logos*, *pathos*, and *ethos*. *Logos* is the art of persuading through the use of logic. MICHAEL R. SMITH, ADVANCED LEGAL WRITING: THEORIES AND STRATEGIES IN PERSUASIVE WRITING 22 (2002). *Pathos* refers to the act of persuading another by using or appealing to emotion. *Id.* Finally, *ethos* refers to the appeal of moral credibility on the part of one engaging in rhetorical debate. *Id.* at 23. Taken together, these elements of rhetoric were thought to bring together the important aspects of persuasion. These elements were the mechanism through which skilled members of a discourse community could persuade others by engaging in debate about complex ideas. These were not really separate ways to persuade but were seen as interdependent aspects of the act of persuasion. As Michael Frost has put it:

> Greek and Roman rhetoricians like Aristotle, Cicero, and Quintilian took a rigorously audience-focused approach to legal persuasion. They wrote voluminously on the topic and on many other aspects of legal discourse and practice.... A substantial part of their analysis ... focused on affective or nonrational modes of argument. In their view, successful arguments depend as much on appeals to emotion (*pathos*) and the advocate's credibility (*ethos*) as they do on logic (*logos*). Moreover, both *pathos* and *ethos* help determine an advocate's organizational strategies and exercise a considerable influence on a judge's decisions. Classical rhetoricians understood and repeatedly stressed that all three modes of argument — *logos*, *ethos*, and *pathos* — were connected and inter-dependent.

Michael H. Frost, *With Amici Like These: Cicero, Quintilian and the Importance of Stylistic Demeanor*, 3 J. ALWD 5, 8–9 (2006). For the ancients, rhetoric was a way to use reason. Rhetoric was also viewed as an important and vital way for us to engage human concerns in a direct and powerful way. See, Anthony T. Kronman, *Rhetoric*, 67 U. Cin. L. Rev. 677 (1999).

Rhetoric has been frequently identified with oratory. In fact, the perception is widely held that rhetoric relates to oral discourse exclusively. Professor Anthony Kronman makes this association in the following passage. But rhetoric as speech is not the heart of what he is describing:

> Speech is the highway of philosophy and science, but it is also an instrument of passion, with the power both to express and to change our feelings. In its role as a tool of reason, speech provides the means for rational deliberation in politics and law. In its role as an agent of feeling, it promotes the emotional transference on which all political loyalties, and hence all politics, depend. Every political regime subscribes to some conception of justice and at the same time demands a certain degree of emotional commitment from its citizens. Speech is the flexible medium in which lawyers and politicians reason about the

> one and cultivate the other. It connects our hearts and minds, and
> the art of making this connection is the art of rhetoric.

Id. at 707. So rhetoric is the art of transmitting the humanness of our public endeavors. It is designed to allow the frailty of our emotions, the contestability of our reputations, and the ideas we represent to withstand the scrutiny of logic and public evaluation.

This is quite a tall order for the field of rhetoric to fill. It is at one and the same time the highest of enterprises designed to allow us to show truths that might not otherwise be observed, and the most human of endeavors illustrating the weaknesses we maintain that keep domains like the law and politics from being precise and rational like mathematics or formal symbolic logic. STANLEY FISH, DOING WHAT COMES NATURALLY: CHANGE, RHETORIC, AND THE PRACTICE OF THEORY IN LITERARY AND LEGAL STUDIES 480 (1992). Rhetoric occupies what Kronman calls an "intermediate space" between the absolute and the purely subjective. Anthony T. Kronman, *Rhetoric*, 67 U. CIN. L. REV. 677, 682–683 (1999). This point is extremely important because it signals the role of rhetoric in its truest sense: rhetoric is an important interface between human endeavors and the desire of the human mind for precision and certainty. *Id.* at 693.

Engaging in acts of persuasion—*logos, pathos,* and *ethos*—allows us to approximate certainty. By persuading others that our positions are defensible, that our arguments are reasonable (perhaps even rational), and that we should be trusted to convey the truth, we are bringing into focus how the human condition mediates between the absolute and raw exercise of political power. Rhetoric is the field that all public debate must occupy. It is not a "field of study" at all, but is instead a field of existence in which we interact with one another. Rhetoric is a practical enterprise, perhaps the most practical. Rhetoric is pragmatic in its purest form.

As you might suspect, this existential characterization suggests that learning rhetoric is not about learning paradigms or tactics that will enable you to "do it well." Instead, this conception of rhetoric is meant to show you how all that has come before it, how all the analytical and practical skills we have discussed (some which do, in fact, lend themselves to the application of formal paradigms) factor into the use of rhetoric as a means of existing and acting in the domain of the law. Rhetoric is not a tool of lawyers. Instead, law is, as Kronman explicitly acknowledges, a domain of rhetoric. It is a domain that depends upon the existence and practice of rhetoric. Without rhetoric, law as we know it could not exist. We simply could not engage the human concerns that law is designed to address without the conduit that rhetoric provides. This is as true today as it was two thousand years ago.

B. Implications for Advanced Legal Analysis and Communication

Contemporary writers on legal analysis and communication are extremely interested in the use of rhetoric. This is a specific application of what has been called the "new rhetoric." See, CHAIM PERELMAN, THE REALM OF RHETORIC (1982). While not abandoning the classical theories about how rhetoric can persuade and about how rhetoric is fundamental to our social enterprises in the way discussed above, the new rhetoric attempts to focus rhetoric in ways that account for the changes in societies that have occurred over the past two millennia.

Legal scholars are so interested in rhetoric because our legal system is a discourse community in which the elements of persuasion are particularly important. Ours is a literary profession, and one that depends on our abilities to convey our thoughts to others in ways that engage and provide meaning. Professor Michael Smith has chronicled the extensive use of rhetoric by lawyers and has also made the case for why we need to be more acutely aware of its proper uses. MICHAEL R. SMITH, ADVANCED LEGAL WRITING: THEORIES AND STRATEGIES IN PERSUASIVE WRITING Chs. 6–10 (2002). According to Professor Smith, by increasing our understanding of how to use rhetoric effectively we can be better at doing the things lawyers need to do well. He does not argue that we need to learn rhetorical strategies as tools to help us be better lawyers. Instead, he maintains that rhetoric will help us utilize our analytical skills more effectively. *Id.*

Smith is implicitly drawing on the metaphor I mentioned above—the conduit metaphor. Using rhetoric is not a trick. The persuasive elements that are captured by the classical rhetorical categories *logos*, *pathos* and *ethos* are present in our work. Learning and understanding rhetoric helps us bring them to the surface so that the analytical work we engage in as members of the legal discourse community can be viewed in their most effective light. The new rhetoric, particularly in the context of the legal discourse community, has embraced the written word as part of our rhetorical enterprise—partially because the written word has been traditionally valued over the spoken word in our tradition. Jacques Derrida, *That Dangerous Supplement*, in JACQUES DERRIDA, ACTS OF LITERATURE (Derek Attridge, ed., 1992). According to Smith, then, rhetoric can and does inform our legal analysis and our legal writing. As you move from novice to expert, you are tasked with seeing how the communications you have with others in the domain engages them and binds them to your task of persuading them; persuading them that your arguments are sound, that there are compelling emotional reasons to adopt your position, and that you have the credibility to be believed.

These three things, derived from classical rhetoric, really do sum up the elements of legal analysis and communication. Professor Smith is correct. Rhetoric can serve as a conduit for our work. If you analyze legal problems fully (with all the analytical complexity that we discussed in earlier chapters), and you craft narratives that will show how your formulation of the legal problem is emotionally compelling (drawing, of course, upon the policy reasons which support your position), you will display the credibility required to be trusted. In a way, then, by following the processes we have discussed in this book, you can bring together your work and display that work for others to see—through rhetoric. This is perhaps the most practical and applicable skill you can master as an expert in the domain—a pragmatic enterprise if ever there was one.

This may seem like a strange thing for me to say. This discussion, perhaps more than any other we have had in this book, probably seems esoteric and abstract. I have not offered any paradigms for you to follow. I have not set out the steps for how you can work *pathos* in to your legal writing or oral arguments. And I have not explained how the new rhetoric can make you a better lawyer. That is because as you bring all your analytical skills together, as you make the progression from novice law student to expert in the domain, all the analytical and communication abilities that you have been developing will culminate in your becoming a member of the discourse community, with all the rhetorical engagements that entails. This is not abstract. In fact, it is profoundly practical.

VI. Conclusion

This chapter is surely a departure from what we have done in earlier chapters. This chapter is meant to serve as a sort of analytical capstone to the more rudimentary and formal topics and skills we have discussed before. This book, in fact, has been designed to propel you forward in your development, to help you move more rapidly from novice to expert. The topics in this chapter are meant to open your mind to more complex conceptual schemes related to legal analysis and communication. To understand them, you must have built a firm foundation in the basics. Upon that foundation you must lay more advanced analytical and communication skills—the kind we saw in Chapter Four. Only then, will the ideas in this chapter be able to truly take root. This capstone is meant to challenge you; to urge you on to deeper appreciation for your craft, and a better appreciation for the work you can and will do.

There is another aim behind this chapter, however. If you have followed the progression of topics carefully throughout, perhaps you can guess what it is. This last chapter is designed to open up your mind to novel (some might say radical) ideas about the U.S. legal system, about law in general even, and the intellectual context which law occupies. The topics we have covered here should show you that law is not a closed and static universe. Law is a dynamic and contextual enterprise that you can have an effect upon. As an expert in the legal system you will not work *in* the system, you will work *on* the system. This is a domain that will allow you to exercise a tremendous amount of creativity, if you view the law as changing, evolving enterprise. The topics here all share one fundamental aspect: each of these complex theoretical notions of law deny that there is any absolute foundation to our legal system or to the way legal reasoning works. Pragmatic legal reasoning, cognitive metaphor theory, narrative theory, and rhetoric are all anti-foundationalist. This means that each of these perspectives allows for the mutability and contingency of human knowledge and our exercise of that knowledge. Our understanding is located in our experience: our practical experience, our logical processes, and the way we interact with one another (through the stories we tell and the rhetoric we use). You should embrace this, as it allows you opportunities that would not otherwise exist. As an expert in the domain, you will benefit from such opportunities. The quicker you get there, the sooner you will see.

Checkpoints

- What characterizes a pragmatic or experimental logic? How does this logic resemble our common-sense ways of dealing with problem-solving? Are there differences? Can you see ways in which pragmatic legal reasoning is useful in your analysis of legal problems?

- Do you agree that metaphors are fundamental concepts by which we all think and communicate? What are the implications for legal analysis and communication if we accept that metaphors are fundamental to our understanding? How can you incorporate metaphors into your legal analysis and communication?

- What does it mean when we say that narrative and story-telling allows you to create a relationship with the reader? How can you help construct such a relationship? Once such a relationship is created, what is your role? What is the role of the reader?

- Why can rhetoric be seen as a culmination of all aspects of legal analysis and communication? What is the relationship between logic, persuasion and credibility? How are these things related to legal analysis and communication?

Mastering Legal Analysis and Communication Checklist

After working through this book, you should be able to answer the following questions:

- ❏ What does it meant to say that your legal education is an entrée to the profession?
- ❏ Why do we learn about the law the way we do in our system of legal education? How do our specific culture and history affect the way we learn the law? Why do other legal systems operate differently?
- ❏ Why is it important to recognize that various actors within the system (clients, judges, lawyers, etc.) interpret legal problems differently?
- ❏ What does it mean to be a member of the legal discourse community? What marks the law as a distinct discourse community?
- ❏ In each of your classes, can you discern what the pedagogical approaches of your professors, and what they expect of you in order to succeed in their classes?
- ❏ What are the comprehensive set of abilities concerning legal analysis and communication that you will have to continue to develop throughout your career?
- ❏ Can you determine what paradigms are being employed by your professors? Are there any that you are using that we have not discussed in this book?
- ❏ What are the paradigms you use meant to teach you? Can you see the connections between the paradigms used and the more advanced abilities you will master?
- ❏ What does it mean when we say that legal education is process-oriented?
- ❏ Is it possible to your use your creativity after you have mastered the basics by using the paradigms your professors teach you? How so? What is the relationship between that creativity and the paradigms we have discussed?

❏ How does one engage in the process of using paradigms authentically? What is the potential detriment of seeing and using short-cuts?

❏ Can you determine the similarities between the various paradigms you have used? What do these similarities tell you about legal analysis and communication?

❏ Can you adapt the basic paradigms that you have learned to suit your needs in new or novel situations? Does the fact that you have learned these paradigms give you confidence to approach unfamiliar legal problems?

❏ Do you understand the differences between formal, informal and pragmatic logic? In what situations might each be useful? Which is most useful to legal professionals?

❏ Can you identify the logical and rhetorical devices that your classmates and your professors use? What about the logical mistakes they make? Can you see such devices or mistakes in the cases you read? What is your assessment of the relative strengths and weaknesses of these logical devices when you encounter them?

❏ When would formal logic be helpful in legal analysis?

❏ Why is inductive reasoning more prevalent in the U.S. legal system? What does it mean when we say that the common law system is an example of inductive reasoning?

❏ How does pragmatic logic differ from the other forms of logic that we have discussed? Do you think that pragmatic logic is more practical?

❏ What is the relationship between rhetoric and legal discourse? Is rhetoric always an element of legal analysis and communication?

❏ What are the ethical or moral responsibilities of members of the profession regarding their use of logic? Do you agree that every member of the profession must police themselves regarding the proper use of logic and rhetoric? Why or why not?

❏ What do we mean by rule-based reasoning? What are the various interpretive techniques used in finding, formulating, and communicating about legal rules?

❏ Can you tell the difference between balancing tests, elements tests, and factors tests? Do you understand which form is best considering your needs and the rules you have found and formulated? How do you make such a judgment?

❏ Why do you think the dominant form of legal analysis and communication in our system is the analogy? What does using analogies and counter-analogies enable you to do?

❏ What is a case law synthesis and how do you construct one? How does synthesizing case law into complex rules allow you to develop rule structures that yield more than the sum of the parts that go into the synthesis?

❏ What does statutory interpretation involve? What are the various approaches to statutory interpretation, how do they differ, and when is each appropriate?

❏ What characterizes a pragmatic or experimental logic? How does this logic resemble our common-sense ways of dealing with problem-solving? Are there differences? Can you see ways in which pragmatic legal reasoning is useful in your analysis of legal problems?

❏ Do you agree that metaphors are fundamental concepts by which we all think and communicate? What are the implications for legal analysis and communication if we accept that metaphors are fundamental to our understanding? How can you incorporate metaphors into your legal analysis and communication?

❏ What does it mean when we say that narrative and story-telling allows you to create a relationship with the reader? How can you help construct such a relationship? Once such a relationship is created, what is your role? What is the role of the reader?

❏ Why can rhetoric be seen as a culmination of all aspects of legal analysis and communication? What is the relationship between logic, persuasion and credibility? How are these things related to legal analysis and communication?

Afterword

Formal education is a difficult and protracted process. You have spent the better part of your life in school. Over the years your teachers and professors have plotted out a progression of lessons and experiences that have brought you to where you are today. Once you enter the legal profession, however, you will have to claim ownership of your continued development and evolution. I have used the theme of progressing from novice to expert in the domain of the law throughout this book. This was done, as I said in the introduction, deliberately. The metaphor of this journey, which has been used by others before me, is an easy one to understand. I have used it here because I find it particularly instructive. It is instructive in two ways.

First, it reveals an insight to the way I have constructed this book. The early sections of this book are designed to assist you as you begin your journey as a novice. Later sections are meant to build upon the early concepts and help you develop more fully formed abilities that will serve you well throughout your career. The last sections in the book, however, are meant to instigate something, to push you beyond the mundane and commonplace. Too often, once we learn something well, when we become good at something, we become hidebound and complacent. The last sections of this book are meant to help you see that no matter how long you are in the profession, no matter how expert your skills become, there are things that you can explore that will stretch your imagination and inspire you to do even more.

The second way this metaphor is instructive is that it connotes something about the work you must undertake to continue this journey. When you claim ownership of this journey, when you begin to chart your own path of development and evolution, you will begin to see things in a new light. You will move beyond the things you have been taught. But you will never lose them. You will see connections where none were apparent before. You will even make your own connections. You can help others to see what you see. Being a professional in the legal system means more than just doing certain tasks. It means being creative in finding new ways to do what others have done before you.

Two other things warrant being said as we close. First, you will have noticed throughout this book that I have used the acts of thinking and writing almost interchangeably. The paradigms we have discussed, the skill set we have developed throughout, and the advanced concepts we explored at the end of the book are all intimately related to analysis **and** communication. For me, it is difficult—if not impossible—to extract one from the other. Accordingly, terms like "legal writing" are somewhat odd to me. To talk about writing in isolation from the analytical component it depends upon elevates abstract and contentless form over function. As you might have gathered from the last chapter of this book, in my view all of the "technical skills" that some try to isolate as elements of writing or oral communication are really just expressions of deeper cognitive and analytical abilities that you are developing.

The last thing I would like you to reflect upon is the theme that ran throughout the final sections of this book: your contribution to the discourse. So often we see our professional lives as being driven and controlled by others. This makes it seem like the work we do, the tasks we engage in, are disconnected from us in some real way, like we are not contributing to the enterprises we are part of. This may particularly be the case early in your career, when the choices about what you will work on will likely be made by others or compelled by circumstances. Even in these situations, however, the sort of analytical model I have discussed throughout this book will enable you to help form and shape the discourse community. It is, in fact, the engagement of this type of connection to the discourse community that I have been urging throughout. Doing your work and following directions are important things for you to do, but you do not have to have a good legal education to work **in** the system. As a professional with independent analytical and communication abilities you can help shape and form the common law; you can work **on** the system as opposed to in it. If you use these attributes properly and productively as a contributing member of the discourse community, it can accurately be said that you have mastered legal analysis and communication. You will have become an expert.

Selected Bibliography

Mark Neal Aaronson and Stefan H. Krieger, *Teaching Problem-Solving Lawyering: An Exchange Of Ideas*, 11 Clinical L. Rev. 485 (2005).

ABA Section of Legal Educ. and Admission to the Bar, Legal Education and Professional Development — An Educational Continuum (1992).

Charles F. Abernathy, Law in the United States (2006).

Ruggero J. Aldisert, Logic for Lawyers: A Guide to Clear Thinking (3d ed. 1997).

_____, Winning on Appeal: Better Briefs and Oral Argument (1996).

Aristotle, The Poetics, in The Rhetoric and The Poetics of Aristotle (Ingram Bywater trans., 1954).

_____, The Rhetoric of Aristotle (1932).

J.D.S. Armstrong and Christopher A Knott, Where the Law Is: An Introduction to Advanced Legal Research (2004).

John Austin, *The Providence of Jurisprudence Determined*, in Philip Shuchman, ed., Cohen & Cohen's Readings in Jurisprudence and Legal Philosophy (1979).

Brook K. Baker, *Language Acculturation Process and the Resistance to In"doctrine"ation in the Legal Skills Curriculum and Beyond: A Commentary on Mertz's Critical Anthropology of the Socratic, Doctrinal Classroom*, 34 John Marshall L. Rev. 131 (2000).

M.M. Bakhtin, The Dialogic Imagination: Four Essays (Michael Holquist, ed. 1982).

Jean Baudrillard, Simulacra and Simulation (1995).

Mary Beth Beazley, *Better Writing, Better Thinking: Using Legal Writing Pedagogy in the "Casebook" Classroom (Without Grading Papers)*, 10 Legal Writing 23 (2004).

_____, A Practical Guide to Appellate Advocacy (2002).

Mary Beth Beazley, Elliott Milstein, John Sebert, and E. Thomas Sullivan, *Is the Tail Wagging the Dog? Institutional Forces Affecting Curricular Innovation—A Panel Discussion*, 1 J. ALWD 184 (2001).

SAMUEL BECKETT, END GAME AND ACT WITHOUT WORDS (1958).

Theresa M. Beiner, *Insights into the Woes of a Profession*, 20 GEO. J. LEGAL ETHICS 101 (2007).

Linda L. Berger, *Of Metaphor, Metonymy, and Corporate Money: Rhetorical Choices in Supreme Court Decisions on Campaign Finance Regulation*, 58 MERCER L. REV. 949 (2007).

_____, *What is the Sound of the Corporation Speaking? How the Cognitive Theory of Metaphor Can Help Lawyers Shape the Law*, 2 J. ALWD 169 (2004).

CAROLE C. BERRY, EFFECTIVE APPELLATE ADVOCACY: BRIEF WRITING AND ORAL ARGUMENT (3d ed. 2003).

BRIAN BIX, JURISPRUDENCE: THEORY AND CONTEXT (3d ed. 2004).

GERTRUDE BLOCK, EFFECTIVE LEGAL WRITING: FOR LAW STUDENTS AND LAWYERS (5th ed. 1999).

BD. OF STUDENT AD., HARVARD LAW SCHOOL, INTRODUCTION TO ADVOCACY: RESEARCH, WRITING, AND ARGUMENT (7th ed. 2002).

Lera Boroditsky, *Metaphoric Structuring: Understanding Time Through Spatial Metaphors*, 75 COGNITION 1 (2000).

DEBORAH E. BOUCHOUX, ASPEN HANDBOOK FOR LEGAL WRITERS: A PRACTICAL REFERENCE (2005).

Robin A. Boyle, *Employing Active Learning Techniques and Metacognition in Law School: Shifting Energy from Professor to Student*, 81 U. DET. MERCY L. REV. 1 (2003).

Mark S. Bransdorfer, Note, *Miranda Right-to-Counsel Violations and the Fruit of the Poisonous Tree Doctrine*, 62 IND. L.J. 1061 (1987).

SUSAN L. BRODY, JANE RUTHERFORD, LAUREL A. VIETZEN AND JOHN C. DERNBACH, LEGAL DRAFTING (1994).

Richard H. Brown, *Social Theory as Metaphor: On the Logic of Discovery for the Sciences of Conduct*, 3 THEORY AND SOCIETY 169 (1976).

KENNETH BURKE, A RHETORIC OF MOTIVES (1969).

STEVEN J. BURTON, AN INTRODUCTION TO LAW AND LEGAL REASONING (1995).

David T. ButleRitchie, *"Objectively Speaking," There Is No Such Thing in the Law!*, 5 DISABILITY MEDICINE 68 (2005).

_____, *Situating "Thinking Like a Lawyer" Within Legal Pedagogy*, 50 CLEVE. ST. L. REV. 29 (2003).

MAUREEN CAIN & CHRISTINE B. HARRINGTON, EDS., LAWYERS IN A POSTMODERN WORLD: TRANSLATION AND TRANSGRESSION (1994).

Emily Calhoun, *Thinking Like a Lawyer*, 34 J. LEGAL EDUC. 507 (1984).

Leah M. Christensen, *The Psychology Behind Case Briefing: A Powerful Cognitive Schema*, 29 CAMPBELL L. REV. 5 (2006).

BRADLEY G. CLARY AND PAMELA LYSAGHT, SUCCESSFUL LEGAL ANALYSIS AND WRITING: THE FUNDAMENTALS (2d ed. 2006).

Fernando Colon-Navarro, *Thinking Like a Lawyer: Expert-Novice Differences in Simulated Client Interviews*, 21 J. LEGAL PROF. 107 (1996).

Byron D. Cooper, *The Integration of Theory, Doctrine, and Practice in Legal Education*, 1 J. ALWD 51 (2001).

EDWARD P.J. CORBETT, CLASSICAL RHETORIC FOR THE MODERN STUDENT, (3d ed. 1990).

EDWARD P.J. CORBETT AND ROBERT J. CONNERS, CLASSICAL RHETORIC FOR THE MODERN STUDENT (4th ed. 1999).

DAVID CRUMP, HOW TO REASON ABOUT THE LAW: AN INTERDISCIPLINARY APPROACH TO THE FOUNDATIONS OF PUBLIC POLICY (2001).

ANTHONY D'AMATO, ED., ANALYTIC JURISPRUDENCE ANTHOLOGY (1996).

Susan L. DeJarnatt, *Law Talk: Speaking, Writing, and Entering the Discourse of Law*, 40 DUQ. L. REV. 489 (2002).

JACQUES DERRIDA, ACTS OF LITERATURE (Derek Attridge, ed., 1992).

_____, *White Mythology: Metaphor in the Text of Philosophy*, in MARGINS OF PHILOSOPHY 212 (Alan Bass trans. 1982).

JOHN DEWEY, LOGIC: THE THEORY OF INQUIRY (1991).

_____, HOW WE THINK (1991).

_____, *Logical Method and the Law*, 10 CORNELL L. Q. 17 (1924).

JAMES M. DONOVAN & H. EDWIN ANDERSON, III, ANTHROPOLOGY AND LAW (2003).

Frank H. Easterbrook, *What does Legislative History Tell Us?*, 66 Chi-KENT L. REV. 441 (1991)

PETER EDGE & GRAHAM HARVEY, EDS., LAW AND RELIGION IN CONTEMPORARY SOCIETY: COMMUNITIES, INDIVIDUALISM, AND THE STATE (2000).

LINDA H. EDWARDS, LEGAL WRITING: PROCESS, ANALYSIS, AND ORGANIZATION (4th ed. 2006).

_____, LEGAL WRITING AND ANALYSIS (2003).

_____, *The Convergence of Analogical and Dialectical Imaginations in Legal Discourse*, 20 LEGAL STUD. F. 7 (1996).

Pamela Edwards, *The Shell Game: Who is Responsible for the Overuse of the LSAT in Law School Admissions*, 80 S.J.L. REV. 153 (2006).

James R. Elkins, *Thinking Like a Lawyer: Second Thoughts*, 47 MERCER L. REV. 511, 520 (1996).

Glenn Erickson & Mark Johnson, *Toward a New Theory of Metaphor*, 18 SOUTHERN JOURNAL OF PHILOSOPHY 289 (1980).

GILLES FAUCONNIER & MARK TURNER, THE WAY WE THINK: CONCEPTUAL BLENDING AND THE MIND'S HIDDEN COMPLEXITIES (2002).

STANLEY FISH, DOING WHAT COMES NATURALLY: CHANGE, RHETORIC, AND THE PRACTICE OF THEORY IN LITERARY AND LEGAL STUDIES (1992).

_____, IS THERE A TEXT IN THIS CLASS? THE AUTHORITY OF INTERPRETIVE COMMUNITIES (1980).

MICHAEL R. FONTHAM, MICHAEL VITIELLO, AND DAVID W. MILLER, PERSUASIVE WRITTEN AND ORAL ADVOCACY IN TRIAL AND APPELLATE COURTS (2002).

DAVID C. FREDERICK, THE ART OF ORAL ADVOCACY (2003).

Michael H. Frost, *With Amici Like These: Cicero, Quintilian and the Importance of Stylistic Demeanor*, 3 J. ALWD 5, 8–9 (2006).

Michael H. Frost, *Introduction to Classical Legal Rhetoric: A Lost Heritage*, 8 S. CAL. INTERDISCIPLINARY L.J. 613 (1999).

IAN GALLACHER, A FORM AND STYLE MANUAL FOR LAWYERS (2005).

BRYAN GARNER, THE REDBOOK: A MANUAL ON LEGAL STYLE (2002).

_____, THE ELEMENTS OF LEGAL STYLE (1991).

Michael Goldberg, *Against Acting "Humanely,"* 58 MERCER L. REV. 899 (2007)

KENT GREENAWALT, CONFLICTS OF LAW AND MORALITY (1987).

G.M.A. GRUBE, ED., PLATO'S FIVE DIALOGUES (2002).

JÜRGEN HABERMAS, THEORY AND PRACTICE (1973).

ALEXANDER HAMILTON, ET AL., THE FEDERALIST PAPERS (1999).

Bernard J. Hibbitts, *Making Sense of Metaphors: Visuality, Aurality, and the Reconfiguration of American Legal Discourse*, 16 CARDOZO L. REV. 229, 235 (1994).

WERNER Z. HIRSCH, LAW AND ECONOMICS: AN INTRODUCTORY ANALYSIS (1979).

OLIVER WENDELL HOLMES, JR., THE COMMON LAW (1991).

DAVID HRICIK, LAW SCHOOL BASICS (1998).

Dan Hunter, *Near Knowledge: Inductive Learning Systems in Law*, 5 VA. J.L. & TECH. 9 (2000).

PATRICK HURLEY, A CONCISE INTRODUCTION TO LOGIC (6th ed. 1997).

Gail A. Jaquish & James Ware, *Adopting an Educator Habit of Mind: Modifying What it Means to "Think Like a Lawyer,"* 45 STAN. L. REV. 1713 (1993).

LINDA D. JELLUM AND DAVID CHARLES HRICIK, MODERN STATUTORY INTERPRETATION: PROBLEMS, THEORIES, AND LAWYERING STRATEGIES (2006).

Mark Johnson, *Mind, Metaphor, Law*, 58 MERCER L. REV. 845 (2007).

_____, *Law Incarnate*, 67 BROOKLYN L. REV. 949 (2002).

_____, *Why Metaphor Matters to Philosophy*, 10 METAPHOR AND SYMBOLIC ACTIVITY 157 (1995).

_____, *Conceptual Metaphor and Embodied Structures of Meaning*, 6 PHILOSOPHICAL PSYCHOLOGY 413 (1993).

_____, *Embodied Knowledge*, 19 CURRICULUM INQUIRY 361 (1989).

_____, *Metaphorical Reasoning*, 21 SOUTHERN JOURNAL OF PHILOSOPHY 371 (1983).

_____, PHILOSOPHICAL PERSPECTIVES ON METAPHOR (1981).

Mark Johnson & Diego Fernandez-Duque, *Cause and Effect Theories of Attention: The Role of Conceptual Metaphors*, 6 GENERAL REVIEW OF PSYCHOLOGY 153 (2002).

Mark Johnson & Diego Fernandez-Duque, *Attention Metaphors: How Metaphors Guide the Cognitive Psychology of Attention*, 23 COGNITIVE SCIENCE 83 (1999).

Mark Johnson & Tim Rohrer. *We Are Live Creatures: Embodiment, American Pragmatism, and the Cognitive Organism*. In Zlatev, Jordan; Ziemke, Tom; Frank, Roz; Dirven, René, eds. (BODY, LANGUAGE, AND MIND, VOL. 1, 2005).

Mark L. Jones, *Fundamental Dimensions of Law and Legal Education: An Historical Framework—A History of U.S. Legal Education Phase I: From the Founding of the Republic Until the 1860s*, 39 JOHN MARSHALL L. REV. 1041 (2006).

R. KATZMANN, ED., JUDGES AND LEGISLATORS: TOWARD INSTITUTIONAL COMITY (1988).

HANS KELSEN, GENERAL THEORY OF NORMS (1991).

Philip C. Kissan, *The Ideology of the Case Method/Final Examination Law School*, 70 U. CIN. L. REV. 137 (2001).

Susan Hanley Kosse and David T. ButleRitchie, *How Judges, Practitioners, and Legal Writing Teachers Assess the Writing Skills of New Law Graduates: A Comparative Study*, 53 J. LEGAL EDUC. 80 (2003).

ZOLTAN KÖVECSES, METAPHOR AND EMOTION: LANGUAGE, CULTURE, AND BODY IN HUMAN FEELING (2000).

Lawrence S. Krieger, *The Inseparability of Professionalism and Personal Satisfaction: Perspectives on Values, Integrity and Happiness*, 11 CLINICAL L. REV. 425 (2005).

Stefan H. Krieger, *Domain Knowledge and the Teaching of Creative Legal Problem Solving*, 11 Clinical L. Rev. 149 (2004).

STEFAN H. KRIEGER, RICHARD K. NEUMANN, JR., KATHLEEN H. MCMANUS AND STEVEN D. JAMAR, ESSENTIAL LAWYERING SKILLS: INTERVIEWING, COUNSELING, NEGOTIATION, AND PERSUASIVE FACT ANALYSIS (1999).

Anthony T. Kronman, *Rhetoric*, 67 U. Cin. L. Rev. 667 (1999).

Thomas S. Kuhn, The Structure of Scientific Revolutions, (3d ed. 1996).

George Lakoff, Thinking Points: Communicating Our American Values and Vision (2006).

_____, Whose Freedom?: The Battle Over America's Most Important Idea (2006).

_____, Moral Politics: How Liberals and Conservatives Think (2002).

_____, Women, Fire and Dangerous Things: What Categories Reveal About the Mind (1987).

George Lakoff, Howard Dean & Don Hazen, Don't Think of an Elephant: Know Your Values and Frame the Debate — The Essential Guide for Progressives (2004).

George Lakoff & Mark Johnson, Philosophy in the Flesh (1999).

George Lakoff and Mark Johnson, *The Metaphorical Logic of Rape*, 2 Metaphor and Symbolic Activity 73 (1987).

George Lakoff & Mark Johnson, Metaphors We Live By (1980).

George Lakoff & Mark Johnson, *The Metaphorical Structure of the Human Conceptual System*, 4 Cognitive Science 195 (1980).

George Lakoff & Mark Johnson, *Conceptual Metaphor in Everyday Language*, 77 Journal of Philosophy 453 (1980).

William LaPiana, Logic and Experience: The Origins of Modern Legal Education (1997).

Terri LeClercq, Expert Legal Writing (1995).

Eve Leeman & Susan Leeman, *Elements of Dynamics IV: Neuronal Metaphors — Probing Neurobiology for Psychodynamic Meaning*, 32 J. Amer. Acad. Psychoanalysis and Dynamic Psych. 654 (2004).

Brian Leiter, ed., Objectivity in Law and Morals (2001).

Karl N. Llewelyn, The Bramble Bush (1951).

_____, *Remarks on the Theory of Appellate Decision and the Rules or Canons About How Statutes Are to be Construed*, 3 Vand. L. Rev. 395 (1950).

Niklas Luhmann, Law as a Social System (1994).

Earl R. MacCormac, A Cognitive Theory of Metaphor (1987).

Neil MacCormick, Rhetoric and the Rule of Law: A Theory of Legal Reasoning (2005)

_____, *On Legal Decisions ad Their Consequences: From Dewey to Dworkin*, 58 N.Y.U. L. Rev. 242 (1983).

John Makdisi, Introduction to the Study of Law: Cases and Materials (2d ed. 2000)

Ellie Margolis, *Closing the Floodgates: Making Persuasive Policy Arguments in Appellate Briefs*, 62 Montana L. Rev. 59 (2001).

Sheldon Margulies and Kenneth Lasson, Learning Law: The Mastery of Legal Logic (1993).

A. Marmour, ed., Law and Interpretation (1995).

Patrick McFadden, A Student's Guide to Legal Analysis: Thinking Like a Lawyer (2001).

Paul E. McGreal, *Slighting Context: On the Illogic of Ordinary Speech in Statutory Interpretation*, 52 Kan. L. Rev. 325 (2004).

Ruth Ann McKinney, Reading Like a Lawyer: Time-Saving Strategies for Reading Law Like an Expert (2005).

Sally Engle Merry, *Legal Pluralism*, 22 Law & Society Rev. 869 (1988).

John Henry Merryman, *Legal Education There and Here: A Comparison*, 27 Stanford L. Rev. 859 (1975).

_____, The Civil Law Tradition: An Introduction to the Legal Systems of Western Europe and Latin America, (2d ed. 1969).

John B. Mitchell, *Current Theories on Expert and Novice Thinking: A Full Faculty Considers the Implications for Legal Education*, 39 J. Legal Educ. 275 (1989).

W.J.T. Mitchell, ed., On Narrative (Chicago 1981).

James E. Molitero and Fredric I. Lederer, An Introduction to Law, Law Study, and the Lawyer's Role (1991).

Myron Moskovitz, Winning an Appeal (3d ed. 1995).

John O. Mudd, *Thinking Critically About "Thinking Like a Lawyer,"* 33 J. Legal Educ. 704 (1983).

Morell E. Mullins, Sr., *Tools, Not Rules: The Heuristic Nature of Statutory Interpretation*, 30 J. Legis. 1 (2003).

Michael D. Murray and Christy H. DeSanctis, Legal Research and Writing (2005).

Richard K. Neumann, Jr., Legal Reasoning and Writing: Structure, Strategy, and Style, (3d ed. 1998).

_____, *Donald Schon, The Reflective Practitioner, and the Comparative Failure of Legal Education*, 6 Clinical L. Rev. 401 (2000).

Friedrich Nietzsche, Beyond Good and Evil (1886).

Laurel Currie Oates and Anne Enquist, Just Research (2005).

Laurel Currie Oates, Anne Enquist and Kelly Kunsch, The Legal Writing Handbook: Analysis, Research, and Writing (3d ed. 2002).

Chaim Perelman, The Realm of Rhetoric (1982).

Stephen R. Perry, *Interpretation and Methodology in Legal Theory*, in A. Marmour, ed., Law and Interpretation (1995).

Terrill Pollman, *Building a Tower of Babel or Building a Discipline? Talking About Legal Writing*, 85 Marq. L. Rev. 887 (2002).

Richard A. Posner, Law, Pragmatism, and Democracy (2003).

Jill J. Ramsfield, The Law as Architecture: Building Legal Documents (2000).

Herbert N. Ramy, Succeeding in Law School (2006).

John Rawls, A Theory of Justice (1980).

Mary Bernard Ray, The Basics of Legal Writing (2006).

Mary Bernard Ray and Jill J. Ramsfield, Legal Writing: Getting it Right and Getting it Written (4th ed. 2005).

Alfred Zantziger Reed, Training for the Public Profession of the Law: Historical Development and Principal Contemporary Problems of Legal Education in the United States with Some Account of Conditions in England and Canada (1921).

Sarah E. Redfield, Thinking Like a Lawyer: An Educator's Guide to Legal Analysis and Research (2002).

Judith Resnick, Processes of the Law (2004).

Paul Ricoeur, *Narrative Time*, in W.J.T. Mitchell, ed., On Narrative (1981).

Edwina L. Rissland, *Artificial Intelligence and Law: Stepping Stones to a Model of Legal Reasoning*, 99 Yale L.J. 1957 (1990).

David T. Ritchie, *Who is On the Outside Looking In, and What Do They See?: Metaphors of Exclusion in Legal Education*, 58 Mercer L. Rev. 991 (2007).

_____, *Using Metaphor in Legal Analysis and Communication: Questions and Answers*, 58 Mercer L. Rev. 1021 (2007).

Kristen Konrad Robbins, *Philosophy v. Rhetoric in Legal Education: Understanding the Schism Between Doctrinal and Legal Writing Faculty*, 3 J. ALWD 108 (2006).

Ruth Anne Robbins, *Painting with Print: Incorporating of Typographic and Layout Design Into the Text of Legal Writing Documents*, 2 J. ALWD 108 (2004).

Tim Rohrer, *The Cognitive Science of Metaphor from Philosophy to Neuroscience*, 6 Theoria et Historia Scientiarum 27 (2001).

David S. Romantz and Kathleen Elliott Vinson, Legal Analysis: The Fundamental Skill (1998).

Kate Ronald, *On the outside Looking in: Students' Analyses of Professional Discourse Communities*, 7 Rhetoric Review 130 (1988).

Richard Rorty, Consequences of Pragmatism (1982).

Thomas Ross, *Metaphor and Paradox*, 23 Ga. L. Rev. 1053 (1989).

Peter Sack & Jonathan Aleck, eds., *Law and Anthropology* (1992).

Kurt M. Saunders & Linda Levine, *Learning to Think Like a Lawyer*, 29 U.S.F.L. Rev. 121 (1994).

Antonin Scalia, A Matter of Interpretation (1997).

_____, *The Rule of Law as a Law of Rules*, 56 U. Chicago L. Rev. 1175 (1989).

Pierre Schlag and David Skover, Tactics of Legal Reasoning (1986).

Deborah A. Schmedemann and Christina L. Kunz, Synthesis: Legal Reading, Reasoning, and Writing (2d ed. 2003).

Uri J. Schild and Yael Saban, *Knowledge Representation in Legal Systems*, 52 Syracuse L. Rev. 1321 (2002).

Nancy Schultz, *How Do Lawyers Really Think?*, 42 J. Legal Educ. 57 (1992).

Helene S. Shapo, Marilyn R. Walter, and Elizabeth Fajans, Writing and Analysis in the Law (4th ed. 2003).

David Shrager & Elizabeth Frost, eds., The Quotable Lawyer (1986).

Philip Shuchman, ed., Cohen & Cohen's Readings in Jurisprudence and Legal Philosophy (1979).

Louis J. Sirico, Jr. and Nancy L. Schultz, Persuasive Writing for Lawyers and the Legal Profession (2d ed. 2001).

Amy E. Sloan, Basic Legal Research: Tools and Strategies (3d ed. 2006).

Kevin H. Smith, *Practical Jurisprudence: Deconstructing and Synthesizing the Art and Science of Thinking Like a Lawyer*, 29 U. Mem. L. Rev. 1 (1998).

Michael R. Smith, *Levels of Metaphor in Persuasive Legal Writing*, 58 Mercer L. Rev. 919 (2007).

_____, Advanced Legal Writing: Theories and Strategies in Persuasive Writing (2002).

Lorne Sossin, *Discourse Politics: Legal Research and Writing's Search for a Pedagogy of Its Own*, 29 New Eng. L. Rev. 883 (1995).

Julie M. Spanbauer, *Teaching First Semester Students that Objective Analysis Persuades*, 5 Legal Writing 167 (1999).

Jean Stefancic and Richard Delgado, How Lawyers Lose their Way: A Profession Fails its Creative Minds (2005).

Robert Stevens, Law School: Legal Education in America from the 1850s to the 1980s (2001).

James Stratman, *How Legal Analysts Negotiate Indeterminacy of Meaning in Common Law Rules: Toward a Synthesis of Linguistic and Cognitive Approaches to Investigation*, 24 Lang. & Commun. 23 (1994).

Ruta K. Stropus and Charlotte D. Taylor, Bridging the Gap Between College and Law School (2001).

Michael Sullivan and Daniel J. Solove, *Can Pragmatism be Radical? Richard Posner and Legal Pragmatism*, 113 Yale L.J. 687 (2003).

Sara F. Taub, Language from the Body: Iconicity and Metaphor in American Sign Language (2001).

Paul Tidman and Howard Kahane, Logic and Philosophy: A Modern Introduction, (8th ed. 1999).

Elizabeth G. Thornburg, *Metaphors Matter: How Images of Battle, Sports, and Sex Shape the Adversary System*, 10 Wis. Women's L.J. 225 (1995).

Robert L. Tsai, *Fire, Metaphor, and Constitutional Myth-Making*, 93 Geo. L.J. 181 (2004).

Mark Turner, Death is the Mother of Beauty: Mind, Metaphor, Criticism (1987).

Arthur T. Vanderbilt, II, An Introduction to the Study of Law (1979).

Christine M. Venter, *Analyze This: Using Taxonomies to "Scaffold" Students Legal Thinking and Writing Skills*, 57 Mercer L. Rev. 621 (2006).

Melissa H. Weresh, Legal Writing: Ethical and Professional Considerations (2006).

Cheryl Rosen Weston, *Legal Education in the United States: Who's In Charge? Why Does it Matter?*, 24 Wisc. Int'l L. J. 397 (2006).

Hayden White, *The Narrativization of Real Events*, in W.J.T. Mitchell, ed., On Narrative (1981).

_____, *The Value of Narrativity*, in W.J.T. Mitchell, ed., On Narrative (1981).

James Boyd White, *Doctrine in a Vacuum: Reflections on What a Law School Ought (and Ought Not) To Be*, 36 J. Legal Educ. 155 (1986).

Steven L. Winter, *Re-Embodying Law*, 58 Mercer L. Rev. 869 (2007).

_____, *What is the "Color of Law?"* in Ray Gibbs, ed., Cambridge Handbook of Metaphor and Thought (2005).

_____, A Clearing in the Forest (2001).

_____, *The Meaning of "Under Color of" Law*, 91 Mich. L. Rev. 323 (1992).

_____, *Death is the Mother of Metaphor*, 105 Harv. L. Rev. 745 (1992).

_____, *The Cognitive Dimension of the Agon Between Legal Power and Narrative Meaning*, 87 Mich. L. Rev. 2225 (1989).

_____, *Transcendental Nonsense, Metaphoric Reasoning, and the Cognitive Stakes for Law*, 137 U. Pa. L. Rev. 1105 (1989).

_____, *The Metaphor of Standing and the Problem of Self-Governance*, 40 Stan. L. Rev. 1371 (1988).

David N. Yellen, *"Thinking Like a Lawyer" or Acting Like a Judge*, 27 Hofstra L. Rev. 13 (1998).

John Zeleznikow, *The Split-up Project: Induction, Context, and Knowledge Discovery in Law*, 3 Law, Probability, and Risk 147 (2004).

Richard A. Zitrin and Carol Langford, The Moral Compass of the American Lawyer: Truth, Justice, Power, and Greed (2000).

Index